Mind Hacking Happiness Volume II

Increasing Happiness and Finding Non-Dual Enlightenment

by Sean Webb

Contact Info:

sean@mindhackinghappiness.com

Published in the United States by CCRSM Press

This book is dedicated to mind spelunkers like you, because you picked up this book.

Also to my wife Whitney and son Declan.

Mind Hacking Happiness Volume II

Introduction

A few things to consider before we enter Mind Hacking Happiness Volume II:

First, welcome to **"the best book on enlightenment currently in print."** I don't know if that's actually true, but that comment was indeed made by an enlightenment researcher who has read well over 100 books on the topic of deep mind, consciousness expansion, and spiritual enlightenment. So I appreciate the comment regardless. I hope you can rate this book as highly as others have.

Next, if you haven't already read "Mind Hacking Happiness Volume I", you may want to read that book before starting this one. The importance of reading Volume I of this series **cannot** be underestimated in regard to its ability to help you understand happiness and the process within your mind that blocks your personal happiness. Mind Hacking Happiness Volume I is the first book of the modern age to explain how **your** personal mind works, how **your** human emotions work, and clearly defines how your mind creates the stuff which stands in the way of your personal happiness. Reading about the concepts outlined in that book will definitely help you better understand the content in this book. Definitely. And it will give you some amazing tools to decrease the stuff that your mind creates that steals your happiness.

That said, book one is just a starting point, and Chapter 1 of this book does review of some of the most critical information presented in Volume I. So if you haven't read Volume I, Chapter 1 of this book will bring you somewhat up to speed. If you are indeed reading this book after completing Volume I, the early review in Chapter 1 will serve as a good refresher before slipping into the deep-water awesomeness that is Mind Hacking Happiness Volume II.

In Volume I, we discussed the science of your mind and the

portion of your mind called {self}, which we showed influenced your happiness every moment of every day of your life. In this book, we move into the deeper secrets of mind and how to move beyond the mind's {self} as a driving component of your life. We discuss some deeper secrets about {self} from the historical religious and intellectual luminaries who have long told us that knowing the secrets to {self} is the **only** possible road to happiness. Here, you'll find a thoughtful consideration of the science of happiness, and explore some of the most profound secrets of your personal human existence. We'll discuss some ancient secrets of the mind that very few people in the world ever discover, and give you hints about how you can uncover those secrets for yourself. You will no longer have to take anyone else's word on how you, too, can hack your mind to be happy any time you wish!

Be forewarned that because a lot of our written human history comes from religious texts, we are going to merge into our conversation some generalities of common religious reference, but we will also retain science and philosophy to maintain balance. You may or may not be surprised that when many of the historic religious figures were teaching about God and finding heaven, they were teaching about the very happiness science presented in this book.

Regarding Your Membership Card to a Very Exclusive Club

You should know that only a tiny percentage of the people in the world know anything about the mysteries we're about to discuss here. In fact, most the people who know about these mysteries don't ever talk about them, because they're almost impossible to talk about. That's why only the ancient philosophers, learned scientists, and persuasive religious figures have spoken about these secrets with any depth of wisdom whatsoever. And it's why, when they did so, they often talked in analogies or parables. So you're about to join a very exclusive club.

Next, you should know I'm not supposed to be telling you what I'm about to tell you. Don't worry, we're not breaking any laws here, but what we are about to do here is highly irregular. We're about to use mass communication technologies to augment the traditional teacher-student model that has been prevalent since time immemorial. In the traditional model, I was supposed to write the first book about the basics of happiness, and the new tricks to reduce your mind's inner pain and suffering, and leave you to take the next step of inner discovery. I'm not supposed to actually talk about the bigger insights that can be found when you dig deep within the mind to a point where it stops and gives up all its hidden secrets. You're supposed to find those for yourself. And while that's only one of the reasons I shouldn't have written this second book, here are my thoughts on that whole giving-you-the-space-to-seek-truth position:

Screw that! That hasn't worked for humanity thousands of years. It's time for those who know to speak up. As a result, I've taken into account all the reasons you and I are not supposed to have this discussion, and I've decided you and I are going to change course. I'm gonna spill the beans to you in a way that incorporates the latest science, which you can check for yourself, and provides you the freedom to make an educated decision about your personal search for truth.

So we're going to talk about the deepest secrets of mind and what it means to be human, and even dive into the somewhat forbidden topics of enlightenment and non-dual awareness. Yes, we're still going to reference science. Yes, we're still going to use some pretty cool analogies and stories where appropriate. But make no mistake, this is where that solid left turn I promised in Volume I happens. Right now. Let's step through the mirror.

What you will find in the following pages is a contemporary description of, and a map to, a state of human consciousness that has existed since before the beginning of written history. This state of consciousness has existed so long that it has transcended the birth and death of languages. It has outlasted the rise and fall of great empires. It has permeated the development and extinction of entire races. It has survived through the creation and destruction of religions. It has even lasted through the constant churning and turmoil of all the cultural evolutions that follow those types of cataclysmic globe-changing events. This state of consciousness is something you can attain. It not only answers every question you could ever ask about your Self and the universe, it opens up new doors of intelligence within you that you didn't even know you had. So strap your{self} in for a ride like you've probably never had before. Welcome to Volume II.

1 A Quick Review about You

Always be on the lookout
for the presence of wonder.

—E. B. White

Okay, let's zip through some of the highlights of Volume I so we can be prepared to talk about the deeper secrets of happiness that I've reserved for this book. But just know that if you'd like the explanations, examples, and supporting evidence for the basis of what we're about to cover here, reading, or rereading, Volume I is your best course of action.

As a last warning, if you haven't read Volume I, this chapter might seem a bit dry as we cover much of the new science of how your mind works in a very short amount of time. So if you get confused with some of the new terminology, chalk it up to picking up a book with Volume II in the title without first reading Volume I. Chapter 2 and beyond will flow much better than this initial chapter.

The Source of Happiness in the Mind

There's a lot more to your happiness than you've been told. And there's a lot less to your happiness than you've been told as well. The secrets of your happiness are very complex, and also very simple. The simplest secret about your happiness is that your happiness comes from your mind - and nowhere else. It is the only place from which your happiness is sourced, and the only place from which your happiness could ever be sourced. Normally, this would be great news, because it means you already have all the happiness you ever need right there within you. The problem, however, is that you don't have control of your mind to be able to create happiness at will. Your mind has tricked you into believing that you need to satisfy it to earn your allowance of happiness. It manipulated you into thinking you need to run around satisfying its mental and physical errands, aligning all the stars in the galaxy until they deliver the conditions your mind requires to present you some happiness through a small slot in a door of your mind where your inner happiness is stored.

That's bullshit, and there is a way to change it. Because although your mind has indeed tricked you into thinking it is in charge of distributing your happiness, there's a particular reason those crazy people who write books about your mind call it **your mind**. And that's because the simple fact is that **you own your mind**. It's yours. And you can learn to control it, if you wish. This includes learning to control when and where your mind gives you happiness, regardless of whether or not you've satisfied its unnecessary and arbitrary requirements. You can indeed alter the process that your mind follows to deliver your happiness. And this is the simplest secret about happiness that almost no one has ever told us.

On the flip side of the coin, one of the most complex secrets about happiness has to do with the process your mind follows to block your happiness and create pain and suffering for you, and how to take control of that process and change it. It's important that you **do** change it because the most recent discoveries in science have uncovered that happiness supercharges your brain and supercharges your life. Although that probably sounds weird, it turns out that our collective belief in the do-better-in-life-to-become-happy model is simply wrong. It's backwards. The science clearly shows that our physiology responds exactly opposite to our assumption, and that our bodies and brain perform best with a be-happy-first-to-do-better-in-life model of living.

Crazy, huh? But it's true. So how do we get to happiness first? Well, first, you have to know how happiness works.

The Mind's {self}

In Volume I, we saw how your mind creates the crap that steals your happiness. We also explored the mechanisms you can play with in your mind to alter that process and decrease your pain and suffering. The basic explanation of that process is as follows:

Your mind is the experience you have because you have a brain. Your brain is your organ of survival. This is why a lot of the thoughts you have are connected with maintaining your safety and measuring your risks. The specific section of the brain connected with your brain's survival charter is called the limbic system. The limbic system spends all day every day analyzing your immediate environment through your senses and thoughts for potential threats. In this scanning for threats process, however, a second question must then be asked: **a threat to what exactly? What am I looking to protect?** This is where the mind's {self} enters the picture. A {self} must be assembled in the brain as a definition of what needs to be defended, so the limbic system knows what to freak out about when it freaks out. When the limbic system freaks out, that's typically called **negative emotion**.

The mind's {self} starts when we are babies, and grows and changes throughout our lives until we die. Science shows our mind's {self} is more than just our body, and includes other people and ideas that are favorable to us. The mind's {self} is basically any idea that the mind points to when answering the question, "Who or what am I?" Our brains take the {self} **very seriously**, because it is the laundry list of stuff that needs to survive into tomorrow, lest it doesn't survive and we die. Your mind's {self} includes your body, the people connected with you, the ideas you hold onto that help define your existence, your beliefs, your memories, and all the crap you own. So when something attacks or threatens or hurts anything on our {self} list, from your family members, to your religion, to your favorite sports team or someone insulting your favorite color, your brain freaks out a little bit. This is why it's easy to understand that almost every thought and experience we have in life gets passed by the {self} to check if that thought is threatening to the {self}. We use brackets around the word {self} to indicate that it's a bunch of shit, and not just one thing. The brackets come from the branch of mathematics called set theory.

{self} Map

Your Equation of Emotion

Your entire nervous system works as a basic comparator. For instance, when your hand gives you messages about something being hot, it doesn't send you a message about the exact temperature of the thing, it simply lets you know the hot thing in question is either slightly or way hotter than whatever temperature your hand was sensing a moment ago. Similarly, when the brain looks to create emotions for you, being part of the nervous system, it compares two things also. The first thing it compares— no surprise—is connected with the map of your mind's {self}, and it's called your Expectation/Preference.

While Expectation/Preference sounds like something you choose consciously, it's not. It's set automatically in the brain because of something within your body called homeostasis. That is your body's natural urge to say, "Everything's gotta be cool. If everything in the body is cool, I'm cool. But if shit ain't cool, some shit is gonna happen to where we make it cool, you dig?" Subsequently, the Expectation/Preference about every little thing on your {self} map is that every little thing needs to be held at status quo or better. So your body has to be held at status quo or better, your family and friends need to be held harmless, your religion and politics need to be hands-off or improved, all the way down to your favorite color being respected. Otherwise some shit is gonna hit the fan in your mind, usually in the form of negative emotions.

The mind takes this Expectation/Preference list connected with your {self} stuff and then compares it to every Perception that passes through your mind, conscious or subconscious. Perceptions come from your senses, but they can be thoughts, emotions, or any little thing. The basic rule is that if a Perception matches the mind's Expectation/Preference about something, a positive emotion becomes the result. If a Perception doesn't match the mind's Expectation/Preference about something, a negative emotion is the result. If either an Expectation/Preference or a Perception doesn't exist about something, no emotion will result.

This comparison is called your Equation of Emotion. It explains every simple emotion you have ever and will ever have, and when multiple Equations of Emotion pile up on top of each other simultaneously, it explains every complex emotion you have ever and will ever have. The strength of Expectation/Preference, plus the intensity of the Perception, determines the severity or strength of the resulting emotion(s). (We will not go into the individual emotion rule sets here to discuss what determines how anger, fear, sadness, worry, etc., are chosen in the mind, but those rule sets exist and are outlined in detail in Volume I.)

The Equation of Emotion

$$EP \, \Delta \, P = ER$$

| Expectation / Preference | Perception | Emotional Reaction |

Knowing the two simple variables mentioned above that create all your emotions gives you the power to alter and adjust those variables and adjust your entire emotional landscape. This can change your life. In addition, simply using your mind to look into your mind at the creation of your emotions in real-time fires some magic circuits in your brain that turn your mental bullshit down in your brain. The science of increased emotional intelligence supports this, and it's been seen live on fMRI brain scans, but the stories from the early pioneers of Mind Hacking Happiness are also proving this out as well. The phenomenon of your brain turning off its negative processing is likely connected with an entire group of studies called the name-it-tame-it studies. You can't help but to turn down your negative crap, because it's a magic phenomenon of the brain we can't yet explain. But, over time, because of what's known as neuroplasticity, you may find this turning-down-negativity effect can become additive. This opens the door to your ability to experience more happiness over time, without changing a thing in your life, except where you point you attention.

A Review of the Control Room of the Mind

Learning about how your mind and emotions work to the point that you can see them operating in real time throws you into the psychological sciences mind space called meta-awareness. Meta-awareness is the space of being able to point your mind's awareness back onto the operations of your mind itself, which is where you land naturally when you realize your day dreaming and need to get back to work. In the space of meta-awareness, you are able to take control of your mind and focus it onto activities that are more beneficial to you and your mind's more efficient operation. This is why I call meta-awareness **the control room of the mind**. Ancient mind disciplines, intense concentration, and even prayer are all about intentionally entering meta-awareness to better focus the mind onto more productive and harmonious activity. When using meta-awareness on a subconscious process such as emotional processing, you slowly gain better understanding and control of that subconscious process. This supercharges and focuses your mind.

There are multiple levels of consciousness in your mind. That's too deep of a subject to go into here, but there's more to your mind than your waking awareness. There's a bunch of stuff going on under the surface of your mind. Your spontaneous ideas come to you from these different levels of consciousness, and almost all the levels of your subconsciousness are working to serve you. They'll serve you even better once you take control of them. Meta-awareness provides you that ability to take control. The meta-awareness space within your mind is the level of consciousness where you can focus and listen to the activity of your mind, and take control of your mind to change what it's doing. This gives you better visibility into your subconscious mind, and more control over your life. The idea and use of meta-awareness to improve life predates written history.

Your Mind's {self} vs. Your True Self

In Volume I we explained that the biggest secret in the universe is about your mind's {self}, because it touches every bit of your mind's processing. The world's leading religious and scientific minds agree that the secrets to everything are contained within the secrets to the {self}. Not only does it fully set one-half of your Equation of Emotion (the EP side), it also influences the other half, your Perceptions. Here's the rub about the {self}: Your mind's {self} is not your actual Self. And because you only interact with your mind's {self}, that means although you think you know your{self}, **you do not currently know your Self** the way the past masters have spoken of knowing Self. Numerous historic masters, from Socrates and Buddha, through Jesus and Muhammad, to Emerson and Einstein, all told us there's a big difference in our mind's {self} and our true Self. And the reality is that most of humanity walks around thinking our mind's {self} is out true Self, which is the world's biggest challenge to world peace, and your biggest challenge to personal happiness on demand.

This is a truth we will dive deeper into later in this book, but as I warned in Volume I, please be aware that this idea that 'you don't really know yourself' may make you feel a bit uneasy, and you may not feel good even at this moment that I just said that to you. This is because your brain actually **requires** what it believes to be an accurate {self} for survival reasons, and it violently rejects the idea that you don't know your{self}, because that idea throws the defense of {self} wiring of your brain into a tizzy. You need to remain mindful of that as we move forward, because it can be a sticking point that inhibits your growth toward happiness if you let it.

Better learning about your mind's {self} and your Equations of Emotion can have a number of positive effects. First, it increases your Emotional Intelligence, which is scientifically connected with more positive outcomes than can be listed here, including raising your IQ, improving your health, reducing your stress levels, making you a better business executive, and making you a better human being. Second, it creates an easy path into the space of mind called meta-awareness, where you can take control of your mind. Third, watching your Equation of Emotion in action turns down your inner turmoil in real time. Fourth, it allows for the transition from feeling the compulsion to follow an emotion to having a choice about following an emotion or not. Fifth, the EoE points out the big control knobs within the control room of your mind, which can be altered to change the output of your mind. Sixth, knowing the EoE gives you a complete understanding of your personal emotional landscape and how to change it at will. Taking control of your mind in this fashion can change the mix of happiness and non-happiness that's created within your mind.

In addition to all that, understanding the mind's whole emotion creation process can be an amazing tool of understanding your own pain and suffering, and also the pain and suffering of others. Carl Jung said, "Knowing your own darkness is the best method for dealing with the darkness of other people." Most importantly, however, better knowing your mind's {self} reveals how the concept of {self} is flawed and that it doesn't truly define you. In truth, although you look marvelous, your mind's entire mechanism of {self} is flawed and ugly, and you need to pitch it in the trash can. That very mind process of {self} is the direct cause of everything in humanity we consider destructive or harmful to ourselves and others. Subsequently, being conscious of your {self} helps you be less destructive to yourself and others. When you learn to take control of your mind and separate from your mind's {self}, you can improve your business prowess, your parenting prowess, your personal relationship capabilities, and your personal capacity to live a happier life. In short, you become a better, more effective, and happier human being.

And if that's all you ever do with the ideas and exercises presented in "Mind Hacking Happiness Volume I", good for you. That stuff can literally be transformational in your life and in the lives of those around you. If, however, you're looking to step through the looking glass to discover the deeper truth about Self by taking a closer look within . . . to seek the truth that the world leading scientific and spiritual luminaries told us is there waiting for you . . . (which is really why you cracked the cover Volume II, isn't it?) . . . then hang on to your hat. Because taking a step toward that more profound truth is exactly what we are about to do.

2 The First Step Toward Deeper Truth—Through the Body

The mind's first step to self-awareness must be through the body.

—George Sheehan, M.D.

One of the coolest studies I've run into in my research for on how to hack the mind to increase our overall happiness and discover the deeper secrets of our Self was one done at the University of Iowa by famed consciousness and brain researcher Antonio Damasio and his colleagues. It was published in the journal "Science" in 1997. It was called the Iowa Gambling Task and involved a couple stacked decks of cards. Here's what happened:

Study participants were asked to play a simple game, where they would pull from two decks of cards. As the cards were pulled one by one, the resulting card value would affect the amount of money the player would receive at the end of the game. The rules were pretty simple. Pull a good card, and the money award was increased. Pull a bad card, and the winnings would decrease. Something the researchers didn't tell the players was that one deck was stacked with a larger number of good cards, accompanied by a smoother but slower ride. The other deck was stacked with a larger number of bad cards with more dramatic swings in both directions. So in effect, one deck gave you money gradually with a smoother ride, and the other deck took away money gradually with more dramatic fortune shifts along the way. There were just enough of a mix of good and bad cards in each deck that it wouldn't be immediately obvious to the player what was going on, but just enough that they would eventually figure out the pattern, and know one deck was good, and one deck was bad. The researchers then hooked up a number of sensors to the study participants to measure heartbeat, skin conductivity, and other measurements that could record their body's physical reactions during the game.

So what did the study reveal?

When study participants started playing the game, they pulled from the two decks of cards, and started to see their winnings go up and down based on the cards they pulled. One deck gave them more money than it took, and the other took more than it gave, but not in a super obvious way. On average, it took 50 pulls from the two decks for the study participants to have a hunch about what was going on with the two decks of cards. After 80 pulls, just about everyone had figured out that one deck was giving money, and the other deck was taking it away. The most interesting part of the study, however, occurred when the researchers looked at the data from the body sensors that measured participants' heartbeats, and sweat on their palms, etc. Because while it took most the study participants 50 to 80 pulls to figure out what was going on . . . (are you ready for this?) . . . it only took their bodies **ten** pulls to know what was going on with the two decks.

The study participants' physiological reactions connected with the emotion of fear indicated that the players' bodies were completely aware of what was going on with the two decks of cards after just ten pulls. It took the players' conscious minds five times as long to even get a hunch, and eight times as long before they were certain of what was going on. But their bodies knew almost immediately in comparison.

This is a hugely significant finding, because the results of this study strike at the heart of our false {self} / true Self riddle outlined in Volume I. They provide scientific support of what the ancient wisdom disciplines and historic luminaries have been trying to teach us for thousands of years: the highest intelligence that holds the answers to life and our existence is found within and through our very own bodies. So it turns out that the biggest portion of the Know Thyself riddle lies within the confines of our skin.

The Secrets of the Body

In keeping with my perpetual promise to be no-nonsense and to the point, I'm just going to come out and tell you; it is here that we have uncovered one of the biggest truths regarding the ancient secrets the world's luminaries wanted you to know. Because the secrets to happiness and indeed Enlightenment itself are found right within your own body.

It's a simple fact that your body contains multiple levels of conscious intelligence. Those multiple levels of consciousness intelligence are where your subconscious thought comes from. It's where your creativity and intuition comes from. It's where your heartbeat, immune functions, and breathing are controlled from. It's where the body can identify two stacked decks of cards five to eight times faster than you can.

What you may not know however, is that there are ways to directly communicate with those multiple levels of intelligent body consciousnesses. There's a way to bring the power of that immense intelligence to the surface of your mind where you can access it directly. Furthermore, when you do communicate with that intelligence, you can gain access to the subconscious knowledge and wisdom hidden within your body which then can enlighten your top conscious intelligence. This is more than hippy bullshit or pseudoscience. It's real science that we'll discuss shortly. To oversimplify for now, access to your deeper intelligence provides the following five benefits:

1. First, because your body and its sensory and thought activity is the largest single item on your {self} map, discovering the deeper truth about your body helps you better understand the biggest component of {self} in the mind that helps create your personal existence. This gives you a lot of power to turn off your pain and suffering process, and create an amazing life for you and those

around you.

2. Second, accessing your deeper body intelligence allows you to see your body as a separate entity. If you experience learning to access intelligence from your body that wasn't yours initially, that puts a noticeable distance in your mind between your waking consciousness and your body. After all, if there's a separate consciousness within you, your mind must acknowledge that separation. So all of a sudden, your body becomes a different entity than you. This extra mental distance helps further free you from your body's tendency to grab a larger portion of your {self} map, thus reducing your pain and suffering as a result.

3. Third, it opens the door to accessing the deep intelligence within your body. There is an amazing amount of wisdom and intelligence within you that is at your disposal when you learn how to access it. Where this gets really interesting is that recent science shows conclusively that life memories are passed down through genetics stored within our cells themselves. And since your body's cells have never tasted death since the moment life began on Earth, always being replicated from other living cells from our moms and dads, your very DNA might even hold memories which date back to when all life began. That might be a stretch, or it might not. Regardless, your cells do hold knowledge and wisdom from before the time you were born. Scientific fact. And you can and do gain access to it.

4. Fourth, accessing your deeper intelligence allows you to discover the secrets of your true Self. This true Self knowledge fills the void that your false {self} leaves when it gets disassembled through the process of inner discovery. This transformative shift happens both gradually and with sudden leaps through epiphanies of insight which come from the mind, and is transformative.

5. Finally, accessing your deeper intelligence allows for an amazing awakening to occur. That pinnacle apocalypse called Enlightenment, which spiritual and intellectual

masters have been speaking of for literally eons, and upon which most global religions are based, is a physiological experience. If and when it does come, Enlightenment comes through your body. So being in tune with the body and opening up the communication channels in your body is critical for you to experience this awakening.

The secrets of the Self references we considered in Volume I, including "Know Thyself / Father's Kingdom is found within / he who knows himself knows God / the value of a human being is measured by the degree which he or she can be liberated from self / to know thyself is the beginning of wisdom" . . . which we framed as the biggest secret in the universe in Volume I, are actually answered within and through your human body. The same body which creates your existence which perceives the universe. The same body that has evolved over millions of years of intelligent development into being what it is today. The same body that God gave you, if that idea is preferable to you. That body holds your answers.

The Wisdom of the Body

Although this "learning-from-within" idea may be new to you, the fundamental idea that you can discover an amazing amount of information about life and your existence through your body is older than written history itself. We know this because the methods used to unearth these profound secrets from your body have existed since before written history. In fact, one of the biggest super-secrets of all the ancient disciplines connected with meditation is that its purpose is to give you a deeper insight into your body. Wait, what? Didn't we say in Volume I that meditative disciplines were actually designed to observe and quiet our mind? Yes. Yes, we did. How very observant of you to bring that up. Okay, so how is meditation now a way of looking at your body instead of your mind? In short, it's actually a way of looking at both at the same time.

It's certainly true that meditative practices center on the mind, and controlling its focus. From a big picture point of view, however, your mind is primarily the experience you have because you have a brain. Your brain is, of course, a part of your body. Therefore, technically speaking, controlling your mind's focus and watching the activity of your mind during meditation is officially controlling and watching the activity of your body's brain. And the disciplines we all use to focus our minds support this deeper truth.

Meditation teachers often instruct their students to focus on their breath (a function of the body). During meditation, we are also told to take notice of any sensations we may feel in the body while meditating. So we acknowledge body sensations and processes while also taking notice of any conscious thoughts in our brains which sometimes arise within our mind which interrupt the focus of our attention. Although we don't often think of it this way, both sensations are actually body activity. Specifically, it's the activity of the living cells within our body doing their thing. And in the core of all meditative disciplines, that is really what we are meant to notice.

It is a well known fact that your body is made up of trillions of living beings. Living beings? Yes. The fact is that your body is a complex system of an almost countless number of cells. And what are cells? They are living, eating, breathing, eliminating, communicating, procreating, dying creatures that come together to create something bigger than they are. For our own psychological comfort level, we typically don't like to acknowledge the fact that our cells are born, live a life, and then die. We don't like to anthropomorphize our human cells even though they literally anthropomorphize us. It is much less complicated for us to believe that our body is either simply who we are as humans, or that our body of cells is a vessel built by God designed to carry around that thing we call Spirit or Soul, our higher purpose of being. Or better yet, it's easiest to not even think about body-cell-life stuff at all. This is because our body makes up a portion of our {self} map, and as we discussed previously, uncertainty about {self} drives our brains crazy. Your brain needs a very well defined {self} to compare perceived threats to, otherwise those brain cells may fail to do their job of keeping you alive.

But not digging deeper into your body is a huge mistake. Just look at how much you've learned about your {self} by simply looking at the basic physiological process of your emotions, and how seeing that process can grant you access to the control room of your mind called meta-awareness. Just think about how much better you understand the creation of your daily pain and suffering based on what you've learned about your mind's requirement to have a {self}, and how the things on your {self} map feed into your Equation of Emotion. By looking within, you now have the most amazing tool of calming your own inner bullshit, because of the science of how your body quiets your bullshit when you focus your attention on that bullshit-creating-process itself. You've learned that overall, your emotions and inner noise is just how your physiology works, and just like you can take control of your arm, you can take control of your brain, which gives you control of your mind.

Now it's time to take the next step, because better understanding the components of your mind's false {self} and where your pain and suffering comes from is only half of the false {self} / true Self story. The other half of that story lies in the deeper realization of Self that can occur when you throw back all the covers within your body that reveal the deepest secrets about your{self} that most other humans have missed for thousands of years. This is the truly transformational part of the process, because what happens in this instant of inner discovery is that the false {self} of the mind gets overwritten with new information. And from that moment forward, our minds start to work differently than they once did because one of its core components has been transformed. Like a computer disk drive full of junk files that slow and muddy the computer's computational capabilities, when that unorganized disk drive is cleaned and overwritten with new data, the whole system operates more efficiently as a result. And the same is true of your mind's {self}. When that {self} gets cleaned out and overwritten with new data, your mind operates at an efficiency level you forgot was even possible. Your imagination goes back to like it was when you were a child. Your thinking-out-of-the-box quotient goes through the roof. Creativity in solving business and life challenges gets increased dramatically. And you get a whole new lease on life, and a whole new level of command on happiness.

To better understand the deeper truth about your body, we should first look at how we all typically see our bodies so we can get a good picture of why we've missed this truth about our bodies our whole lives.

3 The Truth about Our Bodies

Take care of your body.
It's the only place you have to live.

—Jim Rohn

Who or what are you? Are you simply the culmination of your body or are you something more? This single question has plagued man for ages. And no wonder we haven't quite figured it out yet. Because starting from the time we're very young, we are told two completely contradictory tales about our bodies, and both stories get reinforced throughout our entire lives. The first story is that our bodies **are** who and what we are. The second story is that our bodies **are not** who and what we are.

The Message We Get That We <u>Are</u> Our Bodies

The first story of the body being who and what we are starts right after we're born. From the moment we enter the world, we experience our new environment through our body's senses. And the experience of our senses goes where our bodies go as we're carried around from place to place. So we unconsciously make a connection that our bodies are us and that we are our bodies. And these first experiences of sense help cement our physical bodies as the first and most indelible idea on our {self} maps—which, remember, is a definition required by the brain to fulfill its defense-of-{self} charter. But shortly thereafter, we also start to pick up language patterns, and our caregivers start pointing fingers and using different words for different things around the room. When they point or look at us, they use the word **you**, and they give other words to other things around us. So along with our sense-driven feelings about {self}, we also start building conscious ideas of {self}, and these conscious ideas reinforce that our bodies are a large portion of that definition.

This body-as-{self} thing is why later in life, when you see a baseball come flying toward your head, or when I do something stupid like knock a sharp knife off my kitchen counter, letting it fall pointy-edge down toward my bare feet, our bodies freak out a bit with fear and react involuntarily. There's an "oh shit" moment. One half of our Equation of Emotion gets filled with the EP that the body be held at status quo or better, and the other half is filled with a Perception that a threat to the body exists in that moment. And so, true to our definition of fear, and true to how quickly our limbic system takes control of our bodies, we uncontrollably jump a little in reaction to the threat we perceive to our {self} map item of {our body}. Your head ducks out of the way of the baseball, or I pull a muscle in my back trying to jerk my feet out of the way of the falling knife. And those reactions start from the day we're born. There's even a {self}-preserving reaction called the moro reflex you can get brand-new babies to do when they are just minutes old where they flail their arms out away from their bodies to catch themselves if you drop them. (Author's disclaimer: Please do not drop newborn babies to test this. Go watch the videos on the Internet of the moro reflex in action. They actually let the baby fall backward from a sitting position, catching them at the last split second.)

The body-as-{self} story gets reinforced our whole lives. We differentiate between race and skin color, boys and girls, tall and short, fat and thin, etc. We learn to treat people differently based on their physical traits; revering people with superior athletic talents, and politely ignoring people with physical or mental disabilities. In school, the questions we ask as we socialize reinforce the idea that we are defined by the characteristics and actions of our bodies until our body differences create alterations in our personal identities. "How well did you do on the math test?" "Did you guys win that game last night?" Do you think he's ugly or cute?" "Did anyone say yes to going to the dance with you?" Our physical characteristics play into all these answers. Then right about the time we hit middle school Health class, we learn about the brain – another part of the human body. We learn that the brain creates our personality, our intelligence level, and controls the physical capabilities of our body. And because the brain is a part of our body, the message that the body is the culmination of who and what we are is reinforced.

But the reinforcement of this body-as-{self} idea doesn't stop there. Even as adults, our vocabulary as a society perpetuates the idea that our bodies are who and what we are. We hear messages about body weight, hair loss, sexual performance... you name it. "Are **you** fat? Are **you** bald? Can **you** perform sexually? Are **you** at risk of a heart attack? Tonight at 11." These "you" questions are actually questions about our bodies. More accurate questions would be, "Does your body have extra fat stored in it," "Has your body started losing its hair," "Is your body still interested in sexual intercourse," or "Is your body at risk for having a coronary episode?" But by the time we start to hear these "you" messages, we have accepted the fact that we are quantified as everything within the confines of our skin, so we don't even notice the blurring of the lines. Thus, our bodies, and all subsequent ideas about our bodies, become a large item placed right onto the very center our {self} maps. We simply overlook the use of the identity word you when someone is talking about our bodies, because at that point, we've completely swallowed the body-is-the-end-all-be-all-of-existence story hook, line, and sinker.

The Message We Get That We <u>Are Not</u> Our Bodies

The powerfully and constantly reinforced message that we **are** our bodies stands in complete contradiction to the second story we're told about our bodies. This second story tells us we **are not** our bodies, and this story comes from science, religion, and also our bodies themselves.

It's estimated through global polling data that almost 85 percent of us have some sort of faith component connected to a belief in some type of higher power or intelligence in the universe. And whether we're fond of a particular religion or just generically spiritual, a belief in God, or a higher intelligence denotes a belief that we may have some sort of spiritual component which transcends the body in some fashion. So we're not really surprised when we hear from our churches, mosques, and synagogues that our body is just a shell to carry around a portion of us called our soul or spirit. This suggests we are not our bodies, and that when our bodies die, our spiritual portion of our existence goes off to some better place (hopefully), leaving our bodies to rot and be consumed by the Earth. And sometimes our bodies even reinforce this message, presenting experiences that make us feel there is more to our personal existence. They suggest that there's something spiritual about us. We call these spiritual or mystical experiences, where we seem to feel connected to the world and the universe in ways that transcend the body. Science calls these unitive experiences. Surveys show that well over a third of us naturally have unitive experiences that make us feel like there is more to the universe and our personal existence than just our bodies. And well over two thirds of us report having felt the presence of another consciousness around us at some point in our lives.

Now, what science tells regarding these two stories is interesting, because it suggests both that we are our bodies, and also suggests we are more than our bodies.

The Message We Get from Science About Our Bodies

No, science hasn't yet completely proven there is more to our personal lives than our bodies themselves (although science may be well on its way to doing just that, which we will discuss later), but the vocabulary science uses about the body certainly supports the idea that your body is not you. When science speaks about your body, it speaks of organs and functions. It speaks of systems and subsystems. It speaks of structures and autonomic actions. The vocabulary you are taught to use when speaking about your human body talks about your body like it's a machine. The heart pumps blood, the lungs infuse oxygen, and our livers - well, our livers do whatever our livers do. (Our livers metabolize and remove toxins, but you get the joke.) These type of statements might be easily equated to how you might explain the functions of your automobile's various parts. The fuel injectors disperse the gasoline into the cylinder. The exhaust pipes carry the waste out of the system. The computer controls the automatic functions of the car. And this thing honks the horn. Beep. Parents tend to press on the end of your nose when making this sound. Beep.

So if your body is a machine with parts that serve specific functions, as the vocabulary of science suggests, doesn't that fit the narrative that your body is just a wheelbarrow to carry around your spirit? It does. To be fair, many scientists say there is no evidence to support we are anything more than our bodies, and it's their position that all these autonomic systems are the end-all-be-all of what we are, and when they stop, we stop. We'll discuss some new developments in science later which refute this position, but for now, let's stay on task.

So... we are told two stories about our bodies by the world. Which one of them is true? The true story about our bodies is more mind blowing than we could possibly imagine.

The Truth About Your Body

Knowing the truth about your body is important for you, because the biggest part of your mind's false {self} is filled by your physical body and its sensory and thought input. Having a better understanding of the deep truth about your body gives you a better idea about whether or not your body should hold such a large spot on your {self} map. So let's take a closer look at your body and how it works, to help you decide if it should remain in so much control of your {self} map.

In our everyday lives, our senses constantly tell us that our bodies are the lion's share of our existence. When we look in the mirror, we see ourselves, right? We see our arms, our legs, our torso, our face, etc. Behind our face we don't actually see our brain, but we know it's in there somewhere, and science tells us that the brain makes us who we are, right? When we move our bodies, our eyes and our very perspective on the entire world moves right along with our body? All that evidence piled up suggests we must be our bodies.

Even if we try to believe there's something more to that picture, when teachers tell us of a soul, or spirit, or true Self, or whatever term we want to use that day, our brain says, "Nuh-uh! The body is **it**. The body is our {self}. Well, okay. . . our body is **one** of our {self} items, along with all the other ideas we've connected with since... along with our religion, and politics, and opinions, and favorite color. Sure... okay... maybe those other {self} items are a bit malleable, and we can talk about changing our politics some day, or maybe even consider loosening our grasp on the belief our religion is the only path to God. We potentially can change those things from time to time as humans. But we're not gonna be changing bodies anytime soon. So the body is definitely {self}. **Definitely!**" And in hearing that message over and over through our mind's eye, through our emotions, and through our thoughts, our brain becomes that lying politician who repeats a lie so often that we start to believe it. Because we believe it, we start retelling this story to each other, and to our children as they grow up, perpetuating the myth.

But the truth about our bodies is much stranger than the fiction. The fact is that our bodies may themselves be conscious at more levels than we can imagine.

The Consciousness of Our Bodies

In our daily lives, we do not think of our bodies as living creatures. Our bodies are just who we are. We ignore the fact that our body is made up of cells that are alive, so that we never have to face questions like, "Just how alive are they? Do our cells have feelings? Does my body have a separate consciousness than that of my own?" And "If I get plastic surgery or liposuction, could that be considered murder of my cells?"

Seriously though, there is a deep question we do need to ask here, and it has a rather substantial basis in science to support asking it.
That question: "Is there a greater intelligence within my body than the one I perceive as my intelligence?"

It's very easy for us to ignore the fact our body is a bunch of little individual creatures. But ignoring it does not make the truth go away, and in fact if we're on the search within path, we need to take a peek at the pieces that come together within to make us human, and specifically, the conscious intelligence that exists within those pieces.

The fact is that your body is a living conscious entity. It is made up of billions of living creatures. What's more is that those creatures exhibit behaviors that suggest they have their own consciousness, separate of your own. Did you think you were the only consciousness that existed in connection with your body? No, your consciousness is not the only one in there, and we don't have to look very far for proof.

Early on in Volume 1, we did a quick exercise to imagine an elephant, then we made that elephant pink with purple polka dots. And although we'd like to think we just did all that when we saw that pink elephant with purple polka dots, we didn't do any of that heavy lifting. So what provided that image of our pink elephant with purple polka dots in our brains? To answer our own question, what did that was another level of consciousness. It was a level of consciousness sitting right below our waking consciousness that retrieved the image of an elephant, and asked other even lower levels of consciousness to then retrieve the ideas and memories that helped paint that elephant pink and put purple polka dots on it. Psychology doesn't even argue about us having multiple levels of consciousness in our brains. In that discussion, we spoke about the split brain patients that prove the phenomena. The whole science of psychology is based on the study of our multiple levels of consciousness. It's where our creativity comes from. It's where our dreams come from. Scientists have even seen multiple levels of consciousness happening live on brain scanners while performing experiments.

A study done at Carnegie Mellon University showed our multiple levels of consciousness at work under a brain scanner. The study asked participants to make some decisions about cars and other items they were presented with while in an fMRI. But before they were able to make the decisions, the study participants were distracted by a number memorization task they were asked to perform first. The numbers task required the participants' full attention. But the brain scans showed that both the regions associated with the numbers task, and the regions associated with making the decision were firing away simultaneously, working on their respective challenges. The waking mind was on the numbers task. The decision-making task had been taken over by their subconscious mind, aka another level of consciousness. And here's the amazing part: When their subconscious mind was in control of the decision making task in comparison to a control group who maintained a constant focus on the decision task, the study participants who were forced to hand the decision process to their subconscious mind made **better** decisions than the folks who made their decisions without much subconscious input. So the lower levels of consciousness proved **smarter** than our waking consciousness.

Please ignore for a moment that you may not even be the smartest person in your own head. We'll come back to that later as we discuss how to supercharge our brains for optimal output. For now let's stick with the discussion about our multiple levels of consciousness.

So how deep does our consciousness rabbit hole go? We perceive our top-level consciousness, as the consciousness with which we see the world, which we call our mind, and which most of us identify as us. We certainly have multiple levels of consciousness below our top level consciousness, that we call subconscious activity. Science proves that. But where is the bottom rung on that consciousness ladder in our bodies? Where do your multiple levels of consciousness stop as we dig down deeper into your mind and into your body? Do your individual cells themselves have some sort of limited consciousness? Is there a subset of consciousness in the group of cells that beat your heart, or digest your food, or that constrict your pupils when you walk outside into the bright sunlight?

Doctors and other scientists would classify many of our cellular actions as "autonomic" or "involuntary" functions, carried out by the lesser life-forms of cells and cell clusters. They would testify that those functions are directed by electrochemical stimulation provided by the nervous system. "The body just does it. It's programmed to do so. We do not have conscious control of those functions," they say. But what doctors and scientists will not tell you is that both autonomic and involuntary are words we invented to fit a narrative hypothesis about our bodies that has never been proven.

At some point in our history, when the scientists of yesterday were posed with the questions "what makes our heart beat" and "why do our pupils constrict," and "why does the leg jerk when the patella tendon is whacked with a rubber mallet," they didn't know the answers. But rather than admit that they didn't know, which would have been a devaluation to their title of {doctor}, and which then opens up a can of worms about the potential for cellular intelligence and even cellular consciousness, they made up some words that could mask the fact that they didn't know. We still use this same vocabulary today so we don't have to address the fact that these "autonomic" and "involuntary" functions are actually actions initiated by a form of intelligent life that is simply beyond our conscious control. And make no mistake, our cells are very intelligent life-forms. They are so intelligent in fact, it turns out that the nerve cells in our skin can actually do geometry.

Scientists once believed that the nerve cells in your skin were simple signal processors. When something touched your skin, your nerve cells would send a signal that they were being touched, and your brain would collect all the different signals from the nerve cells in that area of contact and figure out the particulars of the object touching the skin, such as shape, temperature, texture, etc. But researchers at the Department of Integrative Medical Biology at Umeå University recently discovered that beyond just when and how intensely something has come in contact with your skin, your skin's nerve cells also perform the geometry to figure out an object's shape and potentially its texture before sending its signals to your brain that something has touched your skin. The cells in your skin talk to each other, performing the same type of calculations done by neurons in your cerebral cortex.

I think that's crazy cool. But there's more:

If the object in question is hot enough to burn your skin, such as when you accidentally place your hand on a hot stove, the message of pain only makes it to your backbone before a nerve cell in the spine initiates a command to start moving muscles in your arm to remove the hand from the heat. In other words, the message of pain never makes it to your brain before the hand starts moving. That body movement command is being given outside of your conscious control. In that situation, beyond any trickery of scientific vocabulary, a living cell in your backbone gets the message that other living cells in your hand are being hurt, and makes the decision to tell the muscles (other living cells) to move your hand away from the heat. Neither you, nor your brain, ever gets a chance to weigh in before your hand starts moving. That deliberate action without your conscious input denotes a decision-making ability by that little cell (or committee of cells) which preempts your own decision making process, thus proving that there is some kind of independent intelligence at work within the cells themselves.

So your body's individual cells are pretty smart cookies, and may well be conscious, making intelligent decisions based on information they have evolved to perceive. But evidence of consciousness may not be limited to just human cells, and if that's true, it would certainly support our human cells are probably conscious. One of the most interesting cases of cells utilizing intelligence to take seemingly conscious action is found outside our bodies. It's called a slime mold.

The Consciousness of Slime Molds

Slime molds are just plain weird. But they're weird in a really interesting way. They're a type of slimy mold (hence the name) that's actually made up of hundreds to millions of single-celled amoebae who simply decide to join together to form a larger organism so they can work together to find food. This group of single celled amoebae then start communicating, which allows individuals in the group to take on different roles in the greater slime mold colony, even though they all have the same exact DNA. They even go as far as to form multicellular reproductive structures, otherwise known as internal organs.

A bunch of single celled amoeba do this.

Without any type of brain or nervous system, these little guys migrate around to find food, utilizing memory that science suggests they cannot possibly have, to accomplish never traveling to the same place twice to find food. Furthermore, depending on the colony's needs, the individual single cell organisms perform unique functions for the group once they join the party. One percent of the amoebae even turn into police, crawling through the greater structure searching for infectious bacteria, consuming that harmful bacteria, then dropping out of the slime mold taking the pathogen with them. This results in the police amoeba's death because they die of the infection they've swallowed, but the larger colony continues on. This is the equivalent of a single amoeba in a slime mold jumping on a grenade to save everyone else. **This is altruism at a cellular level.**

One of the most interesting studies done on these single-celled organisms showed just how smart single cells can be. It came from simply laying out some piles of oatmeal. In 2010, mathematical biologist Toshiyuki Nakagaki of Hokkaido University in Japan laid out oatmeal for a yellow species of slime mold called Physarum polycephalum. He laid the piles out according to where the population centers were located around the city of Tokyo, in ratios that were relative to the populations in those areas. Then he let the slime mold go to work. Within about a day, the slime mold had built tunnels to ferry the oatmeal nutrients around to different parts of the larger organism. The amazing result was that the design the slime mold came up with very closely mimicked the Japanese railway system that humans and computers had designed to ferry people from population center to population center. The kicker was that the differences the slime mold created in its network as compared to the actual railway system, turned out to be **more efficient** than the design the computers and human engineers actually built. So it turns out that, before building the railway system, the engineers should have asked the slime mold first. Slime molds have traveled the Earth for over a billion years, and are still blowing researchers' minds with every study they conduct. To some degree, they act like our human societies do on a much smaller scale.

Of course, this single cell communication ability and intelligence shouldn't come as a surprise to us. Bruce Lipton is a developmental biologist who did a lot of work with stem cell research in the late 80's and early 90s at Stanford University's Medical Center. He wrote a book called "The Wisdom of Our Cells", where he explained how intelligent our single cells actually are. He was one of the group of researchers who helped prove that our human stem cells can become whatever cell they need to be, based on the communication they receive through the cell walls, as instructed by the other cells communicating with it.

This is the type of amazing intelligence that exists at a cellular level in your body. Now, let's go a little deeper to see if we can gain access to some of that intelligence.

The Prodigious Savants

Within our human bodies, cellular intelligence levels go can exponential rather quickly. Derek Amato used to be an average, run-of-the-mill sales guy. Now, he is what science calls a prodigious savant. A prodigious savant is someone with a skill level equivalent or greater than that of a prodigy. Dr. Darold Treffert, a psychiatrist with over fifty years of study on Savant Syndrome, and a consultant for the Hollywood movie "Rain Man", estimates that there are fewer than fifty prodigious savants in the world. Treffert said in a video interview done in 2013, "Some savants are congenital savants. That is, the disorder is present from birth and emerges in childhood or adolescence. In other cases, the acquired savant are [. . .] normal individuals who are typical persons who after some central nervous system incident, such as a head injury or a stroke, have the emergence of some dormant capacity, sometimes at a prodigious level, again, usually in art or music or math, which was not present before."

And that is exactly what happened to Derek Amato. Derek Amato became a prodigious savant in October of 2006 after he missed a diving catch for a football in the shallow end of a swimming pool and smacked his head into the side of the pool, suffering a major concussion. Just five days after he suffered his head injury, Derek discovered he could play the piano. He could play despite never having taken one piano lesson in his lifetime and never having touched a single piano. Today, he can play seven different instruments at different levels of proficiency. But on the piano, he's a natural. In a video done about his newfound talents on YouTube, he spoke of the first time he was exposed to a piano keyboard after the accident, when he visited a music room in his friend's house. "He had this little Casio keyboard, and I just felt for some reason I had to touch it," Derek said. "I felt this energy from this silly musical instrument which simply drew me. And I sat down, after he sat down and took a break, and I just started going. My hands seemed to be doing things I had no idea of, and I had never played a piano. I had never taken piano lessons as a child."

But not only could Derek play the piano, his brain was actually composing complex pieces of music non-stop at speeds that were faster than his hands were able to keep up with.

> I walk every step through my life now with a symphony going on. It's almost as if they're playing for me. It's like every moment I have this beautiful symphony composing in my mind. About two to three weeks [. . .] after I first discovered I could play, then it started making sense, and these shapes, these squares [. . .] they're little tiny black and white squares that go left to right, and it's like a ticker tape [. . .] I always tell everybody, like right now while we're talking, they're going, even during conversation. So I'm hearing this beautiful symphony during our conversation. At the same time, I'm working. I can't catch it all. I can't capture it all.

And these examples of next level cellular intelligence are all over the place.

In India, there lived a woman named Shakuntala Devi, who was a writer and mental mathematics calculator. She could calculate very large numbers in her head without any effort at all. The answers just came to her. In 1977, she was tested at SMU by being asked to give the twenty-third root of a 201-digit number. It took her fifty seconds to answer the question (the answer was 546,372,891). The answer itself had to be confirmed by a Univac computer, for which a special program had to be written. In 1980, she correctly calculated the multiplication of two thirteen-digit numbers that were picked at random by the computer department at Imperial College in London. The answer, somewhere in the neighborhood of 19 septillion, a twenty-six-digit number, was correct, and made the Guinness Book of World Records. In 1988, she traveled to UC Berkeley to have a professor of psychology test her talents. She calculated the cube root of 61,629,875 and the seventh root of 170,859,375 before the professor could even finish copying the large numbers into his notebook. (She answered 395 and 15 respectively.) Devi had no formal education. She was raised as the daughter of a circus performer, becoming a sideshow act at a very young age because of her amazing natural abilities. We call these "natural abilities," when in actuality, they are the activity of our cells solving problems at a much higher proficiency level than we can even comprehend.

Then there's the story of Srinivasa Ramanujan, a man from a poor province in India who had no formal training in mathematics. He changed mathematics as we know it in the early 1900's, individually compiling nearly 3,900 different mathematical identities and equations. He made major contributions to number theory, math analysis, continued fractions, and infinite series, which are all extremely advanced mathematical concepts. His insights into mathematics, most of which would later be proven correct, allowed him to fill three notebooks with mathematical theories based on his own inventions, far advanced from those of the leading European mathematicians of the time. After his death, a fourth notebook was discovered with mathematical theories that even today are being used to explain the activity of black holes.

Where did Ramanujan's discoveries come from? Did they come from his hard work studying previous math discoveries and expanding on them? No. They came to him spontaneously, seemingly out of an intelligence that was much greater than a normal human's intelligence level. They came through him rather than from him. Ramanujan himself gave the credit for his discoveries to being in close contact to what he perceived as God. Of his amazing discoveries, he once said, "An equation for me has no meaning unless it expresses a thought of God." In reality, Ramanujan's discoveries came from the activity and intelligence of his body's cells, which, as we will discuss soon, does not take Ramanujan's God out of the equation for his amazing discoveries. Stay tuned for that discussion. Later in the book, I'm going to spill the beans on how you can get in touch with that crazy level of genius that helped Ramanujan change the world.

From these few examples, it's clear that the highest level of intelligence on Earth isn't really ours, but more accurately belongs to the cellular consciousness operating under the covers of our waking consciousness. When we ask our brain for answers, the answers we receive in our minds don't come from our top level consciousness, they are presented to our top level consciousness from somewhere below our top level consciousness, gift-wrapped with a nice little bow. And according to studies, the more our subconscious gets to weigh in on our decisions, the better decisions we make.

So what can we do with this realization that there is an amazing amount of intelligence within us underneath and separate to that of our waking consciousness? We can move ourselves closer to that intelligence by becoming more in tune with that intelligence through our bodies. This may bring us closer to that same intelligence and make us smarter ourselves. It's a scientific fact that higher emotional intelligence, which is simply a higher level of understanding the operations and reactions of our bodies, has indeed been linked to higher IQ. And a longitudinal study on meditation's affects on intelligence showed that meditators were able to significantly increase intelligence markers over that of a control group during a two-year study. Meditation is all about getting more in touch with the body. So if you want to increase your overall intelligence, maybe you need to be digging deeper into the intelligence of your body. Maybe? Maybe.

And maybe, just maybe, we need to consider that there's a lot more to the story of who and what we are than we've been told.

4 Your Mind Body Connection

When you look at yourself in a mirror,
do you like what you see, or do you
judge your body and use the word
to tell yourself lies?
If you believe that you are not
attractive enough, then you believe a lie,
and you are using the word against
yourself, against the truth.

—Don Miguel Ruiz

We ended the last chapter with a discussion about getting in touch with a higher intelligence within you that is available from different levels of consciousness beyond your waking consciousness. We'll pick up that discussion again soon. First, let's consider the scientific proof that connecting with our bodies does indeed have proven benefits. The fact is that both your mind and your body benefit from a stronger coupling, and science suggests that we all can be healthier people when we intentionally bridge this waking consciousness/body consciousness gap.

Every year, pharmaceutical companies spend billions of dollars attempting to do only one thing; beat the placebo effect. And they are having really big issues with accomplishing that goal. It's the single biggest business challenge of the entire pharmaceutical industry. Half of all clinical trials now are failing because the drug being tested can't beat placebo. The placebo effect is our body's ability to heal itself when we believe we are receiving some type of medicine, even though in reality what we're being given is the equivalency of a sugar pill with no medicinal effect. We don't receive any real medicine, but our body responds like we did. The results can often be what medical science considers miraculous.

This is an excerpt from an article written by science writer (with a neuroscience specialty) Sandra Blakeslee in the New York Times:

> But now scientists, as they learn that the placebo effect is even more powerful than anyone had been able to demonstrate, are also beginning to discover the biological mechanisms that cause it to achieve results that border on the miraculous. Using new techniques of brain imagery, they are uncovering a host of biological mechanisms that can turn a thought, belief or desire into an agent of change in cells, tissues and organs. They are learning that much of human perception is based not on information flowing into the brain from the outside world but what the brain, based on previous experience, expects to happen next.

So . . . going off-script for a second . . . let's take a moment to notice that the Equation of Emotion variable of Expectation/Preference described in Volume I, and recapped in Chapter 1 of this book, is now linked to our body's health outcomes. Okay, onward.

So the placebo effect is caused by what we believe will happen in our bodies as a result of receiving medical treatment. Unfortunately, this also applies to the negative outcome side as well. Studies have shown that people who are told about negative side effects of a drug, but who are then given a placebo, can literally develop the side effect symptoms from taking a pill with no active ingredients, including actually developing hives on their skin. And numerous medical anecdotes include stories of people who have died, presumably because they believed they would, when it was later found they didn't actually have the life threatening illness or condition for which they were diagnosed. It's a fact that women who believe they are prone to heart disease are four times as likely to die than those who don't have the same belief. Regardless of the positive or negative outcome, however, both outcomes are the body's cells reacting to ideas that are introduced by our waking consciousness, which gives the body something it needs to heal or harm itself, without outside intervention. The power of the mind in relation to our bodies' health is substantial.

Dr. Lissa Rankin wrote a book called "Mind Over Medicine" in which she spoke in depth about the placebo effect. Among the various studies she cited regarding placebo, nearly half of asthma patients got relief from using a fake inhaler. More than half of people experiencing ulcer pain found their pain alleviated after taking a placebo. Forty percent of couples suffering infertility got pregnant when taking placebos. And when compared to morphine, one of the strongest pain killers we have, placebos were found to be almost as effective as a real pill when treating pain. Our body's ability to heal itself through the belief circuits of our mind is so powerful that the clinical coordinators of the drug studies done by the pharmaceutical industry are now going well out of their way to attempt to remove placebo friendly folks from their drug trials. They intentionally prescreen people by giving everyone a placebo during a washout phase of the trial. Anyone who has a positive reaction to the placebo is handed their hat on the way out the door and excluded from the study. By doing this, they are intentionally removing people from the drug trials who they think might respond to placebo, which might certainly skew the results toward getting their chemical mixture approved because it beats the placebo effect. And drug companies are keeping all this secret. They refuse to release placebo statistics. Personally, I call that action bullshit, and consider it cheating science, and thus not science at all. I don't think you should be able to weed out people who are likely to respond to placebo, because those people make up the general population, and they are representative of what the doctors are dealing with at the hospital or at their office.

Can the Body Heal Itself?

Setting my personal opinion aside, the fact remains that the mind's influence over the body is substantial enough that it is the main pain point for a multibillion-dollar pharmaceutical industry. So much, that they go out of their way to control for it. An obvious question might be, since there is a proven mechanism within the body that allows the body to heal itself, is there a way to access that mechanism consciously to heal the body willfully when we fall ill? Or better yet, is there a way to get in such a good state of communication with our bodies, or into such a high state of mindful well-being, that we don't get sick to begin with? Science shows that things that get us in better communication with our bodies and which raise our standard measurements of well-being, such as meditation, do increase our immune system responses. One study showed an increased immune system response in subjects after just eight hours of meditation training in people new to meditation. The meditation group was intentionally exposed to a weak flu virus at the end of the training versus a control group who didn't receive the meditation training. Not only did the meditators build up more antibodies against the virus in their blood, fewer of them got sick from the flu, compared to those in the control group, most of whom wound up getting the sniffles.

It's clear that our cells work better when we reach out to make better conscious connections with them. That means there's extra activity going on at the cellular level because of our conscious and subconscious thoughts. To me, as a fan of science and also common sense, that extra cellular activity denotes that consciousness exists at some pretty deep levels into our body's cellular structures. Do a search on YouTube for "White Blood Cell Chases Bacteria" for a video of a white blood cell chasing down a pathogen in a manner that is clearly intentional. Some scientists uncomfortable with this cellular consciousness conversation might say those cells are simply following chemical markers, responding to their internal programming and genetic charter. But what are you and I doing when we go grab a burrito for lunch but following chemical markers (yummy smells emanating from the burrito shop), and responding to our internal programming and genetic charter (eating said burritos so as to perpetuate {self})? Yeah, so maybe our cells are following chemical markers to fulfill their genetic charter, but that doesn't mean they're also not conscious.

Arguments for cellular consciousness are found literally everywhere in the world where living organisms can be found. Science has proven that simple-celled organisms, such as plants, talk to each other, exchanging information, and even sharing resources intentionally. Fungus cells, such as mycelium, communicate with one another, passing information and resources along biological infrastructures that can stretch thousands of miles. In 2009, Bonnie Brasler gave a TED Talk about how bacteria talk to each other in their own chemical language to perform hundreds of different collective functions that one bacteria could not accomplish alone. She spoke of how they even vote on what to do in certain circumstances, following the consensus of the group once the decision is made. They studied a number of different types of bacteria, looking for variances in communication behavior. In her talk she said, "So now what we understand is that all bacteria can talk to each other. They make chemical words, they recognize those words, and they turn on group behaviors that are only successful when all of the cells participate in unison."

It is very easy for us, as members of a race that is overly comfortable in thinking that humans are the ultimate and most intelligent species in the universe, to say the cellular behaviors of our bodies are no more than autonomic processes, or through more diligent minutiae, explain their behavior as reactions to certain chemical environmental variables. In short, it's easy for us say that cells have no individual intelligence, wisdom, or consciousness. But all the scientific evidence points to the contrary; that our cells are indeed conscious. And science also shows that when our higher consciousness, intentions, and expectations get communicated to that consciousness, it can affect the health outcomes of our cells, through the placebo effect, both positively and negatively. So maybe we should look at exploring and strengthening that conscious connection. Maybe? Maybe.

So Are Your Cells Really Conscious?

We can certainly say your cells are intelligent, but what defines consciousness and what makes it possible for your cells to be considered conscious? Spoiler alert: I'm soon going to discuss some pretty cool science that reveals our cells can indeed be considered conscious, and how physical science even connects our cells with a physical mechanism that can source that consciousness. But let's first consider the arguments against the idea of cellular consciousness, just to be thorough and to show how those arguments are flawed.

We need to acknowledge that there is a small group of scientists who believe that consciousness itself doesn't actually exist. In addition, another group of scientists simply hate talking about consciousness - they see it as a topic of non-science. Personally, I see that as a position of non-**sense**.

The reason I think scientists like to deny consciousness and don't like to have conversations about it is because science doesn't yet have the big picture on consciousness figured out, and scientists hate not being able to explain shit. Typically, scientists have an aversion to talking about things they can't measure. As of yet, we can't measure consciousness, or even define what it is. It's for this reason that I think many scientists like to shoehorn consciousness into smaller pre-existing boxes that suggest consciousness is an illusion of other smaller systems, that it really doesn't exist at all, and that it's simply a product of human behavior or an emergent property.

John Searle, a professor of philosophy at the University of California, Berkeley, and one of the world's leading thinkers regarding consciousness, gave an informative TED Talk about consciousness where he refuted all the various arguments that suggest our consciousness doesn't exist. In this talk, he took apart the arguments of behaviorism, which he called one of the biggest embarrassments to science en masse, and he refuted the idea that consciousness falls outside the bounds of science or that it's somehow separate from us in some way. One of the most convincing and humorous examples he gave was when he pointed out the playful argument against the idea that a spiritual consciousness couldn't possibly interact with the physical world. He said, "You wanna see spirituality move something? Watch! I decide consciously to raise my arm (which he said as he started to raise his left arm), and the damn thing goes up." He then went on to explain how many of the various arguments against consciousness are an embarrassment to science. We won't recount the points he made in that video. You can go argue with Professor Searle at Berkeley if you disagree. If that's your goal, I suggest you pack a lunch. Beyond all the philosophical arguments, however, to me the best argument for consciousness is that you are reading this book, and that if I asked you right now if you were conscious you'd probably say yes. But something you should know and consider is that there are some materialist reductionists who would argue with you that you aren't conscious at all.

Materialist reductionists believe that all our behaviors and everything we do are simply a result of a number of happy accidents in physics which piled up to ultimately become humanity. They claim these happy accidents cause our evolution. I believe they come to this conclusion because of a deep misunderstanding of physics, and a deep misunderstanding of consciousness, both of which then collide and cause the materialist reductionists to accidentally hijack the reality of evolution by attaching its activity with the wrong driving mechanism.

Let's back up a second and sort out where science went wrong on our human evolution.

Misunderstanding Evolution

Evolution is a scientifically proven phenomenon, and it obviously has had a huge hand in who and what you have become as a human being. (And by the way, that does not mean God doesn't exist, if you're a spiritual person. And it doesn't mean God didn't create you, either. Stay with us.) That said, I believe there's a big misunderstanding about evolution. The typical evolutionist boils down evolution as the result of atoms banging into each other in ways that things just accidentally happen, including the creation of life here on Earth. Their theory is that after billions of years of atoms banging into each other, life naturally sprang forth and became more complex over time. On Earth, life walked out of the muck and changed randomly over time. Life-forms who experienced spontaneous changes that were conducive to survival went on to mate and continued evolving. The life-forms that experienced spontaneous changes that weren't conducive to survival got killed off, usually winding up as something else's lunch. But from the materialist reductionist's eyes, all the changes were random, caused by atoms banging into each other and mutating our DNA.

Thus, from this perspective, our human bodies and behaviors are all just the result of spontaneous random changes that have slowly occurred throughout the history of the Earth. We humans are simply one of the lucky chains of happy accidents that survived. Our developed human behaviors, which helped us survive along the way have made us the quirky humans we are. But beneath it all, we humans are just a gathering of atoms doing things that atoms do when left to chance. That internal feeling of consciousness we experience… that thing we call "us" . . . is just an accidental development that helped us survive along the way because if we feel we have a consciousness, that gives us the motivation to stay alive. But in reality, we're all just atomic robots wired by a large amount of happy accidents of physics. The fact that we enjoy our consciousness by having barbecues, making and listening to music, and having our earbuds plugged into our iPods while we walk around looking for the next barbecue; all that crap is just a happy side effect of the previous happy accidents of physics.

From my perspective, this intellectual position is a huge misunderstanding of what evolution is, how it works. And besides this misunderstanding now creating a huge false argument against anything we might consider spiritual, it glosses over the one huge mechanism which can better help us understand both evolution, and our human existence as a whole. Evolution is **not** just a bunch of random happy accidents. In actuality, it's an intelligent process intertwined with our cells' consciousness.

Evolution and the Memory of Your Cells

First, let's restate that evolution is real. Evolution within cells has been proven in labs at Michigan State University and now in many other labs around the world. We regular non-scientists can see evolution happening by simply observing that the flu virus mutates every year in its attempts to stay ahead of the flu vaccines we develop. It's a simple scientific fact that the environment outside our cells does create epigenetic changes in our cellular gene expression from generation to generation, and our cells then do change their activities as a result from one generation to the next. These changes are so dynamic that it's even been proven that **life**

memories can be passed down from one generation to multiple other generations through changes in our cells.

Researchers at Emory University exposed a set of mice to the scent of a certain chemical called acetophenone, which smells similar to cherries or almonds. While exposing the mice to this chemical, they administered painful electric shocks to those mice, which created a negative association to that particular smell. When the children of those mice were exposed to that same smell for the first time, without being shocked, they freaked out as if they were in danger just by experiencing the smell. An article from "Scientific American" reported on that study,

> Despite never having encountered acetophenone in their lives, the offspring exhibited increased sensitivity when introduced to its smell, shuddering more markedly in its presence compared with the descendants of mice that had been conditioned to be startled by a different smell or that had gone through no such conditioning. A third generation of mice—the "grandchildren"—also inherited this reaction, as did mice conceived through in vitro fertilization with sperm from males sensitized to acetophenone. Similar experiments showed that the response can also be transmitted down from the mother.

So this science is basically proof of **genetic memory**. It proves that the cellular responses of earlier generations do change the cellular and conscious responses of later generations. This provides a probable mechanism for the theory of behavioral evolution itself. Two cells come together to make a new baby mouse, which carries the emotionally charged memory of mom or dad getting shocked in the presence of a particular smell. And that same science showed that only one cell of the pairing needs the memory. The grandkids got the memory as well. That's crazy cool. The most recent research reveals that scientists have found this same genetic memory phenomenon lasting through sixteen generations in other multi-celled organisms.

But that type of change in behavior is not a happy accident form of evolution. That's a conscious action of those cells to record life experiences and pass down information in a way that increases the survival potential of later generations. Evolution, yes, but a conscious evolution, a conscious response process to an imbalanced Equation of Emotion in the mouse.

So bringing all this back to you, dear reader (because that's the cool part)…

Does this phenomenon of genetic memory apply to you as well as it does the mice? And if so, how far back can this type of genetic memory go in your brain? And how detailed are these memories within the coding of your cells themselves? Could Derek Amato's newfound piano talent, which came after hitting his head, be a product of his genetic memory? Is he a distant descendant of Mozart maybe? It's been proven that our human brain cells are much smarter than a mouse's brain cells, pound for pound.

Researchers at the University of Rochester Medical Center in New York replaced mice brain tissue with human brain tissue into living mice. They made creepy human-mouse hybrids. The human brain cells not only took over the mouse's brain, replicating from 300,000 to over 12 million, those mice wound up being a lot smarter than their mouse brained counterparts. The human-brained mice immediately asked for an upgrade in their living quarters, to include cable TV and individual iPad Minis. Okay, not quite. The human-brained mice weren't exactly doing physics. But their mouse-like behavior was superior in many respects of mouse-like intelligence, such as finding food in a maze and learning new skills. So could this difference in our brain cells being smarter mean our human genetic memories could be more detailed than being passed down the memory of Grandpa being scared from one of Grandma's particularly smelly farts?

The reason these questions are important (Grandma's farts notwithstanding) is because we need to acknowledge that our cells may be consciously storing pertinent information about life itself that we should be trying to gain access to. Because our evolution didn't occur through a bunch of happy accidents. It was an intelligent other-than-you consciousness that created, and continues to create, humanity. That's how we got here. And if we ever wanted to put the last nail in the coffin of accidental evolution to clear the way for consciousness to be our new origin story, science helps us do that too.

The Mysteries of DNA and the Real Driver of Evolution

The really powerful scientific fact that torpedoes the idea that evolution is random, is the simple fact that we, and all cellular life in general, have DNA. Our DNA strands are the instruction set our cells use to create and operate our bodies, including the complexity of our human brain, which is the most complex structure in the known universe. Our human DNA strands have over two billion lines of code. That's a super-complex mechanism of intelligence for evolution to have built alone. Dr. Francis Crick, who was a fan of evolution and who won the Nobel Prize for discovering DNA with his partner James Watson, once calculated the probability that our complex DNA could spontaneously form out of chance through evolution in the 4.5 billion years the Earth has been here. He admitted the chances of evolution creating DNA were similar to that of a tornado passing through a junkyard and leaving in its wake it perfectly assembled and functional jet airliner. So it's not at all likely our DNA could have developed into its current form without some kind of outside intelligent influence. So there's one solid argument against the happy accidents model.

Next, there's a big question that remains unanswered in the materialist reductionist theory of evolution in that it can't explain why life energy exists in the first place, and why dumb atoms build into more complex life organisms over time. What's the purpose? How do atoms slam together to the point where they start taking action that prolongs life? And not just random action, but continued action. I'm all for the possibility of happy accidents, and there may be a few happy accidents in our genetic history, but happy accidents don't just keep happening unless there's an underlying driver that keeps such complex processes such as life going. So what's the driver? What's the underlying mechanism? Materialist reductionists have not yet answered this question, and frankly, they never will if they stick with simple Newtonian physics (the physics of molecules and matter). The answer simply doesn't exist within the realm of Newtonian physics. It's impossible to explain the line of demarcation where dumb atoms start to take the seemingly conscious and nearly mathematically impossible pro-life action of becoming DNA and becoming living cells.

It's here that we are led right back to the existence of consciousness. Consciousness is one of the variables which can address the questions about our DNA, and the underlying mechanism that makes evolution more than a random process. If our cells have access to conscious intelligence, that could certainly explain how they make extremely intelligent decisions that then help create positive evolution. It could also explain from where our human consciousness springs, starting at the cellular level and building up through multiple levels of consciousness (which as we discussed in Volume I is a scientifically proven phenomenon at the levels of our conscious and subconscious minds). It would explain how our bodies react to our top level consciousness' beliefs, which then becomes the placebo effect. And it could certainly explain how leaps are made in human intelligence, such as the amazing human intelligence anomalies we discussed in Chapter 3. In short, if our cells are conscious, beyond changing what you've thought about your{self} your whole life, it would explain a lot of shit.

But we can't just leave it at 'if our cells are conscious'. Because by itself, this 'because; consciousness' answer is weak sauce. If we stopped here, it would simply be a cop-out answer to why everything happens within us, pointing to something we don't yet understand, very similar to what religious folks say when they try to explain stuff about life they can't explain and say, "because; God." So we're going to stop with the mere speculation. We're going to discuss the science that shows the hard link between our cells and the only bit of science that has been inextricably linked with consciousness (which by the way, may lead us right into a scientific explanation of God). And so… a bit deeper into the rabbit hole... we go. Right toward the door to enlightenment.

5 The Physical Link Between Your Cells and Consciousness

Think with the whole body.

—Taisen Deshimaru

As I shifted into second gear, my sleek red motorcycle felt like it was going to launch itself out from under me as I enjoyed the beautiful dance of internal combustion being translated into the torque that was now accelerating both of us quickly toward sixty miles per hour. I was returning from lunch on a lightly traveled side street of an industrial park in suburban Atlanta. I tried not to make it a habit of using excessive acceleration while riding in Atlanta traffic, mainly because Atlanta traffic is dangerous enough on a sport bike even without adding a speed factor. But sometimes when the conditions were right, I simply couldn't help it. Today, the conditions were perfect. It was a beautiful summer afternoon, and this road was designed for stealing a moment to experience the brute force acceleration this bike could generate. The road had only one driveway on it for about a half mile, and otherwise, was a straight shot to the next stop sign, and was usually completely deserted.

Before I tell you about the accident, which of course by this point you know is coming, I attribute my need for speed to my dad. He was a pilot in the military and a bit of a daredevil. He used to fly airplanes under electrical power lines, and bounced the plane's wheels off the tops of train boxcars. He told me all about doing hammerhead stalls, barrel rolls, snap rolls, and flying upside down in an open-air cockpit with a single seat belt to hold him from falling to his death. I never became an airplane pilot, but riding this particular sport bike seemed not too far off that mark. It was pure adrenaline. The police officer who showed up at the accident scene determined that speed was not a factor in this accident, but my love for the speed of that motorcycle certainly was, or I wouldn't have been riding it that day. Now to the accident . . .

As I crested the first hill that blocked the view to the rest of the road, I saw the single business park driveway which accessed this lonely stretch about 150 yards ahead in the distance. A car was entering the road, turning across my lane into the opposite lane. Business traffic. Crap. Time to slow my roll. I eased off the throttle and stopped accelerating the bike. It was a good decision. Behind the first car that pulled out, there were a couple other cars waiting to enter the roadway also. Oh well. I guess I wouldn't be experiencing the bike's raw acceleration into third gear on the way back from lunch after all.

As I coasted a bit and neared the driveway where the remaining cars were now moving forward toward the road, I watched for eye contact from the second driver. He was looking the other way to check for traffic coming from that direction, so I wasn't getting any eye contact from him. This made me nervous as I drew closer to his car. As a motorcycle rider, you're taught, and it's even somewhat instinctual, to watch for eye contact from other drivers to make sure they see you coming, even if you have the right of way, which I did. Regardless of traffic laws, one mistake from another driver could mean the end of your life on a motorcycle. So I was looking pretty intently for that eye contact.

As my bike approached the position where the road and driveway intersected, his car was still moving forward, and he was still looking the other way. "Look left. Look left!" I almost shouted it. He never looked left. I started to grab the brakes. Before I could do anything else, the car accelerated out into my lane before the driver ever turned his head to look in my direction. At the last second when he finally did look my way, and he saw the sleek red motorcycle that was now skidding into the side of his car, his eyes got as big as saucers. He tried to accelerate, but the front wheel of my motorcycle caught the back bumper of his car. The bike high-sided, and catapulted me like a rag doll, over the car's trunk and into the air. Fortunately, my body missed hitting the car itself, which probably saved my life. Unfortunately, the last thing I remember before waking up to the ambulance siren approaching was looking down at the pavement as I was traveling about forty miles per hour about ten feet above it, hearing my motorcycle bounce down the roadway behind me. My last thought was, "This is probably not going to end well."

When I came to, I opened my eyes and realized I was lying on my back on the hot pavement. I saw the beautiful sky, and some trees, and a lady leaning over me. She seemed to be looking right in my eyes, but I forgot that I had a tinted visor on my helmet, so when I opened my eyes she couldn't see that I'd opened them. When I moved my arm to open my visor and get some air, she nearly jumped out of her skin. "Oh my God, I thought you were dead," she said. "No, no. Don't move. The ambulance is here." "Ambulance? Oh yeah. I had a motorcycle accident."

As they loaded me into the ambulance, a police officer jumped in the back to ride along. Somewhere in the process, my wallet had been thrown from my pants pocket, and the officer wasn't sure who I was or even if I had a license. As I lay on the gurney on the way to the hospital, the officer was trying to fill out a report and get my information. "What's your name?" he asked. Oh, well, that's an easy question, I thought. I went to answer him, but when I went to that place in my mind where my name was held, it wasn't there. In that moment, I didn't have the slightest idea what my name was. "Um, wow! I don't know," I said. So he nodded and tried another question. "Do you know where you live?" I thought for a second. I couldn't remember that either. I shook my head in confusion. This blew my mind. "Where do I live? Who am I?" "Well, you were out for a bit," he said. "Give it a few minutes. Maybe it will come back to you."

During the ride to the hospital, the officer and I chatted about how people forget things after accidents. He seemed like a nice guy. He told me a couple stories. I felt like he was the type of guy I'd probably meet for beers after work. After a few minutes, I piped up with my name like it was the name of some trivia question answer I'd forgotten. "Sean," I exclaimed. "My name is Sean." He wrote it down. When we got to the hospital, another officer delivered my wallet and license to the first officer, since they'd been found at the scene of the accident. He filled out his report, handed my wallet to me, told me how to get a copy of the report for my insurance company, wished me well, and left.

After some X-rays, the doctor came in and gave me his assessment. "I looked at your helmet. It was scratched in six zones, so you should have a broken neck. You don't. From the eyewitness reports of the accident, you probably should have multiple broken bones, but all the X-rays we took were negative. You're built like a rock. You probably have a concussion, and you're definitely gonna be sore for a few days. Here's some Lortab. Go home and lie on the couch."

What was interesting to me was that by about an hour after the accident, I'd remembered everything about my life and most of what happened leading up to and directly following the accident, including the fact that my favorite motorcycle was now totaled. But directly following the accident, I could have told you none of it. Right after awakening from the crash, I had a sense of what it was like to be me, and overall I felt like the same person who is sitting here typing out these words, but I had no idea who I was beyond that moment. None of the ideas connected with my mind's {self} would come to me when I went mentally looking for them. I knew that I was the type of person who'd go have drinks with the officer assisting me, but I couldn't tell you the name of a single bar near my house. Or where my house was, for that matter. Or what color it was. Or even what city it was in.

So was I conscious in that ambulance? Yes. But how conscious was I? This very question outlines one of the big problems we have in discussions about consciousness. How do we measure or even define it?

**

We're presented with a rather big challenge in our efforts to uncover the deepest secrets of happiness by connecting with our multiple levels of consciousness when we look at our consciousness with a scientific eye. This is because the word consciousness applies to so many different facets of being alive and perceiving experiences. Discussions about consciousness can easily get confusing. Sometimes the term consciousness means being self aware. Sometimes it means knowing the subjective experience of our senses. Sometimes it just means not being asleep. When we're talking about our bodies and the operations of our bodies, however, there's a basic idea about consciousness that science is honing in on. It's an idea connected with the simple fundamentals that science often uses as a basic measuring stick of organic life. Here's the definition: Something can be said to be conscious if it has the ability to sense itself, perceive its surroundings, and make decisions based on those perceptions about its following actions.

I think this basic definition fits the experience of our daily waking consciousness. We can certainly sense ourselves. We can also sense what is going on around us. And it's true we can and do make decisions, based on those first two perceptions, about what we're going to do next. But what's cool is that this definition also explains the activity of the smaller organisms within us that create our body and thus help create our greater consciousness. Not surprisingly, this particular definition happens to be plucked from the world of biological science for something called **autopoiesis** (auto-po-ee-sis). Autopoiesis is the word used to explain the life-creating and life-perpetuating activity of our cells. But as we'll soon see, it turns out to be a pretty good definition for consciousness overall.

In Greek, the word auto means "self," and poieses means "creation" or "production." So together the single word autopoiesis means "self creation" or "self production." Dr. Neil Theise contributed to an amazing video on YouTube explaining autopoiesis by introducing the founders of the idea, Chilean biologists Maturana and Velara, and explaining their idea of autopoiesis in simple terms.

> They defined life using this approach that says something is alive that has a bounded structure, that has a porous membrane dividing inside and outside, that there are

processes of sensing what is outside, integrating that information, processing it, and then responding. And everything that's alive does that, whether it's a single celled organism, or something that's as complicated as us, or whales, or dolphins, or elephants, or ecosystems potentially.

He continued, "So they said wherever you find life you find mind. It's not about a nervous system, it's about being alive. And even a single cell has a very simple form of mind."

Dr. Theise went on to discuss his work in complexity theory and how smaller individual life-forms then self-organize into larger scale structures (like our friends the slime molds do to survive, and like the cells in our bodies do to survive). He made the comparison that cells self-organize into human bodies, human bodies self-organize into cities, cultures, and political systems, which then self-organize into societies and countries. He made parallel examples of this phenomenon happening everywhere in nature, with ants self-organizing into colonies, birds self-organizing into flocks, and fish self-organizing into schools, all acting together in unison to better serve the survival of the group. He said this type of blanket behavior implies that self-organizing systems can exist in hierarchies. After making this point, he shared the observation that our cells which self-organize into our human bodies are in turn made up of biomolecules that self-organize into our cells. And of course, biomolecules are just atoms which have self-organized into those molecules. And atoms themselves are made up of subatomic particles which have self-organized into the protons, neutrons and electrons of those atoms. And so on, and so on. So this pattern continues until we get down to the realm of quantum physics.

The reason this is important is because it's when we get down into realm of quantum physics that we find a science with a proven connection to consciousness.

The Quantum Physics Consciousness Connection

Normally, when you hear someone starting to talk about quantum physics and consciousness, you should probably get up and run as fast and far away as possible. That's because usually the person talking doesn't know much about consciousness or quantum physics, and thus doesn't know what the hell they're talking about. They are most likely either spewing some nonsense they've been told by someone else, they saw some ridiculous pseudoscientific video about it somewhere, or they've misinterpreted something they've read. Scientists call this going **woo-woo** because it's the sound people make when they board the crazy train. Pull on the train whistle: Woo-woo! We are not going woo-woo here. At least not entirely.

That said, when we invoke quantum physics into any discussion about consciousness, we are definitely wading into some pretty strange waters. And there is no way we can avoid wading into those waters. Because when we're faced with the pile of evidence which starts with (1) the curious existence of our own consciousness, (2) the fact that quantum physics is indeed inextricably linked with consciousness; (3) the undeniable observations that conscious life activity occurs in our bodies just above the molecular level; and (4) the issue that we can't identify exactly how, why, or where our seemingly dumb atoms come alive to create pro-life activities... given all those weird facts... we need to be open to the possibility that the mechanism for conscious life comes from below the level of the atoms themselves. Thus, bringing quantum physics into a discussion about consciousness isn't woo-woo. It's a required step in the scientific discovery process to understand something we don't yet understand. And as we'll will soon discuss, science is now proving that our human cells may have a direct link into the realm of quantum physics. But let's not get ahead of ourselves. First, let's back up a minute.

So what the hell is quantum physics?

What the Hell is Quantum Physics

If you've heard the words quantum physics before, but don't yet know anything about it, basically stated, quantum physics is the branch of physics that explains what goes on at the atomic particle level underneath the physical world of our universe. In comparison, Newtonian physics (aka classical physics) attempts to explain the realm of physical matter, like the stuff you can reach out and touch all around you right now. Quantum physics attempts to explain the invisible energies that become particles, which become atoms, which then create matter. With classical Newtonian physics, balls bounce, rain falls, and a farts can be lit on fire. With quantum physics, particle energy comes together to create the carbon and hydrogen atoms that can become the flammable ass-methane, but there's an additional catch in quantum physics. The carbon and hydrogens of the ass-methane molecule only come together if there's an observer around to observe it being lit. So without an observer, there is no fart to light on fire. Cue the frat party.

All joking aside, quantum physics is indeed that crazy. We'll touch on quantum activity a bit later in the book, but in general, quantum physics supposes, and proves, that quantum particles like photons and electrons can actually exist in two or more places at once, that they can disappear and reappear in different places instantly, and that these smallest of small energies can behave both like particles and like waves, depending on what you're looking for, and don't pick how they are going to act until you look. Quantum physics is so crazy weird, that quantum experiments have been proven to show their effects through impossible distances in space, and even backwards in time, where the result of the experiment was recorded **before the experiment had been completed**. And this kind of crazy time-traveling reaction held true with experiment conclusions, that even when after the result was recorded, the experiment in play was chosen randomly by a computer. And the prerecorded results match the outcome of the randomized experiment, backwards in time. Every. Single. Time. And continues to do so every time they do it. That's some crazy shit.

And before you actually say, "That's crazy," or "That's impossible," that's exactly what most quantum physicists say after they've concluded their experiments and look at the data. It caused Nobel physicist Neils Bohr to once remark, "Anyone not shocked by quantum mechanics has not understood it." Quantum physics is exactly that shocking because it deals with entangled particles that interact over infinite distances at speeds that Chinese scientists have estimated occur at over 10,000 times the speed of light, and which instead of choosing one or the other exclusive paths to a measurement device, choose both simultaneously. According to Newtonian physics, that's impossible. But it's child's play in quantum physics and happens every time certain experiments are performed. The science of quantum mechanics once caused quantum physicist Richard Feynman to say, "Do not keep saying to yourself, if you can possibly avoid it, 'But how can it be like that?' because you will go down the drain, into a blind alley from which nobody has yet escaped. Nobody knows how it can be like that."

The craziest part, however, is that quantum physics experiments have also proven conclusively that some type of conscious observer needs to be in the loop for the energies that create matter to even become matter at all. Quantum physics calls this "the collapse of the wave function by the observer". But what those fancy words boil down to is that if there is no observer around to observe these minuscule energies in action, they don't nail themselves down to doing any one thing in particular, opting instead to being all potential outcomes simultaneously, waiting to resolve to doing something until an observer becomes present and observes the outcome. It's only then that all the previous possibilities resolve to one cause and effect reality and history gets written backward in time to create the causes of how the outcome came into being. Otherwise stated, science has proven that for energies to be able to become something we consider real, an observer has to be around to see it, or it doesn't happen, and only when an observer is around to see it does reality actually become reality. And as much as there are a few physicists who would love to argue the semantics of the words I used there, theoretical physicist John Wheeler stated it plainly: "No microscopic property is a property until it is an observed property."

Nobel physicist Eugene Wigner said of this quantum physics connection with consciousness, "When the province of physical theory was extended to encompass microscopic phenomena, through the creation of quantum mechanics, the concept of consciousness came to the fore again. It was not possible to formulate the laws of quantum mechanics in a fully consistent way without reference to the consciousness."

We could spend a few chapters of this book discussing the experiments that prove all this crazy stuff, but we'd just be reinventing the wheel by doing so. Other books already exist that explain it much better. The best scientifically factual book on this subject I've found, which discusses the connection of quantum physics and consciousness, is called "Quantum Enigma", by Bruce Rosenblum, who was a professor emeritus of physics at University of Southern California, and Fred Kuttner, an MIT grad and Physics Lecturer at UC Santa Cruz. In it, they write,

> Quantum theory is the most stunningly successful theory in all of science. Not a single one of its predictions has ever been wrong. Quantum mechanics has revolutionized our world. One third of our economy depends on products based on it. However, this physics can look like mysticism. Quantum experiments display an enigma that challenges our classical world view. The world view demanded by quantum theory is, to borrow the words of J. B. S. Haldane, "not only queerer than we suppose, but queerer than we can suppose."

Rosenblum and Kuttner later go on to explain all the various interpretations of quantum physics, and how not a single one of them leaves out a connection with consciousness. They also point out how some physicists don't even know of this enigma, or that they think it's been solved when it hasn't. About that, they wrote, "In teaching quantum mechanics, physicists (including us) minimize the enigmatic aspect in order not to distract students from the practical stuff they will need to use. We also avoid the enigma because it is a bit embarrassing. It's been called our 'skeleton in the closet.'" But it's a real skeleton, not an imagined one.

An alternative book for you to peruse, which has just a bit more woo than "Quantum Enigma", is called "Biocentrism", by astronomer Bob Berman and stem cell researcher Dr. Robert Lanza. Although I personally think the book oversteps the connection of quantum physics with individual consciousness a bit, on the whole "Biocentrism" does a great job in explaining the individual experiments which proved the quantum physics connection with consciousness in very simple terms.

At the end of the day, quantum physics focuses on the itty bitty energies that make up our known universe. But because quantum physics makes the rules for the Newtonian particle physics that create our whole universe, that means we, as humans, live a quantum based existence. And consciousness may be at the root of it all.

Bringing It All Home

But more than being just a crazy theory, here's the really wild part of this discussion, and where our mind-bending science makes the transition from the laboratory into our heads (literally). It's also where we finally come full circle to the likelihood of cellular consciousness. It turns out that the cells that make up our bodies and all other life on the planet are partly made of these things called microtubules. Why are microtubules important?

Microtubules make up our cells. They create the cellular membrane of our cells, they create the life sustaining material inside the cell which falls outside the cell's nucleus, and they play an important role in a number of internal cellular processes. We wouldn't have cells, or even life on this planet at all, without microtubules. Microtubules make up the critical part of the cell walls on our neurons, becoming the entire reason our neurons can make the weird shapes they do in interconnecting to thousands of synapses. So without microtubules, we wouldn't have a brain. Microtubules provide the infrastructure for those receptors and emitters, and even create the neuronal synapses themselves. Without microtubules, our cells' communication channels wouldn't exist. We wouldn't be able to think, feel, or exist without the activity of microtubules. And why is this important to point out?

[And here comes the first huge bombshell of this book that no other book on the planet has ever pointed out to you.]

It turns out that science has just recently proven that our microtubules interact with quantum field vibrations.

Yeah… that same quantum field, which touches all space and time simultaneously, which seems impossible and hard to wrap our heads around. The reality may be that the quantum field itself is wrapped around our heads, or at least the cells in our heads. Because now there is physical evidence that the cells in our heads have a mechanism to directly interact with the realm of quantum physics, to include all its backward-and-forward-in-time strangeness, and for which impossible spatial interactions are child's play.

A research group at the National Institute of Material Sciences in Tsukuba, Japan, confirmed that the microtubules in the brain, specifically, are effected by quantum vibrations, and may, in fact, be the basis for "electrical oscillations of the brain that are correlated with conscious awareness." Mic drop. But really, it's not my mic to drop. To be fair, this human consciousness model was first suggested back in the 1980s by quantum biologist Stuart Hammeroff and emeritus professor of mathematics and physicist at the University of Oxford Roger Penrose. They've been working on it for a while. It turns out they may be right.

Because of the nascency of neuroscience, for a long time it was a mystery to neuroscientists how gamma waves could even exist in the brain because they were thought to be electrochemically impossible, too fast for the brain to create and process. But they've learned a lot about gamma waves since then. If you recall, gamma waves were previously thought to be meaningless brainwave noise. Now they are understood to be the most effective and beneficial waves we have in our brain, integrating many information sources into the information we need to utilize. And, that turns out that turns out to be a very interesting fact when we start talking about the topic of neuronal quantum vibrations. Because the vibrational frequency of our quantum connected microtubules is directly within the gamma waves spectrum's wheelhouse. So from a scientific perspective, the implications of this little discovery are staggering. But it's implications with consciousness are particularly so.

Although science has yet to check the microtubule vibration in other cellular life outside our brains, cellular life everywhere has microtubules. In the grass outside. In the plants and trees. In the insects. In the animals and brains of those animals. Even our own body's non-neural cells are made from microtubules. So the odds are quite good all our non-brain cells interact with the quantum field as well. In fact, scientists are just now finding evidence that the olfactory nerves in our noses reference the quantum properties of molecules to determine what odor signals are sent to our brain. It turns out very different molecules have similar odors due to having similar quantum properties, and very similar molecules have very different odors due to having very different quantum properties. Our nose employs quantum tunneling to tell the difference. Quantum theory is even being used to better explain the energy efficiency of photosynthesis in plants, which has been a mystery to Newtonian physics. And because all cells everywhere have microtubules, it's possible that cells throughout all of nature interact with the quantum field, and every living thing is connected with consciousness.

Okay, so I went a little woo-woo for a second there. But can you blame me? It's actually a potential reality.

Going super woo-woo for a moment, we could suppose that a potential direct connection to the non-local characteristics of quantum activity can now explain the statistically significant findings that have shown things like ESP do actually exist in some people. Or maybe now we can explain the experiences of past lives or alien encounters. Personally, I like to refrain from jumping neck-deep into fringe subjects that can potentially have numerous explanations, but I also like to keep my options open. So we must acknowledge that there is a scientifically valid path that may explain things previously identified as pseudoscience.

That said, one of the most informative conversations I had about keeping a healthy distance from jumping too early into explanations of proof was when I spent a number of hours sitting with John Clauser, having some beers at the Berkeley Yacht Club as we talked about the hard science of quantum physics and its potential implications in our everyday lives. Clauser is the Wolf

Prize in Physics awardee who proved quantum entanglement to the world through laboratory experimentation. That discovery helped confirm quantum theory for the world and may eventually lead to quantum communications technologies and quantum computing. To say he's a smart guy would be the understatement of the century. He is a stickler on being a dedicated critic and skeptic of scientific discovery, because of all the bad science that's being conducted by the medical and biology communities in particular. His position on quantum physics affecting our brains was certainly non-committal. He was pretty certain entanglement itself couldn't be overly influential. Admittedly, we didn't discuss the new science of quantum interaction in microtubules, or the new discoveries about the very common brain atom phosphorus making entanglement within our brains possible, but his attitude about following the data keeps me grounded with a healthy skepticism until someday we know for sure.

That said, if my foray into quantum physics taught me anything, it's that probabilities run the universe. And so, after going all that way to come full circle to our original question of whether our body's cells are conscious or not, considering the latest science to answer that question, I think there is a high probability that the answer to that question is a resounding "Yes, we are conscious, thank you very much for asking. Hold my beer while I deliver this pile of oxygen atoms." Of course, I could be wrong about that, and we need to acknowledge that possibility, too.

Now let's go really woo-woo to ask some cool questions: Could this mechanism that connects us to the quantum field be what Ramanujan (see Chapter 3) tapped into to be able to explain mathematics well beyond what the mathematicians of his day could explain? The solutions just came to him, remember? Could this microtubules-create-all-cells thing be the reason all cellular life reacts the same way, and why all life seems to be universally connected? Do our cells, including our brain cells, have some direct connection to the magic which governs physics and creates our entire universe, literally transcending space and time, and not as just some hippie bullshit saying? There's more evidence to come on this.

Getting Back to Happiness: Realizing What the Bigger Picture Means to Our Understanding of Self

So why did we take this rather long multi-chapter tangent into the body? Why did we dig into the science of our bodies to point out the fact that we are made of living cells, and that those living cells are in command of an intelligence we can't possibly comprehend? Why did we need to consider that those cells are likely to have a consciousness that is separate from our own, and that those cells seem to be wired into the crazy magic of the universe called quantum physics, which is inextricably linked to consciousness?

We took this little stroll for a number of very good reasons that make sense, knowing what we now know. First, taking a closer look at your body gives you a better understanding of the biggest portion of your mind's {self} map, which contributes to all your inner turmoil. By digging into this deeper reality of your body, and seeing the multiple levels of intelligence and consciousness below your waking consciousness, you can see there's way more to know about the intelligence and consciousness that underlies your existence. You can see beyond the two simplistic tales you've been told: the body is just who and what you are, or the body is just a shell that carries your Spirit or Soul. Taking a tour through the science of what is **you** takes you one big step closer toward the deeper truth of the Know Thyself riddle.

How this ties back to happiness, is that catching a glimpse of the reality of the single biggest item on your {self} map, you can now start to see your emotional reactions for what they are - a process of your body, not a process of your true Self. This realization can take you across the bridge from "I am my body" to "I have a body." It can take you from "I am my thoughts and emotions" to "My body has thoughts and emotions." Certainly your body/brain does greatly affect your mind, but from this firmly rooted place of an on-demand meta-awareness ("I am not completely my body"), you now have the potential to choose **how much** your body affects your moment-to-moment life. This is the first step in traveling from compulsion to choice with regard to what emotions and internal reactions you wish to allow, rather than letting the body's subconscious reactions run away with the show, forcing you to deal with them. Going from compulsion to choice was one of the benefits we mentioned of the Equation of Emotion in Volume I. This is the first huge step of getting your mind on the leash and in control. As a bonus, because you now know your ideas of your body have been wrong all this time, you know your {self} map in general might not be entirely trustworthy. This is a giant leap toward your personal inner peace.

Second, seeing the body as a separate but connected consciousness, you can start to consciously move your body out from the center of your {self} map. Instead of being caught up in the drama of a negative internal reaction, you can now tell yourself, "This negative emotion is a reaction of my body." This one move engages your brain's internal wiring to reduce the severity of your emotional pain and suffering through the name-it-tame-it circuits. And don't forget, it's the pain and suffering sourced from your brain about your general life bullshit that bugs you and steals your happiness. By seeing your body as not entirely you, and more as a physiological process, that separates you a bit from your body's pain and suffering and noise, and drops you into meta-awareness where you can change what is going on in your mind. These repeating moments can allow you to better balance your emotional input with rational thought, rather than have the emotional process hijack the whole show during times of stress.

This process of redirection creates a regenerative feedback loop in your body because you are constantly refocusing away from the negative reactions of your body back to an equanimity. Equanimity reduces your stress and positively affects the health of your body, as proven by the placebo effect, and it strengthens the calmness in your mind through the work of neuroplasticity. The whole process becomes a big positive snowball effect. Out of negativity. Into equanimity. Even in moments when your mind is angry, or sad, or afraid, if you maintain the small gap between your awareness and your mind's reaction, you can potentially also be happy right along next to the negative reaction because of the small mental separation. This is a step on the path to Nirvana, that wondrous place where absolutely nothing can steal your mojo. This type of shift helps reduce the physiological severity of your negative emotions because your {body} is continually pushed further and further out from center of your {self} map. This becomes additive yet again. So in effect, seeing your body as less who and what you are and transitioning into something you have and are connected to, helps your brain's own wiring make you more and more calm over time.

Third, it's clear our cells are smarter than we are, given that they can identify a stacked deck of cards five times faster than we can, they can spontaneously give some people answers to mathematical challenges with ease, they can allow some people to sit down and play a piano without training, and regardless of whether we individually have any special talents passed down by multigenerational cellular memories, the fact is just two cells from our own bodies can join together and assemble another entire human body from scratch in just nine months. That's a crazy level of intelligence. But now that you can start to see the multiple consciousness levels within your body, you can start to consider the possibility of gaining access to the massive amount of intelligence hidden within your body which transcends your own waking intelligence. And with this, we are increasing your intelligence in the worst case scenario, and knocking on the door to Enlightenment in the best case scenario.

And speaking of Enlightenment, the fourth benefit you can get from accepting the consciousness in your body and moving your body out of the center of your {self} map is that you have the space to discover your true Self. This is the other half of the false {self} true Self riddle. We'll discuss more on this topic later in our discussion on Enlightenment. That magical mystical ancient phenomenon called Enlightenment comes to you through your body. Understanding the internal landscape of your body, and knowing the deeper reality of your body's inner workings, gives you a much better idea about how to attain Enlightenment than you've ever had in the past.

In summing up this discussion about your body, there is a much deeper truth to your human existence than what you've been told. There is a profound meaning to the messages of the past masters who told us to look within ourselves for that deeper truth. There's a reason the world's meditative disciplines are all connected with using, observing and communing with our bodies, even if the meditative discipline asks us to enter our mind, which we can now see as largely an activity of our body's brain. If we consider ourselves rational human beings, believing material science had a hand in creating our existence, it would be irrational and ignorant for us to assume that the quantum field which governs the universe, and which is inextricably connected with consciousness, isn't also connected with life energy. If we would consider ourselves religious or spiritual, it would be pompous for us to assume the founders of our religions didn't understand the most complex science in the universe and exactly how it connects to us. "Look within yourself," they said. "We are all connected," they said. Lastly, as fans of common sense, it would be downright silly for us to assume any human experience we have, including the spiritual kind, doesn't come through our physiology in some way that can be explained by science. Are our bodies not built by the Divine? Then why would the Divine abandon that same model when it comes to spirit? Explaining how spirituality might actually exist scientifically doesn't make it less holy or spiritual. In fact, explaining it may just make it easier for us to tap into as a species moving forward. I hope.

One Last Thing on Consciousness

As a heads up, I need to geek out on some science for a second, so for you less sciency folks, jump to the end of the chapter, or excuse this slightly geeky tangent for a moment. There's some fundamental science to discuss with the haters of the last few chapters.

As mentioned in Volume I, there are some scientists who disagree with these ideas about the potential for our cells to have consciousness. They believe simple Newtonian physics and atoms running into each other can explain all our behaviors, and that our top level consciousness is an illusion of experience piled on top of other conscious layers that exist at lower levels in our brain, which only seem to give us consciousness and **free will**, which is our ability to make decisions. Let's now discuss what I think these scientists are missing.

In Volume I, prominent atheist and neuroscientist Sam Harris provided us with some pertinent science on {self}, which helped explain all our individual emotions about all sorts of stuff on our {self} maps. Sam Harris also wrote a book called "Free Will", and identifies himself to be in the group of scientists who believe we don't have any. While he continues to formulate experiments that uncover some pretty amazing stuff, Sam and I differ in our thoughts about consciousness and free will.

Typically, scientists in the 'we're-not-really-in-charge-of-ourselves' camp base their arguments on experiments done by Dr. Ben Libet, initiated in the 1970s. Libet's work was focused on measuring brain activity before, and during the process of, making what we consider a conscious decision. Specifically, while we already knew at the time that our brain signals precede a physical action like pushing a button with our finger, Libet was interested in finding out if brain signals also preceded the 'decision we made' to push that same button. He devised some experiments where some letters flashed in succession on a screen, or people looked at the second hand on a clock, and study participants could then report the moment they originally **felt** they had decided to press the button. Did the brain activity of making the decision occur before the person **felt** the conscious awareness of actually making the decision?

In short, of course it did. What Dr. Libet found was that there were brain signals preceding the moment a person **felt** like they made a decision to take action. In fact, follow up experiments showed that they could predict someone pressing the button 7 seconds before they felt like they'd decided to, AND they could even predict which hand, right or left, the participant would use to press the button. So it seemed, at that moment, that humans had no free will. At least at our conscious awareness level, anyway. It seemed that every decision we made was predetermined by the cells in our brains making decisions for us, which we were then only made aware of 0.7 to 7 seconds later. So from that perspective, it seems clear that we have no free will. Our atoms in our cells made the decisions for us based on their atomic states at the moment the decision came due. If this is extrapolated, all our decisions, from whether we have bacon and eggs or cereal for breakfast, to who we vote for on election day, are made by a physical process within our brain that only informs us about it afterward. Therefore, our conscious free will can be considered an illusion, and similarly our consciousness itself can be considered an illusion. Done and done. Right?

Not quite.

[First, I'm going to skip the discussion on the two variables that were left out of this work, which are the uncertainty principle, and consciousness, because there's a bigger flaw in Libet's work to ponder. And before we get all… "what's consciousness got to do with it?"… there isn't one interpretation of quantum physics that is independent of consciousness. And since the quantum field touches absolutely everything through all space and time, then consciousness touches absolutely every part of the Newtonian physics that materialist reductionists suppose make all our decisions. Without taking into a variable which is clearly connected, we can literally throw the materialist reductionist theories out the window in regard to both consciousness and our free will. But again, we don't even need to go that far with the argument.]

The argument against consciousness and free will actually falls apart earlier, when we take a closer look at the experiments of Libet that scientists use to suggest we don't have free will. Because the simple fact is that all the experiments done by Libet, and everyone else who followed, didn't actually measure the point at which the study participant truly exercised their free will. The reality of these experiments is that each and every one of the study participants who participated made the decision to press that button at the moment they agreed to participate in the experiment in the first place. And there's more than a simple semantics argument going on here. Because the fact is that the study participants received the opportunity to make their decision, and their instructions for the experiment, through the filter of their conscious awareness. They were made aware of their option to either participate or not participate, and how to participate through their ears, which passed through their top level of awareness, which then passed down the information from above. The rest was programming the brain to respond as expected in the experiment, which they then carried out.

All the rest of the experiment after that first moment of decision was simply the participant programming their subconscious cells to act in a manner that was in accordance with the instructions they received from Dr. Libet, and allowing their brain cells run that program by performing the experiment per the instructions they received. So of course their brain cells could be measured making decisions about pushing the buttons before they were pushed and the subjects' conscious awareness was alerted that the decision had been made. Those subconscious cells were only doing what they were told by the higher conscious awareness that was involved in the decision that everyone play along for Dr. Libet's experiment. When the electrodes were attached, the free will had already been exercised. It was that first moment of learning about the experiment that the decision had been made to press any buttons, regardless of how many times they wound up pressing them.

What would be really interesting would have been to see the results of someone who agreed to do the experiment but then went rogue (without the potential instruction to do so), and decided not to press the button at all in comparison to someone who had followed the directions. "Fuck your buttons. I'm not pressing them. Let's see what happens to your results now."

Although consciousness is a little more complex than how we're talking about it here, I think we've covered the basics of how science such as Libet's has missed the boat on free will. The long and short of it is that, wherever it resides in our physiology, I believe we do have free will. And I think science will eventually get to the point of proving it once we better understand the quantum consciousness connection. What's really going to bake some atheist scientists' brains along the way is that their very mathematical model most likely proves the existence of God. More on that later.

A Quick Reflection

Could the link between our brain cells and the quantum field be the scientific explanation to those things which we consider spiritual?

Could this beyond-time-and-space link to our personal consciousness be what explains the scientifically proven phenomenon of things like extra sensory perception, and past life experiences?

Could this explain the operation of things like our creativity, or the ability to link to superhuman intelligence which pushes the boundaries of scientific discovery?

Could this link be the very mechanism which allows for humans to experience spiritual enlightenment, something which we will explore more in depth before the end of this book?

Stay tuned. That discussion is coming.

6 Yup, It's Final— Our Pets Are Conscious and Have Emotions

> Emotions are the gifts of our ancestors.
> We have them and so do other animals.
> We must never forget this.
> —Mark Bekoff

Personally, I think if you can't find a perfect moment in the companionship of a good dog, you're not gonna find a perfect moment anywhere. Right now, I have two dogs. Both are fourteen years old, and I've had them since they were six weeks old. Their names are Aggie and Patch. Aggie and Patch are German Shorthaired Pointers, which were bred to be hunting dogs. My dogs have never hunted anything but table scraps and the occasional squirrel while outside running around. They are members of one of the more highly intelligent breeds, although this has been both a blessing and a curse at times.

Patch can get into almost any container engineered by man. Our dog food container with the twist top lid? No problem. Our Milk-Bone snack holder with the dual snap closure? He helps himself regularly. One of the best dog gates money can buy to keep the dogs in the kitchen at night? Puppy's play, as far as Patch is concerned. If he wants to come upstairs and sleep next to, or even on the bed, you're not stopping him. He's too smart.

I once saw Patch convince Aggie to abandon one of her dog treats through a very complex ruse so he could steal it. One day while Aggie was gnawing on a soup bone I'd brought home from the grocery store, Patch ran into the front room of the house, paused, then barked once like he saw something out the front window. There was nothing there. After barking at nothing, he then immediately turned around and headed back toward the room in which Aggie was enjoying her soup bone. Aggie, having heard Patch bark from the front room, and being the protective watchdog type, dropped her bone and was, at that moment, racing to the front room, barking to chase away whatever Patch was barking at. Patch took the long route to the bone through the foyer. He claimed the bone at the same moment Aggie made it to the front window, barking out at nothing. Aggie remained in the front room for a good two minutes, looking around trying to figure out what Patch had seen. I don't know if she ever grasped the full picture. It was obvious Patch knew what was out there - the opportunity to get Aggie's bone was out that front window. And he was right. Aggie just couldn't see it.

Definitely don't underestimate Aggie, though. She's no dummy. One time we took the dogs to a dog park in Atlanta where we had set our bags down upon a hill far away from the crowd so we could play with the dogs and our son. While we were playing, I noticed a woman had sat down on the hill close enough for her to reach out and touch our bags if she wanted to. That seemed very odd to me. The hill was empty, except for our bags and that one lady. She seemed to be reading a book, doing her own thing, but she had sat down close enough for a stranger to possibly assume the bags were hers, and not someone else's in the park.

Not three minutes later, I spotted Aggie. She was sitting directly **in between** the lady and our family's bags on the hill. I thought this was strange. At the dog park, she usually never stopped roaming and running, exploring and playing. Sitting next to our bags was atypical behavior. I called to her. She didn't move. This was also atypical behavior. I called her again. She didn't budge. So I walked over to where she and the lady were sitting. As I knelt down to Aggie to find out what was up with her, only when I got within a few inches of her did I hear that she was almost inaudibly growling under her breath. She was letting her eyes drift in the direction of the lady sitting strangely close to our bags, growling in her direction. She had put herself in watchdog mode. She thought something might be amiss about that lady sitting so close to our bags.

Now . . . it's at this point that some scientists would try to tell you I'm trying to anthropomorphize my dogs. That's the scientific way of saying I'm applying human characteristics, human behavior, and even human thinking into my dogs' actions and reasons for acting. Many scientists think our pets are just dumb animals driven by animal tendencies, devoid of our thinking and reasoning capabilities. But considering the nervous system, how life works, how cells work, and knowing that the animals of the world are made out of the same cellular model we are, we know those scientists are just plain wrong. Intentional deception in animals has been highly documented, as in Patch's case. And emotional intelligence and something called theory of mind, which is one subjective mind's ability to understand that other creatures have subjective minds also, has been proven in animals. We'll discuss some science shortly.

Getting back to that hill, Aggie had attached to our family's bags as a portion of her sense of {self}. The same science proven at UIUC by Tiffany Barnett White, that humans can attach to abstract ideas and items as part of {self}, had clearly occurred in my dog. And now her limbic system was sensing a threat to an item on her {self} map (our family's bags). Her action to plant herself in the path of the lady next to our bags was simply an action to defend what she now saw as {her bags} sitting on that hillside. From her perspective, a stranger sat down too close to her stuff, and she was going to do something about it. Clear and simple. Her actions that day are just how the nervous system works. And dogs certainly have nervous systems. We can't deny that.

This same mechanism that Aggie exhibited that day by connecting with our family's stuff and moving to defend it is the same mechanism dogs use to defend the families they attach to and who care for them. It's the same brain activity pattern Jim Coan at UVA discovered. They connect their human caregivers to part of their {self} map. It's not necessarily us they're defending when that stranger comes to the door, it's their brain's understanding of {self}. This pattern is, of course, congruent with all of nature. Whack a bee's nest, you're gonna get stung. Find yourself in between a mama bear and her cubs, and you're in for a mauling. Those things are part of the creature's unconscious {self} maps. So if our dogs and other animals in nature follow this universal pattern of mind to defend {self}, which is a function of the nervous system, what does it mean regarding animals experiencing emotions?

It means that animals feel emotions as much as we do, limited only to their sense of {self}, and the complexity of their Perceptions. Period. Science supports this conclusion through multiple peer reviewed published studies, and our model of emotions in Volume I informs us exactly why animals have variations in their complexity of emotion as compared to us humans. In 2012, a group of neuroscientists converged on the University of Cambridge and signed a document titled "The Cambridge Declaration of Consciousness in Non-Human Animals." It clearly stated, "The absence of a neocortex (something humans have that many animals don't) does not appear to preclude an organism from experiencing affective states." The words affective states are what science calls emotions. As a result of the compounding science, New Zealand passed a law recognizing that animals are sentient beings and have feelings, banning the use of animals in testing cosmetics and other products, and negating many laws permitting the treatment of animals as objects or property.

Does this mean that animals have the full suite of emotions we humans do? Probably not. We'll touch on the limitations of animal emotions in a moment, but even admitting that there are limitations, animals have been proven to have some pretty complex emotions, and maybe even some strange talents of mind that humans have long forgotten.

As little as ten years ago, scientists didn't even test the cognitive and emotional intelligence levels of animals, but in the last ten years that has changed dramatically. And what they are finding is changing brain science almost weekly. Elephants for instance, have been found to be highly intelligent, being able to use tools to accomplish tasks, and to be able to spontaneously work in cooperation with each other to solve difficult problems. Beyond just cognitive intelligence, however, they've been found to have a high level of emotional intelligence as well. Elephants have been shown to exhibit empathy for each other, consoling each other on the death of their elephant relatives. Science tells us that empathy is on a high rung on the emotional intelligence ladder, and requires a mental capability called theory of mind, which until recently scientists assumed was uniquely human. Elephants usually reserve this grieving and consoling behavior for losses within their own kind. But one of the most extraordinary instances of this behavior came when two herds of elephants lost one of their favorite humans in 2012.

Lawrence Anthony was an international conservationist in South Africa, who, because of his ability to rehabilitate wild elephants, was nicknamed the "Elephant Whisperer" by animal behaviorists globally. He had rescued multiple elephants from destruction, even saving some from the Baghdad Zoo during the invasion of Iraq in 2003, and moved some of them to a reserve in Zululand, South Africa. He seemed to have a special connection with his elephants. They trusted him. They behaved more calmly in his presence, even backing down form a near rage in one instance where human and elephant lives were both at stake. He detailed this account in his book, aptly titled "The Elephant Whisperer". Upon his untimely and unexpected death from a heart attack in 2012, thirty-one elephants who lived closest to him, and who had not walked to his home near their reserve in well over three years, spontaneously trudged in a twelve-mile single-file funeral march to his house overnight. They stayed for two days without eating anything. Then, just as spontaneously as they showed up, they turned around and went home. That's not only an emotional display, there was obviously some kind of non-local connection that allowed those animals to know Lawrence Anthony had died. From twelve miles away. Crazy cool stuff.

This published study behavior and the story from South Africa show us something very important. It shows us that these elephants work within the same model of mind that we do, and emotionally speaking, they create a {self} map which can include both animals and people, and lead to expressions of both empathy and compassion. So their nervous system cells work the same way ours do. There is no question elephants can become angry, and afraid, and sad. There are thousands of examples of those reactions being documented. But now we also have science that shows both dogs and horses read our emotions from our facial expressions and postures. This denotes emotional intelligence in those animals. Other studies conclusively show that dogs can become jealous, dolphins and chimps can experience happiness and grief, ants unquestionably experience fear, and they can even experience something as complex as self doubt. A bonobo in Milwaukee saved and distributed its Paxil subscription, becoming the first known primate drug dealer in the world, and also proving that bonobos have theory of mind capabilities, knowing those pills will affect his friends the same way they affect him. If that weren't impressive enough, chimpanzees have been proven to have meta-cognition, which is the ability to think about what you're thinking about, which is a form of meta-awareness, which then also suggests they can probably think about what they're feeling. Koko the famous multilingual gorilla in California, to whom researchers taught sign language, often has conversations about her feelings. And before we attempt to assume brain size creates the level of potential emotional and cognitive complexity, both chickens and mice-sized prairie voles, both who have teeny tiny brains, have been proven to experience empathy, which requires both emotional processing, and theory of mind activity.

In a TED Talk given in 2011, leading neuroscientist Antonio Damasio told us that the proto-self exists at the level of single celled life-forms, and a core-self exists in numerous multicellular creatures, including animals. Humans and numerous intelligent animals have an extended self where life narrative enters the picture. In his book "Self Comes to Mind", Damasio said he considers emotions internal programs that urge us into action. Now that emotions can be seen as a basic function of the nervous system, we can see the complexity of emotions in animals comes down to the same two variables it does in humans. It's simply the complexity of the variables in the animal's mind that determines the complexity of the emotions in the animal themselves. The more complex the Equation of Emotion is in an animal, the more complex the emotions are. This is limited only by their {self} map and their cognitive abilities. The more complex their {self} map is, the more stuff there is to get upset about in their world. The more complex their perception process is, the more ways they can perceive things which interact with their {self} items. Who knows if they can stack up complex emotions by stacking up Equations of Emotion on top of each other. Who knows whether they get the subtlety of your sarcasm when you tell them they got a great haircut, even though the groomer butchered them and they look just like Ozzy Osbourne. But it is certain animals of all shapes and sizes have emotional reactions to life events. It's just how the nervous systems in Earth creatures works.

So when you're certain your cat is holding a grudge for a few days because you did something wrong, like give it a bath without its permission, you're probably right. When you feel like your dog stole one of your favorite shoes again, just for the sole purpose of playing a joke on you, and laughing internally while you look for it, you're probably right. When you assume the bee that stung you did so because they were having a bad day, well, maybe not. There's a limit to animal cognition. But if you get angry about factory farming treating animals horribly, not letting them move around or breathe fresh air, because you think they have feelings, too, and that regardless of whether we decide to consume them for food, they should be treated with dignity and reverence throughout that whole process . . . um, yeah . . . I gotta side with you on that one.

My question is what could the potential negative emotional states of plants and animals be doing to their health before becoming the food we eat? It can't be good.

7 The Basics of Happiness

I am determined to be cheerful and happy
in whatever situation I may find myself.
For I have learned that the greater part
of our misery or unhappiness is determined
not by our circumstance but by our disposition.

—Martha Washington

Okay, so it took us seven chapters into Volume II to get to our first chapter explicitly on happiness in a set of books with "Happiness" in the very title. How did that even happen? Well, it happened because without first understanding the mechanisms within you that create your happiness, and the mechanisms within you that steal your happiness, you are doomed to fail miserably at the task of increasing the happiness levels in your life.

Without a proper understanding of how happiness is created, you would have continued running around your whole life trying to set the individualized external conditions that you thought would flip the little magic switch inside your mind where - poof - happiness then occurs. Because it's easy to be fooled into thinking that happiness works that way. Our external conditions can seem to make us happy. We see an amazing sunset on the horizon and we feel happiness. We experience the warm embrace of a loved one, and we feel happiness. We get that raise in pay at work, or buy that new electronic gadget, or take that fancy vacation where we get to experience some really cool shit, and that little man at the switch in our brain decides that the correct conditions are now set, and 'click', our happiness occurs. And we feel it. It's real happiness. So that must be how it works, right?

But now you know different.

You know it's not **really** the external conditions that make you happy but the magic within your own mind which makes that occur. While it is certainly true that external conditions can influence your mind into happiness (I am not going to tell you that if you win the lottery, it isn't going to make you happy - something like that is going to make you happy for a time), the reality is that the external conditions weren't the source of the happiness. Your mind itself was the source.

But a question remains. What other ways besides setting external life conditions are there to activate happiness? What if you could skip the setting-all-the-external-conditions crap and simply turn on happiness without all the extra effort? What if there was a way to trip the happiness switch inside you manually that you would never need to worry about setting life's conditions anymore, and you could simply enjoy whatever happened, whenever it happened?

Would you even do it? Or would you continue chasing the things you thought would make you happy and just accept it as part of the process? Because if that is the choice you make, there is no doubt you will be chasing happiness your whole life, and you will never be a master of it.

The Happiness Question

I was giving a talk at the University of Georgia one Saturday morning in front of a group of student entrepreneurs and I asked that room full of young people the following question: "What would make you happy?" There was a telling silence at first, but eventually, hands started rising above the crowd. "I want to be successful in business," one young man said. "I'd like to graduate," another person said. A young Indian woman spoke up and said, "I just want my parents to be proud of me." Another girl said, "I think I'd like to raise a family, and be able to provide for that family." After a short pause, a guy in the back row piped up, "I'd like to beat Florida this year." Because Georgia and Florida have a huge rivalry, everyone laughed in agreement. The answers that came from the crowd that morning about happiness were all over the map. And while my small informal survey was in no way scientific, those types of answers are typical to what is reported on formal surveys about happiness. When people are asked what things they think will make them happy, the answers can range from making a lot of money, to finding a good mate and raising a family, to traveling the world in search of adventure.

Buddhist monk and happiness expert, Matthieu Ricard, wrote in his book on happiness,

> Ask any number of people to describe a moment of perfect happiness. Some will talk about moments of deep peace experienced in a harmonious natural setting. Of a forest dappled in sunshine. Of a mountain summer, looking out across a vast horizon. Of the shores of a tranquil lake. Of a night walk through snow, under a starry sky. And so on. Others will refer to a long awaited event. An exam they've aced. A sporting victory. Meeting someone they've longed to meet. The birth of a child. Still others will speak of a moment of peaceful intimacy with their family or loved one. Or of having made someone else happy. The common factor to all of these experiences would seem to be the momentary disappearance of inner conflict. The person feels in harmony with the world and with herself.

In Chapter 8 of Volume I, there's a simple definition of happiness that is in sync with Ricard's observation, and lays out happiness in relation to your mind's Equation of Emotion: Happiness occurs any time you experience a Perception on one side of your Equation of Emotion that balances with the Expectation/Preference of anything on your {self} map from the other side. In other words, when your Perception about something matches your Expectation/Preference about that something, you get happy. Matthieu might call this "a momentary disappearance of inner conflict." But being more than a momentary disappearance of inner conflict, this new, more specific definition of happiness based on your mind's {self} now explains exactly why you feel happy about your favorite sports team winning the big game, or your political candidate winning the election, or why you get happy when you find some forgotten money in a laundry pants pocket. It's indeed a cessation of inner conflict, but it's also a tad more. In that moment, both sides of your Equation of Emotion are in balance with something on your {self} map, meaning something you individually care about is at stake.

On the darker side of happiness, this same basic definition also explains how someone with a deranged sense of {self} can find happiness by inflicting pain and suffering on other human beings. The act of inflicting pain might make them feel powerful, which matches with their Preference. Or how a businessman can be happy about the demise of a major competitor because of his business Preference, even though the competitor's failure includes the layoffs of thousands of people. Or how a military general can be pleased with a missile strike that meets the mission objective, but kills innocent children in the process. The variation in our {self} maps explains how very different things make different people happy.

While our new scientific definition of happiness proves accurate, and happiness is a simple function of our nervous systems, and knowing this truth allows us to make our lives much happier by tweaking some things in the control room of our mind, this new basic definition of happiness is just the tip of the iceberg when it comes to the whole happiness story. It turns out that there's a bit more to know about happiness.

The simple fact is that up to this moment we have completely misunderstood what happiness is, how happiness occurs, and what it takes for us to be happy on a long term basis. The happiness that our bodies create is so amazing that we spend most our lives chasing the things we think will deliver it. Aristotle called happiness "the only goal we always choose for its own sake, and never as a means to something else." Epicurus said, "One must practice the things which produce happiness. Since if that is present we have everything. And if it is absent, we do everything in order to have it."

Chasing Happiness

One of the deepest truths in our lives is that we are always chasing happiness for ourselves or those we love. If we go to work, it's to make money so that we can buy food and shelter to provide for our happiness. If we surf the Web, or watch TV, or go to a concert, or go see a movie, what we are looking for there are moments of happiness. If we go outside for a walk to work out our life's most complex problems, we are looking for the eventual resolution of those problems, which brings happiness. Even if we intentionally start an argument with someone to defend our position on something, ironically what we are striving to achieve is our eventual personal happiness. When we play with your kids, we are looking for happiness. When we go to vote in an election, we are looking for happiness. When we buy a new car, or get a new haircut, or take a new job, or go on a diet, or move to a different home, or go on vacation away from that home, or purchase new clothes, or purchase a new anything for that matter, we are looking for happiness.

As a species, on a grand scale, we organize into societies, create farming systems, take jobs, and create laws to achieve happiness. We accumulate worldly items, create global trade, and develop international relationships. All for happiness. We form bonds, develop interpersonal relationships, and start families, all for happiness. Thus, it's not a stretch to say that attaining happiness is our main motivator. And we do certainly act like it's our main purpose, engaging in the never ending chase of trying get our mind to flick that invisible little switch. That switch which provides that one feeling within our human existence for which there seems to be no equal. It is the pinnacle. It is the ultimate. And the quest for it underlies all our life's goals.

What happens in our bodies when we experience happiness proves that achieving happiness is a worthwhile goal.

The Effects of Happiness on Our Physical and Psychological Health

When you're happy, the cells in your body react in specific ways which decrease stress, improve your health, and even prolong your life. When you're happy, your cells reduce their production of stress hormones like cortisol, which have been linked to countless life threatening health conditions, not to mention a few debilitating ones like arthritis and dementia. In addition, happiness increases production of positive hormones and neurotransmitters such as oxytocin, serotonin, and dopamine, all of which improve your health, improve your overall mindset and help your brain work more efficiently. Happiness triggers the release of endorphins, which are natural internal pain killers that reduce your aches and pains, and have been shown to improve overall mood. When you're happy, your immune system works better. Your circulation improves. Your heart rate and blood pressure go down, reducing your risk of heart attack and stroke. Over time, happiness stimulates brain growth in your prefrontal cortex, which is the section of the brain which helps you think better, and helps regulate your negative emotions, removing the factors that block you from experiencing more happiness in the future. So happiness is not only beneficial to your body and mind health, happiness actually creates changes in your body that make it easier to experience even more happiness.

The compounding science that happiness makes us healthier human beings overall prompted Dr. Derek Cox, a director of Public Health at the National Health Service in the UK, to state, "We've spent years saying that giving up smoking could be the most important thing we could do for the health of the nation. . . . And yet there is mounting evidence that happiness might be at least as powerful a predictor than some of the other lifestyle factors that we talk about in terms of cigarette smoking, diet, physical activity, and those kind of things." Wow. Maybe the national news should have a disclaimer on the lower edge of the screen like those that appear on packs of cigarettes. **Negative perceptions of the world caused by this newscast have been proven to be hazardous to your health.**

Happiness Improves Our Peak Performance

Numerous studies have shown that happy people are much more productive than those who are not. Happy people have been shown to work better with others in all types of professional environments; so they make better team members and coworkers. In addition, happy people are more creative, they tend to fix problems rather than complaining about them, and are more optimistic when facing tough challenges. Happy people have more energy, sleep better, are more highly motivated, and they have been proven to learn how to adapt to new challenges faster than their non-happy counterparts. Happy people worry less about making mistakes, which may be because studies show that happy people actually make fewer mistakes, and they make better decisions in complex situations. In short, increasing happiness should be the first thing you do if you want to increase your personal performance.

How to Learn to Know Happiness

Happiness is so important on so many levels, yet we know so little about it. Well, personally speaking, I say **no longer!** From this point forward, our understanding of happiness is not going to be as clouded as it once was, and our quest for happiness isn't going to be as blind as it has been. It's time to reveal the details of exactly how your happiness works, so you can take command of it within your mind, and take ownership of it within your heart.

First, we'll review something you need to know about happiness in relation to your new perspective on emotions, then we'll cover some details you need to understand about happiness to develop a deep lasting happiness rather than just a short term bump. Later in the book, we'll consider the deepest mysteries of effortless happiness, and the extremely secret path to potentially attaining the never ending happiness and blissful state called Nirvana. A warning that we may temporarily strip some of the romance and mysticism out of happiness, but trust that we'll put it right back in shortly.

Let's start with discussing one of the big problems we've discovered about happiness.

Happiness Is Fleeting—And Why Happiness is Fleeting

They say that happiness is fleeting. And just like all of our other emotions which wane over time, they're right. When you experience things in your life that make you happy, after a while you get used to those things. And when you get used to those things, they no longer make you as happy anymore. Science calls this phenomenon **hedonic adaptation**, and at its core hedonic adaptation occurs because of how our nervous system works.

If you recall, when we introduced how all our emotions work as an output of our nervous system (which includes our brain), we explained our nervous system as a big comparator. It measures the differences between things and reports on that difference. So when a change occurs, like a new smell enters our awareness, or a new taste, or sight, or sound, or touch, or even a new thought, we notice it. It gets pushed up from our subconscious attention into our conscious awareness. And sometimes our new awareness comes with some emotional information attached. Noticing a gas leak in our home can trigger the emotion of fear, for instance. But once the new information has been processed, or our nervous system gets normalized to the new variable, and it quits reporting it to us. After a short period of no change, there is no new difference to report, and no more need to create associated emotions. Just like our nose becoming accustomed to a gas leak after a short while, which can then kill us, this same pattern is also true of our happiness. Another elegant insight from Matthieu Ricard's Happiness: A Guide to Developing Life's Most Important Skill:

> Savoring a delicious meal is a source of genuine pleasure, but we are indifferent to it once we've had our fill, and would get sick of it if we'd continue eating. It is the same with a nice wood fire. Coming in from the cold it is a pleasure to warm ourselves by it, but we soon have to

move away if we don't want to burn ourselves. Pleasure is exhausted by usage, like a candle consuming itself. It is almost always linked to an activity, and naturally leads to boredom being repeated. Listening rapturously to a Bach Prelude requires a focus of attention, that minimal as it is, cannot be maintained indefinitely. After a while fatigue kicks in and the music loses its charm. If we'd be forced to listen for days on end, it would become unbearable.

Master Ricard also mentioned a study of lottery winners revealing that for most, after their unexpected windfall of receiving millions in cash, it took only a year before they returned right back to their pre-lottery happiness levels. The money and all the things it brought them didn't make those lottery winners any happier after only one year. In fact some winners, after learning that the money they so yearned for previously didn't deliver the long-term happiness they expected, actually wound up being less happy than they were before winning the money, even falling into depression although they were still rich. This is because our nervous systems normalize and stop sending signals after a while. This is why we jump on the happiness treadmill of chasing ever increasing positive changes in life in an attempt to rekindle happiness. When our previously happy life starts to get stale, it becomes time to get more money, or a better car, or a better house, or more vacations, or maybe even a different spouse, or have children with our existing spouse when the relationship loses its charm . . . whatever it is that we think will make us happy again.

Chasing Happiness . . . and Failing

This hedonic adaptation phenomenon within us is a double-edged sword. It drives us to improve our technologies, catalyzing our creation and innovation, ensuring we get used to those creations and innovations after a short while, and then pushing us to continue creation and innovation. But it's also what provides the requirement for an ever increasing profit model in our board rooms and on Wall Street, with ever increasing levels of success and ever increasing levels of greed. This hedonic adaptation mechanism is why money can't ever buy us happiness. We get used to the money or items we acquire after a short while, and we wind up right back where we started on the happiness meter. This weird belief that happiness can be attained by adding money or items of value to our {self} maps is the basis for all the faulty {self} help approaches that promise to increase our happiness by teaching us ways to attain the material items we think will make us happy. "Do you want to make more money? It's not really work if you develop your downstream network." Or here's a popular one: "Have you made your vision board yet?" "You just need to ask the universe for your new car." Yeah, not only is all that stuff bullshit, if you believe in that kind of general approach to attaining happiness, you're on the never ending happiness treadmill, and you're destined never to get off, and never to be completely happy. Sorry for that bad news.

This whole realization about our nervous system and hedonic adaptation could be horrible news for all of us, if there weren't one more important happiness detail; there's a second type of happiness available to us that is more meaningful and more permanent. Let's talk that type of happiness.

Our Two Types of Happiness

Science splits happiness into two different forms. The first is called **hedonic** pleasure, which refers to the sensory experience of enjoying specific things. Hedonic happiness is eating a meal we love, or looking at a painting we appreciate, or loving the new car we just purchased, or watching our favorite team win the big game, or having sex, because orgasms rock. Hedonic happiness is the temporary fleeting type of happiness. Some hedonic happiness events last longer than others, but all of them eventually ebb over time.

The second type of happiness is called **eudaemonic** happiness, which is a deeper level happiness than the simple sensory pleasures of hedonic happiness. Eudaemonia is the more profound feeling of well-being that is experienced at our core, and which is independent of any one specific event. It's most commonly defined as our inner levels of "human flourishing," and its word roots literally translate to "good in spirit". I personally call hedonic happiness by the word 'happiness, but I point to eudaemonia by using the word 'joy". For our purposes, we'll call hedonic happiness **shallow happiness**, and call eudaemonic happiness **deep happiness**. I think that analogy compares well with other things we enjoy in life. Take for instance, shallow short term relationships versus deep meaningful relationships. Shallow sense of purpose versus deep sense of purpose. Shallow chocolate cake versus deep chocolate cake. Yummy.

In contrast to our shallow more temporary happiness, which is simply the pleasurable emotion we experience as the result of a balanced Equation of Emotion in our mind, our deeper eudaemonic happiness is a more profound feeling connected with our whole existence being in tune with the world. I consider eudaemonia as the opposite of depression. Depression isn't just sadness, it's a profound depressed state of mind and body connected with an overall feeling that life sucks, and it may not get better any time soon. Depression can grip you and not let you go, even if you experience a few moments of happiness while you're feeling depressed. The deep eudaemonic happiness is the same thing, except on the happiness side. The deep happiness of eudaemonia is more than just happiness. It's the immense joy of existence that eclipses any instance of our shallow happiness, and like an oak tree, if it's rooted deeply, can't be easily swayed by fleeting negative thoughts or emotions. Thankfully, the deep happiness of eudaemonia can grip you and not let go as well. And life feels awesome when it does.

Now, before we assume hedonic shallow happiness and eudaemonic deep happiness are just the same type of happiness expressed at different intensity levels, the differentiation between our shallow and deep happiness dates back to ancient Greece, and modern science even proves they're different from each other. Aristotle considered the deeper happiness of eudaemonia "the chief good; the end towards which all other things aim." This makes for great Greek philosophy, but is there any real evidence we can review? It turns there is. Science has measured the difference between the shallow happiness of hedonia and the deep happiness of eudaemonia at a cellular level within our bodies. So it turns out that our cells know the difference between our two types of happiness.

In 2013, and again in 2015, Barbara Fredrickson, Kenan Distinguished Professor of psychology at the University of North Carolina at Chapel Hill led two studies that seem to show our cells actually change their gene expression when we are experiencing the deep happiness of eudaemonia, but when we're experiencing the shallow happiness of hedonia, not so much. The researchers at UNC and UCLA were specifically looking at a set of immune system gene expressions that our cells alter, based on what they experience at the cellular level (otherwise known as epigenetics). The study showed that people who have high levels of deep eudaemonic happiness had "very favorable gene-expression profiles in their immune cells. They had low levels of inflammatory gene expression and strong expression of antiviral and antibody genes." In comparison, people who scored highly in shallow hedonic happiness showed less dramatic, but still positive results. So it seems our cells may even know the difference between our shallow hedonic happiness and our deep eudaemonic happiness.

Although it's good to know deep happiness may be better for us on a cellular level, it's clear from our own experience that our deep eudaemonic happiness is just better, period. It's nice to experience the happiness of looking at a beautiful sunset, but I'd never trade that for the majestic awe of feel-good amazement I experience in sensing that sun I'm looking at is just one of a countless number of stars in the universe, and I'm lucky enough to have inhabited a human body on a planet which lies the perfect distance away from this very star, on a planet that developed a self-sustaining ecosystem, with air, water, and oxygen in perfect proportions for me to be able to enjoy that beautiful sunset. The hedonic happiness portion of that situation is, "Cool, look at the pretty sunset!" The eudaemonic happiness portion of that situation is, "Holy shit, this moment and my whole life are a miracle of pure perfection!" Personally, I'd rather have the latter feeling more.

At the top end of the hedonic happiness scale, where the shallow happiness meter gets pegged is the place called **perfect happiness**. It's temporary, but it's a cool place to be. You can be perfectly happy with a new car, or a piece of cheesecake melting in your mouth. On the top end of the eudaemonic happiness scale where the deep happiness meter gets pegged is the place called **bliss**. You can't get stuck in perfect happiness. But you can get stuck in bliss. It's what some ancient texts called Nirvana, but there are tons of names for it from all over the world. We'll talk more about this soon. For now, let's look at what you can do to increase both types of happiness.

Increasing Your Happiness

So the one question we have not yet collectively answered for you is, "how do I increase the overall happiness levels in my life?" Or more specifically, "how do I hack my mind to actually increase deep happiness within me, and not just increase my pleasure or decrease my inner pain and suffering?"

Well, first, in order to learn how to do anything, including how to increase your happiness, it's helpful to refer to the adult learning model. The adult learning model has four levels of development, which are; (1) **unconscious incompetence,** (2) **conscious incompetence,** (3) **conscious competence,** then finally (4) **unconscious competence.** Level one, unconscious incompetence, is the space of not even knowing what it is that you need to know. It's when you don't know what you need to learn to become better at whatever you want to do. So learning what you don't know is what gets you from level one to level two. The second level is conscious incompetence. Conscious incompetence is when you still can't do what you want to do, but at least you know what you need to do to get to where you want to go. Level three, conscious competence, is when you actually start succeeding at what you want to do because you're focusing on it and working at what you've learned. The final stage, unconscious competence, is when you no longer even have to think about how to do what you want to do, you just do it. It's lights-out mastery at that point.

Volume I provides the knowledge you need about increasing happiness to move from level one to level two on taking command of your happiness levels. That book teaches you what it is that you need to know, telling you how your mind works and how to use that information to reduce your inner mental bullshit that blocks your happiness. While it's nice to have a goal to increase your deep happiness of eudaemonia, you first need to acknowledge that using the strategies outlined in Volume I are actually **required** to help increase your happiness. Reducing your inner bullshit can be compared to removing the flat tire on your car before you attempt to put on a good tire in its place. If you have a flat, you can try to put the good tire on over the flat tire all you want, but if the flat is still on the car, you're not going anywhere.

So you need to take the time to perform the task of consciously identifying the things on your mind's {self} map. And you need to make an effort to consciously look at your mind's Perception patterns on a moment-to-moment basis. You need to regularly perform an internal Equation of Emotion Review to throw yourself into meta-awareness so you can take back control of your mind more frequently when it's causing trouble. And finally, you need to add some quick and deep mind hacking activities into your daily routine to strengthen your mind and get it more under control over time. This will get your mental bullshit under control, enabling your name-it-tame-it circuits, and building plasticity over time. There isn't a quick fix to increase happiness that will have you immediately living in a world of sunshine and rainbows filled with unicorns who shit marshmallows. This is a process. You're working **against** all the past effects of your brain's plasticity in its habits of creating negative shit to deal with. Roman philosopher Seneca pointed out, "The mind is slow in unlearning what it has been long in learning." Seneca was a smart dude. So understand that creating the environment for deep happiness is a process.

But the cool thing is that following that process and taking the next step to practice what you learned in Volume I will move you effectively and efficiently from level two, conscious incompetence, to level three, conscious competence. To give you the tools to move you from level three, conscious competence, into level four, unconscious competence, we'll explore two branches of focus.

The first branch, which we'll introduce here but speak of later, has to do with silencing your mind, and getting your mind to process fewer Equations of Emotion overall. This is the path toward inner peace. Some ancient masters called this developing the state of **no mind**. Contemporary teachers sometimes discuss this concept as making fewer judgments about yourself and others. The idea of having fewer wasteful and negative thoughts within the mind has long been connected with the idea of being liberated from our pain and suffering. This branch is the path of mastery, and we will discuss it later in the book.

The second branch of focus—and this is where you start to learn some next level shit—involves mind hacking variables on both sides of your Equation of Emotion, which increases your happiness levels immediately. Since the hacking tools you learn here will help you move into your mastery level happiness work, this second branch is where we'll start.

When looking to hack the variables in your Equation of Emotion to increase your happiness, you need to understand how each variable impacts your shallow hedonic happiness levels, and your deeper, more permanent, eudaemonic happiness levels. Let's start with a look at your Perceptions.

Changing Your Perceptions: The Power of Positive Thinking

Changing your mind to think more positively is definitely one of the requirements to creating a happy life. Even when you get to the level of happiness mastery, where your mind is much more silent than it would normally be, if your mind's non-silent times are filled with negative Perceptions, it's harder to hold on to your positive mojo. Although we're about to see that thinking positive isn't the biggest piece of our happiest puzzle, it is a required piece of it. You need to be able to teach your mind to look for the good in life rather than what it is wired to do, which is to look for potential threats against you. In addition, when dealing with other people around you, which is something you do a lot of the time, you need to teach your mind to be able to see things from other people's perspectives, so you can better understand where they're coming from, and so you can bridge the gap between your Perceptions and theirs. This can ultimately reduce the amount of conflict you experience when dealing with others.

As a warning, seeing the good in life is not easy work. Our brains are wired to notice the threats in life first, and the brain circuits that notice threats work much faster than the circuits that notice beauty, love, and things connected with our higher human virtues. It turns out anger and hate generate much faster than happiness and love in our brains. Thankfully, science has shown that we can rewire how our brains process and react to things in our world. By consciously choosing how we see the world, we can literally rewire our brains in both form and function. And yes, science proves it. A quick example of how our brains change as a result of how we use them are the studies done in the UK regarding something called, "The Knowledge".

The Knowledge

Even if you've never been to London, you may imagine that as one of the world's major cities, street traffic there can be congested at times. And because it's such a popular city for tourist and business travelers, there are thousands of cabs operating in and around the city at all hours of the day. To ensure London's traffic issues are not compounded by adding in a bunch of wandering cab drivers with mediocre knowledge of the city's routes and traffic patterns, London requires that new cab drivers pass a test before getting approval to drive a cab. This test is so comprehensive and daunting, that it has its own scary name. It's called The Knowledge.

London is a huge and complex city, but it's also very old. In the larger metropolitan area it has 25,000 winding streets built on top of ancient horse paths, some of which are one-way-only streets and some of which change their traffic patterns at different times of the day. Beyond that, the city has 100,000 points of interest, and it has 325 main routes that connect the various points around the city, including government buildings, major businesses, tourist attractions, hotels, hospitals, houses of worship, pubs, restaurants, etc. In order to ensure cab drivers can get from place to place in the most efficient way possible, while dynamically routing themselves around spontaneous traffic snarls that could pop up anywhere at any time, London cab drivers are required to memorize the information contained in The Knowledge. No GPS. No pulling the map out while driving or asking the passenger how to get where they're going.

As a result of this rather tough memorization requirement, it takes the average applicant four years of study and seven attempts to pass the cab driving test. It turns out that in studies of the cab drivers' brains who passed the test, numerous MRI brain scans revealed that the gray matter portion of their brains associated with learning and memory physically grew in size as a result of their memorization activities. How they used their brain changed how their brain was shaped. In addition, new white matter glial cells (the communication lines) in that part of the brain grew dramatically. The net result was that the way the cab drivers' brains communicated and functioned changed based on what the cab drivers did with their thoughts and actions. This was an amazing discovery, and it's now been duplicated all over the brain. It turns out that thinking about how to play a piano piece without actually playing it can not only improve the person's later performance of that piece, but thinking about and playing the piece makes the portion of their brain associated with hand and finger coordination grow in size and increase its interconnectivity. And, of course, this neuroplastic phenomenon isn't limited to our brains learning about how to drive around the city of London or play the piano.

When you consciously decide to change your Perceptions about the world from one moment to the next, you are using your conscious thought to change the communication patterns in your brain. This pattern becomes more permanent and subconscious over time. So when you consciously manage your Perceptions, such as choosing to see the good in a situation instead of the bad, you are using your brain's existing wiring to hack your Equation of Emotion to give you a more positive emotional experience, and you are training your brain to create those positive patterns more and more often so that your positive tendencies become more ingrained over time. This one step can make you a happier person overall, no matter where you start on the happiness ladder. Psychology calls this type of approach "reappraisal". Us regular folks call it taking lemons and making lemonade.

So there's no more hiding behind the thought, "I'm just a negative person." Or, "I'm wired to be pessimistic." Because science has proven that a bullshit excuse. While your genetic tendencies can have an impact on you if you leave them alone to do their natural thing, the fact is you can change your negative mind behavior if you choose to. You can consciously turn your negative thought patterns off by intentionally deciding to see things in a more positive light, and keeping your focus on the positive when your brain wants to go negative. And by doing so, you will be slowly strengthening the brain circuits that create positive thought, and eventually, the negative circuits that help create your inner bullshit will starve to death. Science calls that atrophy, but it's a real thing. The brain circuits we don't use get pruned, just like muscles we don't use get weaker over time.

Personally, I think it's time that you killed off some of your negative brain parts with some positive thinking. This practice of seeing your rainy days as opportunities to stay inside and play your favorite video game not only creates a positive Perception you can enjoy, it diminishes the potential for a negative emotion to arise if you focus on the rainy day part. In Volume I, one of the stories I told was about teaching my son to focus on sharing the joy of his opponent's win in air hockey rather than wallowing in his loss. It's worked great for him since. But it's a learned action. He's actively hacking his Perception. And I need to remind him sometimes. It's tough. His brain is wired to be pissed and disappointed when he loses. Thinking positively doesn't come naturally. That said, if you can train your brain to be more positive, that mental action can make all the difference in the world when dealing with your natural brain wiring.

The Ugly Alternative

The alternative to not developing these skills in your mind is simply to let your negative emotions flourish uncontrollably, which creates negative effects in your body and mind. So positive thinking is definitely something you need to learn. I can tell you as someone who started with bad brain wiring and who used to struggle with negative thoughts, emotions, and even depression, it does get easier to think more positively over time. Thinking positively and looking for the good in every situation changed the patterns in my own brain, which then became habit, thanks to plasticity. Now I see the positive first, and I get to decide if the negative Perception should even get an ounce of my attention.

Thanks to plasticity, the more you practice positive thinking, the quicker and stronger your positive thinking habits get, until the process of seeing the positive in life seems to happen automatically. As a bonus, this talent keeps your mind from developing negative thought patterns, which could eventually pull you out of the deep happiness of eudaemonia, should you achieve it. So maintaining a pattern of creating positive Perceptions for yourself is a required tool you should have. That said, you should also know that positive thinking has limitations.

Changing Your Perceptions: The Limitations of Positive Thinking

Consciously changing your Perceptions has effects on both types of happiness. Because your Perceptions feed your mind's Equation of Emotion, every positive Perception you create that agrees with an idea of {self} is going to bump your temporary hedonic happiness meter and create some hedonic happiness for you. Period. Such moments create opportunities for you to experience moments of complete happiness on the high end of that meter. Those happy feelings do create positive outcomes in your body and mind. According to studies, health improvements will most likely occur. In these moments, positive emotion hormones get pumped into your blood stream. Your stress levels decrease. Consciously cultivating those hedonic happiness moments with positive thinking is great. That said, changing your Perceptions doesn't increase your eudaemonic happiness, but it can stop it from decreasing if you're in a high state of well being. Actually increasing your eudaemonic happiness is a bit more complicated. And so here, we run into one of the limitations of positive thinking.

Changing your Perceptions can't really increase your deep eudaemonic happiness for a few reasons. First, your mind sometimes run out of energy to think positively because your brain is wired to look for threats. It's what science calls your **negative bias**. From a nature's ecosystem perspective, the life organisms that are quicker to identify threats live longer and go on to mate. You're fighting millions of years of evolution there. So even in the instance where you've practiced increasing your happiness, and plasticity has changed your thought patterns to be more positive, sometimes life's bullshit comes at you so incessantly, your mind eventually runs out of positive vibes, and simply gives in to say "fuck it, okay, this sucks. OMG, let's go be depressed." Second, if you learn to consistently create positive Perceptions, but you're still plagued with a complex {self} map in your mind, that makes it even harder for deep happiness to be achieved by managing your Perceptions alone. Because if you have a lot of shit on your {self} map, and you try to manage your Perceptions associated with that long list, it gets exponentially exhausting. There are simply too many Perceptions to reappraise. Studies have shown we only have a finite amount of mental resources during the day to redirect our minds in this fashion. So the more complex your mind's {self} is, the quicker you run out of positive energy.

Lastly, we pointed out very early in the book that your mind's {self} is your false self, sometimes called your ego, and that it's only an idea of what your mind thinks is you. As we discussed the science of {self}, we uncovered that your mind's {self} isn't really an accurate definition of you. It's simply a set of ideas that are completely malleable. And beyond the ancient sages telling us so, we personally verified that your mind's {self} is a mental illusion.

So how deeply happy can you become when you're running around changing your thoughts in an attempt to satisfy an illusion? When you engage in that activity, you're playing the game of the man behind the happiness door who only provides happiness from behind that door in small increments when you've aligned the stars in the universe and your Equation of Emotion is balanced. That's not turning the key and kicking in the door of happiness to stroll in whenever you want to. That's manipulating the same old system that operates under the rules you want to break.

Although thinking positive and looking at the good in life does keep your mind from going all emo on you, dying its hair black, and locking itself in it's room with a sign that says "KEEP OUT, thinking positive is a crutch", thinking positive is indeed only the oil in your happiness engine that keeps the engine operating smoothly. It's not the engine itself. It's not the way you get to happiness where happiness then becomes your way.

So if altering your Perceptions of the world doesn't move your deep profound happiness meter, what does get you into your deepest most profound happiness? The answer to that question is found directly on the other side of your Equation of Emotion. On the other side of the Equation of Emotion across from your Perceptions lies your Expectations/Preferences about things that are associated with your mind's {self}.

And so it's here, again, that we are led right back to the {self} for our big answers on happiness.

8 Happiness All Comes Back to {self}

> Happiness depends upon ourselves.
> —Aristotle

In Volume I, and in brief reviews throughout this book, we shared numerous examples of the world's ancient luminaries and leading thinkers who told us that the secrets to a perfect life are connected with knowing about the {self}. Along that suggested path, we discussed the scientific findings on the {self}, what ideas make up your mind's {self}, why your definition of {self} is required by your brain, and how having a {self} impacts your moment-to-moment emotions and daily life experience. We discussed that when left to its own devices, your brain always retreats back to its default activity connected with thoughts about the {self}. We looked at how consciously simplifying {self} can reduce your personal pain and suffering. And we argued that every one of humanity's failings is clearly connected with the unconscious defense of {self}.

The {self}

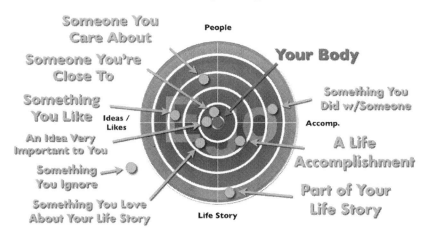

And so here we stand in our discussion of the deepest most profound levels of happiness, which the world's greatest philosophers called "the chief good," and around which we've shown all human activity gravitates, and we are led right back to the doorstep of the {self} for our answers.

So is this where I make the super-obvious remark that in order to increase your deep happiness levels you need to change yourself? Yes. Yes, I think it is. And I know what you might be thinking, "Did this guy just take me through a book and a half of mind bending bullshit, to Aristotle and back, with pit stops at fMRI studies, cellular consciousness, and quantum fucking physics, for him to now tell me that in order for me to be happier I need to change myself? Are you fucking kidding me right now?"

Feel free to throw something. I won't tell anyone. ;-)

Yes, it sounds ridiculously obvious to say that if you don't have complete control of your mind to draw forth deep seated happiness at will, you need to change something in yourself to get that. But to be fair, now you know exactly what we're talking about when we say the words "change your {self}," and now you know exactly why that generic message that everybody uses but never explains can actually be proven scientifically accurate. But there's one other hugely important reason you needed to go all this way before coming back to the realization you need to change the {self}.

And that reason is that the {self} hates to change.

The Mind's {self} Resists Change

I'm absolutely not going to pull any punches with making this particular point. It's a fact that you picked up this book because you had an interest in increasing your happiness through this new approach of hacking the mind's mechanisms that both delay and provide your happiness. You knew that whatever was in this book would require you to change something about yourself. Maybe you'd need to change the way you thought about things, or the way you did things to be able to find the magic key to the happiness door, which you could then kick in whenever you damn well felt like it. But what you didn't know, even at the moment you were admitting maybe you needed to consider making a change, was that even at the moment you selected to read this book, there was something within you already resisting everything you would read within these pages, and resisting any change you would then try to make. It resists you any time you pick up a {self} help book. It's partly why many of us read one {self} help book after another and never wind up getting any {self} help.

Because the thing within you resisting your {self} help, resisting making any changes at all, resisting you increasing your deep eudaemonic happiness, is your mind's own {self}. Because your mind's {self} **hates** change. And I mean that literally. In Volume I, we basically defined hate as the reaction of your mind saying, "your very existence threatens my sense of {self}". That's what hate is. It's why Boston Red Sox fans hate the New York Yankees, and vice versa. It's why the Palestinians hate the Israelis, and vice versa. And it's why picnics hate rainy days. And vice versa. The one side's very existence threatens the sense of {self} of the other. When the mind's {self} is forced to confront and address the potential need for this thing called **"change"** - by definition that "change" threatens what the {self} is at the moment.

The very existence of a suggested change threatens the {self}'s sense of {self}. That matches our definition of hate perfectly. Thus, when the mind's {self} looks at change, it generates the fear and anger based emotion of hate deep down within us. Bottom line, every time you offer the opportunity for the {self} to change within you, with your good intentions, and your reasoning, and scientific studies, and all the other crap you want to try to pile on top, the mind's {self} takes one look at that change and says, "fuck that noise! I'm not changing shit."

That's why changing your {self} is hard. That's why it requires so much work. But don't worry. We're gonna hack that.

From our brain's perspective, the fundamental reason we hate change is because when something around us changes, that change could pose a threat to us and needs to be evaluated immediately. For instance, when someone walks into the room in which you're sitting, that new person changes your immediate environment. So your eyes instantly want to look up to see who just walked in. You want to check to see if it's someone friendly, or if it's your dead neighbor from next door, because as you expected, the zombie apocalypse has started with you as its first victim. Seriously though, this basic reaction is the reason some people don't like when new neighbors move into the neighborhood bringing with them a foreign religion. Their minds see that as a change in their environment which could threaten {self}. So they start peeking out their curtains to assess this new environmental change and decide what the most decent human way is not to like them. It's an unconscious function of the human nervous system run amok within our society. And this whole threat to {self} mechanism is why our minds hate changes in our environment.

An even worse kind of change, however, is when the mind's very definition of {self} changes. When that happens, that's when the internal shit really hits the fan. Alarm bells and whistles go off, red lights start flashing, and every bit of the mind gets put on alert. This occurs for a very specific reason. Changes occur frequently in our environment, right? Just taking a drive down the road can give us that experience. So our minds are accustomed to checking for threats within our environment. These aren't usually a big deal. But if we change something within the walls of our mind's definition of {self}, that changes the whole ballgame for our mind. The action of changing even a single idea of {self} changes the fundamental list of things that the mind must protect against threats... **and not only with every single Perception that our mind creates moving forward... but also for all the past Perceptions it's already checked and cleared.**

So this creates a pile of paperwork for the mind, not to mention, the brain has now been found negligent at performing one of its primary tasks; if something has to change in {self}, that means the brain had the wrong definition of {self} this whole time, and you were in jeopardy the whole time because of that mistake. It's like a huge scandal that the mind wants to cover up, and what better way to cover it up than admit the mistake never happened in the first place, and that the change in {self} does **not** indeed need to occur. Besides, changes in {self} can be confusing, so we should just leave that alone.

This is what is happening when you're sitting in the restaurant thinking, "Steak? Yeah, I love steak! Wait, I forgot. I added {I'm on a diet} to my {self} map yesterday. Does that mean I can't order the steak, and I need to get a salad instead? Or I could do the lasagne? Oh wait, that's got too many carbs. Crap. I hate this new diet thing." With just the one little change, it creates a ripple effect that changes everything moving forward, and everything we've experienced in the past. This is why the mind particularly hates making changes to the {self}. Changing {self} changes the list of what it needs to protect from threats. And that's why the mind typically wants to avoid changes in {self} at all costs.

You need to understand that your {self} resists change at every step of the way, so you can use this knowledge to your advantage. The great warrior and General Sun Tzu, who wrote the timeless book "The Art of War", once said, "Know thyself, know thy enemy. A thousand battles, a thousand victories." In this case, both entities within that quote are your mind's {self}. And by knowing what your mind's {self} is, and how and why it operates, you're now set up for victory against the {self}'s resistance.

Changing the Mind's {self} to Increase Happiness

In the last several paragraphs you learned that the mind's {self} hates change because when the {self} changes, it changes everything from the mind's perspective. But this fact also brings with it a very powerful realization: If you can indeed find a way to change your {self} in your mind, that changes absolutely **everything** in your mind.

Earlier we discussed how your mind creates your entire life and even your perception of the world around you. So when you change something that is so fundamental to the mind - when you change one of the first things the mind assembles after you were born - when you change the very definition of your existence itself - it changes your mind, and thus your whole life from that moment forward. From a process standpoint, when your mind's {self} gets changed, the list of {self} items that the limbic system has to check for threats gets changed. This can alter and even remove certain fears, angers and sadnesses from your life. When your mind's {self} changes, your {self} associated thoughts within your default mode network change as well. Remember from Volume I that the default mode network is firing when your {self} thoughts are humming. So when your {self} changes, your inner narrative changes for the 47 percent of your waking hours that your mind wanders—for the rest of your life. When the {self} within your mind changes, your entire life's motivation, including all of your actions, and even how you sustain your happiness changes right along with it.

When you change your mind's {self} it changes the whole game of life.

So how can you change your {self}? How do you change the whole game of life in your mind so that your happiness levels can increase in a meaningful and sustained way? The answer to that question comes in two parts. The first part is what you can do to hack the {self} consciously. The second part is what you can do to hack the {self} at a subconscious level. And you need to do both if you want any lasting effect.

Hacking the {self} Consciously

So how do you hack your {self} to increase your happiness levels? Well, you could certainly rip a page from Volume I and go through all the extraneous crap on your mind's {self} map, and decide which things you've cared about for too long that you can toss off your map and no longer care about. In other words, you could start with a little mental house cleaning. Here's a hint: When reviewing the things you're attached to, it's better to keep things like {the health of your body} and {fostering caring relationships with your family and friends}, and ditch things like {celebrity gossip}, {online politics}, and maybe even {the evening news}. You can hack the {self} consciously by telling your{self}, "I am no longer a person who cares as much about daily politics." And until election time comes around again (which unless you're a billionaire or run a major corporation is just about the only time you'll ever be able to do anything about something you disagree with), you will be less bothered by the daily noise of the political machine of your nation. The more things you can get off your mental plate, the more space you will have for happiness to develop and flourish.

But don't forget to dig deep with this process. Look at releasing or changing some of the things that you have long thought make up who you are, which fall near the center of your {self} map, but maybe don't need to anymore. For instance, if some of the positions in your party's political platform give you mixed emotions, give your{self} a break from politics for a while and reconsider your affiliation. Give your {self} some space. Or maybe you've been going to a particular religious service for a while out of a feeling of obligation or tradition. If this is true for you, stop going for a while. See if you get called back to it.

If anything you've been doing in life doesn't ring true in your heart, go explore other options and take other actions. Call everything about you into question. If your life includes cultural influences that you feel restrict you and keep you from living a happier life, ditch those cultural rules. If you're in a bad relationship that you haven't ended because the thought of being alone is scarier than ending it, end that relationship. Make room for something else. If you hate your job but you haven't quit because you need the money, cut your expenses and go find another job or another field of work. If there are ideas on your {self} map that are causing problems in the relationships you have with your family and friends, you may have to take a tough look at those, and/or maybe stop defending those ideas of {self} with your family and friends. Your mind's {self} is an invented illusion. Don't let it hurt others or your{self} because you take this illusion too seriously. This is your life. It's your mind's attachment map, and while it does affect you, you can decide what makes the cut and what doesn't, and thus what affects you and what doesn't. You can sculpt your life if you decide to. Change your life to ring true to your deeper Self.

Clearing things off your {self} map is one way to consciously hack your mind's {self}. Another way to hack the {self} is to **add** a couple particular ideas that help the {self} promote happiness. This could include adding to your {self} map the idea {I'm going to start each day by stopping to be thankful for three things I experienced yesterday}. Or you could add the idea {I'm going to be compassionate to other people's inner turmoil because they are as much a victim of that pain as any pain they make me a victim of}. Those are nice thoughts to attach to {self}. But this wouldn't be a next level book on happiness if I left you with just those. So one of the newest ideas I've got for you to try is going to be one of the toughest ideas you'll ever contemplate. But if you want more control of your mind, this is one of the most effective ideas you'll ever learn to love. The idea you need to add to your {self} map is that you love the idea of constant change.

The sound of screeching tires on pavement. The sound a record needle makes when it's scraping all the way across an LP vinyl record. The sound of Homer Simpson when he releases one of his iconic "Doh" noises. These are the types of inner noises your mind makes when a stranger suggests you should start liking the idea of constant change. Did we not **just** get done discussing how our minds **hate** change for reasons that are connected with how our brains work? Yes, yes we did. But regardless of how much our minds hate change, the most basic fundamental characteristic of the whole universe is that it constantly changes. In fact, the only thing in the universe that doesn't change, is that everything in the universe is in a constant state of change.

The Greek philosopher Heraclitus once said, "No man ever steps in the same river twice, for it's not the same river and he's not the same man." What Heraclitus meant when he made this statement comes down to the basic science of the universe. If we take a snapshot of an entire river from beginning to end at the moment you first step into it, the second step you take is into a different river compared to the first. Between the first snapshot and the next, a number of changes will have occurred. The water will have moved downstream a bit. A number of pebbles or sand particles near the bottom will have drifted as well. Fish will have moved. The very position that river holds in the universe will have changed, thanks to the spin of the Earth, and the fact that the Earth is constantly orbiting the sun. So from one perspective, nothing about that river will be the same as it was. And in the same way, with blood moving around your body, cells making changes within your body, you moving your body's position, and different molecules filling the air in your lungs with each new breath, you're not the same person between the first step and the next. Even if you hold the thought that your mind makes you who and what you are, your mind has moved in thought from one moment to the next. So even your mind has changed.

Every year, we celebrate our birthdays and the anniversaries of various events based on where we are on a calendar we built that is connected with our orbit around the sun. But we never take into consideration how the sun has moved, hurtling through its orbit around our Milky Way galaxy, and how our galaxy is moving in relative space, and that we're absolutely nowhere near where we were last year at this time in the relative cosmos. Although we've been marking time on a calendar which repeats year after year, the reality is that we've been on a constantly changing one-way journey through time and space our entire lives. We're spinning at over 1,000 miles per hour, and traveling around the sun at about 67,000 miles per hour, which itself is traveling 447,000 mph around our galaxy. Good luck at guessing how fast the galaxy is traveling.

From last year at this time, your body has changed, your mind has changed a bit, the people around you have changed, and things in your environment have changed that have helped change you. So from then to now, you're a different person than you were a year ago. So change isn't just a fundamental rule of the universe, it's also a fundamental rule about you.

So consider for a moment that you could actually add {I embrace change} to your {self} map. I realize that may be a stretch. It's tough to imagine ourselves as people who embrace change because our brains are hard-wired not to like change, and our body's natural response to change is to increase our stress response. But the fact remains that if you can consciously make the shift to be more accepting of change, and even go to the crazy extreme of expecting change to occur regularly in your life, that one little shift is certain to increase your levels of happiness. Expecting change to occur in your life fills the EP side of your Equation of Emotion with the fact that change is coming. Always. So when that change does come, your Equation of Emotion will be more balanced, even if that change temporarily sucks. The change was coming anyway, but now at least with expecting change to occur at some point, you're less sad if it's a less than favorable change, and if it's a good change, you're even more happy about it.

Taken to the extreme, if you were more embracing of change in your life, that encourages your curiosity flourish about what's going to be different today than it was yesterday. You could start to enjoy the little differences you notice in all the things going on around you from day to day. You could like meeting new strangers to see what fun could be had in the short moments of everyday life that you spend with them. You could find yourself loving how the rest of your life is going to be full of surprises, and even if some of those surprises aren't that awesome, that amazing thing called "change" is certainly coming again tomorrow, so no worries, any bullshit you experience will be temporary.

Can you see how making that small addition to your {self} map might help your happiness levels?

It's a simple fact that the universe doles out change in a never ending metamorphosis, so this new perspective could help the universe create one Perception after another that is more pleasing to you. When change comes, you expect it, so it increases your hedonic happiness levels through a more balanced Equation of Emotion. And because your entire mind's {self} now senses a deep connection and harmony with the most basic fundamental characteristic of the universe itself, your deep eudaemonic happiness starts to flourish now, too.

It's silly, in a universe that serves up change in every single moment of its existence, that we would let our minds recoil from change, when the reality of our existence is that everything always changes. If we learn to embrace those changes, that very shift in our minds become a source of happiness for us any time something changes. When a happy moment comes, we can be happy that the positive change occurred. And we can be just as happy when that happy moment fades, because that fading happiness creates a space for more change and different experiences of happiness to occur. In addition, when a sad, angry, or fearful moment occurs, we can be grateful that when those moments pass, our next ones will be that much more enjoyable.

Sure, the idea of embracing change can be challenging, but we don't need Captain Obvious to remind us that changing how things work in our minds is a required part of making our life awesome by hacking our minds to create that reality, and consciously adding {I embrace change} to our {self} maps might just be one of the conscious mind hacks we need to consider to bring more happiness into our lives.

These are just a few ideas for consciously hacking your mind's {self}. But let's now discuss where the real power to change our lives lies.

Hacking the {self} Subconsciously

Hacking the {self} consciously is an effective approach to hacking your {self}, but frankly it can also be hit and miss process. For instance, if you try to add something onto your {self} map which is in conflict with something else on your {self} map, that internal conflict can sabotage your attempted change. It takes a lot of dedication and willpower to make conscious changes to the {self} that stand the test of time. What is more effective, is entering the control room of your mind to change {self} on a **subconscious** level. Don't let that idea scare you. Contrary to how it sounds, this is when hacking your {self} gets a lot easier.

Hacking your {self} subconsciously happens when your mind rewrites your {self} because of something it experiences through meta-awareness. In Volume I, we discussed that when you learn to turn your attention back onto your mind itself, it shifts your awareness into meta-awareness, where you watch your mind and understand why it's doing what it's doing. In Volume I, we explained how performing an Equation of Emotion review can put you into meta-awareness, but other mind disciplines do this as well. Activities which fall under the umbrella of meditation disciplines do this specifically. One of the huge side effects of this awareness shift, where you get to see your mind from the space of meta-awareness, is that when you see your mind operating from that higher level of awareness, you can actually **feel** that distance between your awareness and your mind. On a conscious level, your experience of seeing your mind operating from a short distance spotlights the fact that you aren't just the operation of your mind. You're that awareness too. After all, you can't see your mind unless there's some sort of separation between you and your mind, which means your mind isn't the entirety of your conscious existence. Now… while this is a cool curiosity for your conscious mind, your subconscious mind takes the discovery of this separation from mind **very** seriously.

When your subconscious mind experiences the distance between your awareness and the activity of your mind, it immediately acknowledges the separation between you and what it previously defined was you. This is an important point for you to understand, because it's your subconscious awareness that creates your **feelings** about stuff. It's where the feelings of your emotions comes from. And in this particular case of existing in meta-awareness, your subconscious is creating the feeling associated with the space between your conscious awareness and your mind's activity. But your subconscious is also ultimately responsible for assembling of your mind's {self}.

What this means is that the little epiphany that "there's more to you than you realized just a moment ago" now requires your subconscious mind to rewrite its definition of {self}. Discovering that you are more than the old {self} now requires a newer {self} to be created. A {self 2.0}, if you will, that includes your newly discovered awareness outside of your mind's {self}. This makes the outer boundaries of {self} bigger and more inclusive than what they were just a moment ago. Your mind says, "I'm responsible to keep this definition of {self} thing up to date. But now I've just experienced there's an awareness that is separate from what I had previously defined as {self}, until just a moment ago. So now I need to change the {self} to include the larger picture that it is more than just the ideas that I had assembled previously. I need to include that new awareness thing somehow." And so the mind rewrites {self} to include that awareness feeling, and the bounds of the {self} expand outward to include the old idea of {self}, **and** our awareness of that {self}.

Now… leaving that there for a moment, the fact is that when this shift happens, it helps us live a calmer, more emotionally balanced life. Why is that so? One of the best analogies I can think of to explain why this meta-awareness experience helps you is to imagine your {self} as a puddle of water outside on the ground somewhere. Imagine a puddle of water large enough to float a couple of toy boats in it. The puddle of water is your mind's {self}, and the toy boats represent things on your {self} map. If we were to throw a life problem into that puddle, in the form of a decent-sized rock, that life-problem rock is going to make a big splash in your little puddle. Depending on the size of the rock, it might make a splash so violent that water could splash up out of the puddle, making you feel smaller, and it may even sink one or both of your boats. If you feel small and the problem feels large, that moment of turmoil can be catastrophic.

Now imagine expanding your puddle out to be a small pond with the same two toy boats floating in it. Now your {self} seems bigger, but without any more stuff on it. Throwing that same life-problem rock into your larger pond will now only create small waves in relation to the pond. Your boats might rock a bit, but they're not going to tip over because of the smaller waves. So the same sized life-problem affects you less. Now let's expand your pond out to be the size of a lake, keeping your same two boats. If you throw the same life-problem rock into the water of your {self}, you will hardly even notice the ripples, and the toy boats will be completely safe. You can now even handle splashes from the biggest life-problem rocks.

Expanding your puddle of {self} is what happens when the subconscious expands your mind's {self} outward to include your awareness that you are more than your mind's {self}. You become bigger without adding any more attachments to your mind's {self} map. The same effect can be experienced when you consciously try and hack your {self} by telling your{self}, "I am bigger than my problems." Repeating this phrase over and over, "I am bigger than my problems, I am bigger than my problems, I am bigger than my problems," can sometimes help you feel bigger in relation to whatever problems you are currently facing in life. Just reading it makes you feel bigger doesn't it? It pushes the walls of your {self} out a bit for a short time, even if it's just for a few minutes to handle the crisis you're currently thinking about. Using this affirmation is the temporary conscious hack analog to the permanent hack of feeling the expansion of mind that occurs when you realize through inner experience that you are more than your mind's {self}.

Psychologist Amy Cuddy delivered a TED Talk where she told us about a physical hack that can do the same thing. In that talk, which at almost 40 million views, is one of the most popular videos on TED.com (go watch it if you haven't already), Amy told us about the feedback loop that our physical bodies have to create perceptions that our minds acknowledge and react to. She mentioned how smiling can create feelings of happiness, and she also discussed how power poses, where we expand the size of our bodies by spreading out our limbs, can decrease the levels of the stress hormones we create by 25 percent within just two minutes of performing the pose. In comparison, the people who made their bodies smaller in non-power poses experienced a 15 percent increase in stress hormones. So it turns out that making our bodies seem physically bigger creates the feedback loop that makes our mind's {self} bigger. Amy said in that talk, "So two minutes leads to these hormonal changes that configure your brain to be either assertive, confident, and comfortable, or really stress reactive, and feeling sort of shut down." Knowing that our bodies are on our {self} map, this completely makes sense to me.

Ironically, this is the same thing that happens when we add the idea of a belief in God to our {self} maps. In particular, the thought of {God doesn't give us more than we can handle} can be a very powerful idea of {self}. When people see themselves as part of something bigger, their {self} seems bigger in comparison to what it was before. And just as seeing our minds from meta-awareness pushes the {self} boundaries out a bit, the idea that we're connected to a consciousness bigger than our own does the same thing. So when we have a faith in something bigger than ourselves, we seem to handle more than someone who does not have a faith. And science shows that people of faith do live a bit longer, and are a bit happier in life than those without that belief. That said, I used the word 'ironically' at the beginning of this paragraph, because this idea of God is usually introduced to us through a particular religion, which brings with it a ton of attachments we are then required to add to our {self} map. This complicates things. These additional {self} ideas that come along with the dogma package sometimes become a more a destructive force than a helpful one in our lives. This is how religion becomes a negative force globally while remaining a positive force personally.

I think the problem of dogmatic attachment is why most global religions had originally included meditation as a core practice of their religion (and many still do). Meditation expands our {self} boundaries. Meditation is a practice of meta-awareness, which illuminates the space between conscious awareness and the mind's activity. And it's in this moment of present awareness, your mind hiccups and realizes you are more than the simple {self} it thought you were a moment ago.

Now… from a scientific perspective, there are over 1,400 studies that show how meditation is beneficial to our health and well-being. Meditation trains the mind to be quiet, which results in fewer Equations of Emotion being processed. It changes the {self} on a subconscious level through expanding our {self} beyond its old boundaries. And so your {self} expands outward. Your puddle of {self} gets bigger, and you can handle bigger life-challenge rocks.

So hacking the {self} subconsciously comes down to entering meta-awareness purposefully and letting your subconscious notice and feel the difference when you're in that space. You can use a meditative practice to do this. Or you can use your new understanding of mind and the observation of your Equation of Emotion in your moment-to-moment awareness. Or you can use both. Meditation typically has to be done with some time set aside, but monitoring your mind through the Equation of Emotion Review can be done all day, every day, wherever you are. When an emotion starts to arise, you simply ask yourself what particular attachment of {self} is in play, and what Perception you're having that's interacting with that attachment. Using both meditation and mindful conscious awareness is super powerful. It's the ultimate mind hacking strategy.

When looking to hack your {self}, it's best to give your mind the opportunity to have a realization about {self} at an experiential level. Experiences from within change the {self} in dramatic ways immediately and without resistance. There is no committee, no review board, and no discussion when {self 2.0} is created within. That change in {self} is not just another idea of {self} that's introduced by some book, which you then try to convince your {self} is beneficial. That's your mind seeing its flawed idea of {self} with its own inner eye, and saying "oops, I better fix that." The mind tends to believe the things it senses and experiences from within. This is when the {self} gets rewritten in a small but extremely beneficial way, up through large changes with huge benefits. Oliver Wendell Holmes said that a mind that is stretched by a new experience can never go back to its old dimensions. This is what he was talking about.

Bringing this full circle back to your search for happiness . . . a newly updated and more accurate {self} means having a different {self 2.0} map feeding into your Equations of Emotion. This allows you to experience increases in both your temporary hedonic happiness and your deeper eudaemonic happiness. True to everything presented in this book, your entire emotional landscape can change as a result to a change in {self}. But unlike consciously removing things from your {self} map, this subconscious change of expanding {self} is a more dramatic change. Let's look at why this is so and what exactly happens in your mind when this expansion occurs.

***

If you remember when we first talked about the {self} map, we said that stuff closer to the center is considered higher value {self} stuff than other stuff that falls farther out on the map. All our life's decisions and motivations come from where things fall on our {self} map. In Volume I, when I had the decision to save my son or my cell phone, the thing that was closer to the center of my map won that contest. Similarly, your next buying decision will be completely determined by what fits better with the ideas of {self} that fall closest to the center of your map. Price, product benefits, brand ideas, and even the aesthetic value of the logo and packaging, will all get measured against what's most important to you.

Well, when your mind creates its new {self 2.0} map to include the experience of your awareness beyond your mind, the mind's {self 1.0} crap no longer holds the very center of your map. This crazy new experience of **the awareness beyond your mind** gets awarded the center of your new {self 2.0} map, pushing {self 1.0} out a bit to make space. It happens that way because your subconscious mind creates the feelings associated with the new experience of you watching your mind. And at that moment you became more than just your mind. You are your mind and whatever awareness that is watching your mind. All of that is now you.

So your mind adds your awareness that seems beyond your mind to your new {self 2.0} map. And because it's an experience from within, your mind's {self 1.0} stuff gets pushed out from the center of the map to make room for your new understanding of you. Your {self 2.0} map gets written starting with your conscious awareness at the very center, surrounded by your old {self 1.0} crap. Yes, unfortunately, this old {self 1.0} stuff still makes it onto the new map, because it's all that you've ever known. So the crap that used to annoy you still annoys you, but because it's farther out from the center on your new {self 2.0} map, at least it annoys you less.

Remembering our puddle-to-pond-to-lake analogy, this is how meditation chills us out:

1. Our {self} map grows in size without adding any more individual {self} ideas that could wind up ruining our day, which helps us become bigger than our problems.
2. We discover a more accurate definition {self} that now includes an awareness that can be elevated above the fray.
3. All the rest of our {self} crap, including even the sense that we are our bodies, gets pushed out from the center of our {self} map, which reduces our negative bullshit about those things on our {self} map (because things farther out on our map affect us less, and now everything on our previous {self} map is pushed farther out than before, thanks to our experience while in meta-awareness).

Any time you enter meta-awareness, be it through a meditative practice such as yoga, contemplative prayer, or mindfulness meditation, or through the conscious awareness activity of performing an Equation of Emotion Review, you're not only being separated from your mind's bullshit, becoming a witness to it rather than a victim of it. When you can take control of your mind, you can know that your waking awareness isn't completely a result of your mind. And at the point you become practiced at seeing your mind's {self} from a short distance away, you start to realize your mind's {self} actually isn't you.

This is the deepest unspoken secret of all the world's religions. And it's what the scientists and philosophers pointed to when they spoke of this being the beginning of wisdom. This idea that the mind's {self 1.0} is not really us is the doorway to knowing {self 2.0}. Knowing {self 2.0} not only makes life better for us, but it opens the door to discovering {self 3.0}, otherwise known as Self with a capital S, otherwise known as our true Self, sometimes called Spirit. And this is where life can become perfect. This is knocking on the door of the very deepest secrets of {self} that the world's ancient masters wanted you to know.

Hacking the {self} subconsciously is the easiest way to go from {self 1.0} to {self 2.0}, and it's the **only** way to go from {self 2.0} to {self 3.0}, otherwise known as the discovery of the true Self. This is when your experience of inner discovery rewrites the {self} in ways your conscious mind could only dream of. Thus, the most effective changes you can ever make to your {self} will need to be done at the subconscious level, through meta-awareness practices.

It is for this reason that you need to develop a practice of getting into meta-awareness. So you can most easily hack your {self} for higher levels of hedonic and eudaemonic happiness. Meditate more. Do more yoga. Do more earnest introspection with the model of your Equation of Emotion and the variables that feed your pain and suffering beyond just reading these Mind Hacking Happiness books. Be able to see your mind in operation from a short distance from within your mind, so you can eventually separate from the pain and suffering that your mind creates as part of its process to defend {self}. Learn to see your {self} for the mental illusion it is. That is the path to true and lasting happiness.

In the beginning of Volume I, I promised to show you the path to the place beyond happiness. I said I would not only show you the way to happiness, but that I would show you how to get to the place where happiness is your way. While I can't take you there myself, because it's a journey that can only be done alone, I'm about to explain to you the secrets of Enlightenment, the ultimate expansion of {self} through subconscious hacking.

9 The Basics of Spiritual Enlightenment

> He who knows others is wise.
> He who knows himself is enlightened.
> —Lao Tzu

[As a heads up, in this chapter we're going to slow down a bit as we roll into this most ancient mystical topic to give it the reverence it deserves, especially as we start to initiate this new discussion on the potential science that makes spiritual enlightenment possible and replicable. If you're new to the concept of enlightenment, this will be a good way to start our discussion. If you're familiar with the concept, it will be a good way to proceed forward in adding science into the mix of ancient wisdom, and mind exercises we've covered thusfar.]

Now that you've learned exactly how the deep mind hacks of conscious and subconscious changes to {self} can increase your deep eudaemonic happiness, you don't have to just swallow it when that long-haired California hippie says, "**Dude,** you should **totally** meditate." Yes, California hippies even call females "dudes". To dig deeper into that topic, in this chapter we're going to peek into the deepest subconscious secrets that can be uncovered from within, which are usually referred to as Spiritual Enlightenment.

The Door to Enlightenment

Picture, the following scene: You're standing in front of an ancient wooden door that has been framed into the side of a very remote mountain. Behind this very door lie the ancient secrets of life and the universe that the past masters all tried to teach us, but which we weren't ready to hear, or that we simply misunderstood. These are the secrets to opening **your** mind to a Truth long forgotten by humanity, waiting to be rediscovered. Secret capabilities of human mind that are so powerful, when they surface in someone, they get written into history. They open your mind to its full potential, to its full intelligence, and gives you access to both the conscious and subconscious realms which create your reality, and which can transform your world. Behind this door lies access to the deepest hidden secrets of your mind that you can use to control your mind to a level you've never experienced before, and thus control your life at a level you never thought possible. Behind this door are the secrets of being everything you wanted to be; a super business person, a super warrior, a super parent, a super lover, a super leader, and even the potential to be superhuman. Behind this door are the secrets of transforming your{self} into being a super-chill, fearless badass, who isn't afraid to make your life whatever the hell you want it to be, and being someone who can bend the entire world to your will. Behind this door are deepest secrets of human Self.

As you look at the door, you can see the names of previous masters who have passed through this door engraved in the wood. You look, and immediately see the rebelliously scrawled inscription, "Jesus was here." Then you see a smaller but very cleanly carved "Muhammad." And as you look, you see them all. Some names you recognize. Others you don't. There are thousands of names. Plato. Buddha. St. John of the Cross. Lao Tzu. Krishna. Aristotle. Dōgen. Seneca. Bahá'u'lláh. Descartes. Albert Einstein. Carl Jung. Gandhi. Alan Watts. Eckhart Tolle. They're all over the place. There's a knife sticking in the door for new names to be inscribed. It's sticking through a Jimi Hendrix sticker. Over the doorway there's a sign. It reads, "Welcome. This is the doorway to your deepest mind. There is no latch. You must figure out how to open it for yourself. Please be warned that if you enter here, anything is possible, and you should know sometimes God stops by for tea. If you enter and find your way back out, you will know everlasting happiness, and life will be one playful experience after another, even if the shit is hitting the fan. Your name will be automatically added to the door as you leave."

This scene isn't just imaginary bullshit. It's real. You are actually standing at that door with what you are about to learn. Now, I can't lead you through that door. You have to figure out how to open it and step through it yourself. It's a solo trip. But I can tell you how others have opened it, and I can share with you some of the things you're going to find in there, which might prompt you to try to open the door and enter. We're about to have a very open and honest discussion about the topic of Spiritual Enlightenment so you can know exactly what it is, how it works in the mind, the associated science, the reason it seems to be able to turn regular people into world class sages, the reason it removes all of our pain and suffering when we discover it, and how you might one day experience enlightenment for yourself. I'm even going to share with you my first person experience of what it's like to pass through the door of an enlightenment experience, and come out on the other side. And what it's like to live day to day after that experience.

First, An Admission

Before we move forward, you should know that I'm not supposed to tell you any of what I'm about to tell you. In the world of enlightenment, the first rule of fight club is that you don't talk about fight club. In addition, the second rule about fight club . . . well, you get it. I kid about this a bit, but in all seriousness, there are going to be more than a few masters from various traditions who don't think you and I should have this conversation. They would remind me that telling you outright about my perceptions of enlightenment might later taint your perceptions and create expectations, and even inhibit you from finding enlightenment yourself. Though my fellow liberation teachers are completely justified in making their point, because the fact is that there **are indeed a lot of good reasons that I should not be telling you what I am about to tell you,** please understand that we are going to completely ignore every one of those good reasons and spill the beans anyway.

For the record, here are those reasons:

Reason #1
The first reason I'm not supposed to speak to you so directly about this topic is because it can add attachments to these ideas within your mind. The fact is that everything I am about to tell you about enlightenment may become an attachment in your mind about the topic of {enlightenment}. But enlightenment only truly occurs with the release of all attachments of the mind, and a complete dissolution of {self}. So adding more attachments of the mind and piling on more ideas associated with {enlightenment} technically leads you in the wrong direction. So if you take what I say here and make it an attachment to the idea of {spirituality} or {religion}, you'll be farther from attaining enlightenment than you ever have been. So know that you should hold anything I say here at arm's length and not make it part of you.

Reason #2
The second reason I'm not supposed to speak to you about this stuff is because of the expectations it can give you about your own development of mind, which can be counterproductive to your development. As I tell you about the potential levels of attainment others have achieved, you might set the expectations in your mind that you should attain that same level of understanding or experience. This can lead you completely off the path, because if you practice for a while and fail to attain the same experiences or benefits as others have, you can become disappointed and dejected and cynical about your own growth. This is the equivalent of going to the gym and working out for a couple weeks with little improvement, then walking by the magazine rack in the grocery store to see a slim and muscular workout model on the cover and think, "Holy shit, I'm never gonna get there. Why even bother?" And this is a real danger.

Sometimes that door of deep mind on the mountain opens quickly. Sometimes it takes years of standing there, practicing to open it. If the ancient door of deep mind doesn't open for you right away, embrace the incremental improvements you experience by simply being on the path and practicing. Remember the health benefits that studies show come with inner peace practices. Notice and appreciate the small but beneficial improvements in your mind you experience along the way.

There is some good news which offsets this ancient risk, however: It's the modern age now. With the brand new meta-awareness tools from Volume I, the scientific perspective on Enlightenment, the amazing communications technologies that link us all together, and the many approaches to enlightenment, I think you have a real shot at developing your enlightenment skills.

Reason #3
The third reason I'm supposed to remain quiet has to do with the limitations of language itself. When it does come, Enlightenment comes as a result of inner experiences catalyzed by mind, and then afterward, it becomes a stream of experience. And here's the rub; experiences can't be fully explained in words. You can tell me what it's like to perform your favorite hobby or activity, including what you're thinking when you do it, and the body sensations you feel while doing it. But unfortunately, our language is limited, and I would have to perform your hobby with the same level of knowledge or skill that you have to completely grasp your experience. And even then, because I'm not you, my experience won't be the same as yours.

Similarly, enlightenment is not something that can be understood by your thinking mind after an explanation. You can't understand it from reading a book. You can't get it by thinking about it. You can't just figure it out. You have to get your mind into a very particular state of consciousness, experience it, and become it. It's an experiential thing.

That said, while it's true that I could never explain to you another experiential thing, such as plunging your hand into warm swirling water (because to do that would take an infinite assembly of words and analogies to try and explain to you the combined concepts of warm, wet, and swirling, which you would never ever understand with your thinking brain), **I can however**, lead you to a pool of warm swirling water and tell you how to plunge your hand down into it. Boom! Instant and complete understanding for you through your own experience. So my wish here is not to provide an explanation of the answers you seek, but to be that guide who teaches you the path to get where you attain the internal experience yourself.

Reason #4
The fourth reason I'm not supposed to tell you these secrets is because when you learn them, you may just stop your search. Your intellectual curiosity may be quenched, and your mind's false {self} might say, "I've learned enough about enlightenment, I'm good." This is because of what happens to the {self} during the enlightenment process. It gets demoted quite a bit. Almost to nothing. Your **you** of {self} becomes less important. The needs of those around you (and the world, for that matter) becomes more important. You become rather {self}less. And right now, your **you** of {self} rules the roost in your mind. It thinks it's most important portion of you and wants to remain that way. (Remember that your brain is wired to defend your {self}, and you can't help it.) So your {self} does not give up that centralized power easily. And that {self} within you will indeed create feelings of fear and uncertainty for you to deal with if you decide to search for enlightenment. (This is one of the other hidden reasons I'm not supposed to tell you about this stuff – we're supposed to sneak up on your ego. We're not supposed to give it a warning that we're gonna take it apart.) Giving your mind's {self} (aka your ego) a warning makes it want to whisper in your ear; "How will this enlightenment thing affect my religion? And what does my religion think about enlightenment?" And "Who will I be afterwards, if I attain enlightenment? Should I even be searching for enlightenment?" This is where your mind's {self} starts working against your efforts like it never has before. Warning your mind's {self} about what may be ahead gives it ammunition to use. You'll need to manage this, but hanging on to the idea that you want to know the truth beyond all your mind's thoughts is your path to pushing through any resistance or fear your mind puts in your way.

Ignoring All the Reasons

Why am I ignoring these reasons to remain quiet about

enlightenment? Quite simply, history has failed miserably in leading people to enlightenment. It's the most important topic in the world, and the most important transformation that can occur in a single human's lifetime, and the simple fact that enlightenment is even possible has died out almost completely in the intellectual record of society. As of late, it's been slowly making a comeback, and maybe the fact the word enlightenment was included in the title of this book is why you picked it up. But it's time we lit the fuse on this rocket in earnest, and took a lot of the mystery out of this topic for good.

It's a simple fact that in our world almost no one understands enlightenment. Worse than that, very, very few people teach it. And even fewer know the upper limits of perfection of mind that can be attained. I want to change that. Currently, we're an entire world of the blind leading the blind when it comes to how to live individually happy lives and how to let others live individually happy lives as well. We're a bunch of clueless idiots about the path to complete and lasting inner peace, which then results in world peace. I'm pretty sure a superior math teacher wouldn't stand around and let other math teachers tell you that multiplication and division are the apex of mathematical achievement. Because although you can certainly plan farms and feed people with that subset of mathematical knowledge, the best math teachers know if you learn calculus, it can take you to the stars. So I'm not going to stand around and let some other happiness teacher tell you that life has to be all ups and downs, and that a deeply rooted eudaemonic happiness that accompanies a sustained and on demand inner peace can't be attained. **It can be attained. It is entirely possible through working with the mind. There's way more to know about your existence than you currently understand.** And you need to know that. Because it can and does change your life and make it awesome.

There are ancient words in every language and religion for what I'm about to discuss with you. That means what we are about to discuss exists across cultures and religions, and it has existed for quite some time. The idea exists globally because it is built into our physiology. You can consider it something God put within us to find, if that idea pleases you. It's a natural human experience and quite possibly an all sentient life experience. And it's the thing that the world's most recorded and immortal minds told us was the most important thing to find.

So getting to you finding it, let's get to a few basic questions about enlightenment so you know a little better what it is we're talking about.

A Few Questions

Question #1: First, why do we call what we are about to discuss "Enlightenment" or "Spiritual Enlightenment"?

Answer: Great question! I'm glad you asked. The reason we call it "Enlightenment" is because we use the word enlightenment to express a gain in knowledge about something. For instance, when we learn about concepts in math or science, we can say we are more learned, or enlightened, about math or science. This translates to any topic. When we learn about basket weaving, we can say we're enlightened about basket weaving. In this same vein, we call this experience "Enlightenment" because it gives use more information about ourselves and our connection with life than we've ever had before.

The term "Spiritual" is often associated with "Enlightenment" for two reasons. First, the knowledge we receive during enlightenment usually conveys information about things that we perceive as being beyond the natural limits of the physical mind and body. The source of the enlightenment experience also feels very existential, as if it comes from outside the physical boundaries of mind and body, yet it is incredibly personal and part of both. Second, as we'll discuss in Chapter 10, because enlightenment seems like a beyond-body-and-mind perception, enlightenment has it's historical roots in the teachings and writings of several religions. This doesn't mean that enlightenment is only for those who believe in a spiritual plane or 'God' as defined by a particular religion - it's not. Enlightenment exists independent of religious belief as a physical phenomenon. But the word "spiritual" often gets included with enlightenment because of this historical connection.

Question #2: We just mentioned something about gaining knowledge from within. What's that all about?

Answer: If you remember our discussion about the knowledge we gain about our mind when we have the **experience** of noticing we're not our mind, and if you also remember our discussions about exceptional levels of human intelligence coming **through** the exceptionally intelligent humans rather than **from** them, well, when we're discussing the phenomenon of Enlightenment, we're talking about those same two phenomena being mixed together in an internal awakening of wisdom and intelligence that defies explanation.

When talking to people, I've tried to describe my experience (which I will share with you shortly) as tapping into, and becoming one with, the mind of God. During moments of Enlightenment, we learn things we didn't even know we could learn. In those moments, we understand absolutely everything there is to know in the universe, and as a bonus, although much of this infinite knowledge eventually fades, we **do get to keep some of that wisdom and knowledge** moving forward. And a lot of what we get to keep is **world changing shit.** And all of what we get to keep is life changing shit, without a doubt.

Now... before you pass judgment that this idea is completely friggin' crazy, and doesn't really happen within the mind, hold that thought. We're about to look at just how far back this idea goes in written history, showing us that it's a phenomenon of human existence. In addition, we've already touched on the science that makes enlightenment possible, and we'll soon discuss the effects enlightenment has even had on modern science. So chill on rejecting the idea out of hand. Besides, if you reject the idea that there's a deeper intelligence within you, you're denying all future instances of your own inspiration and creativity because those don't come from your waking consciousness either. And you wouldn't want to do that to your{self} would you?

Derek Amato's sudden prodigious savantism with his piano mastery after hitting his head shows us there's a ton of amazing stuff our minds can do that we had no idea they could do. One of the craziest mysteries of our minds, which we have yet to begin to understand, is how information can exist somewhere within our deep minds that, when we access it, can deliver wisdom and knowledge to our conscious mind and actually add to our conscious knowledge. This new knowledge and wisdom component is the very essence of Enlightenment, and why indeed it's even called "Enlightenment".

Enlightenment Is Experienced Differently In Different People

Because our human physiologies are different from each other, our personal capacities to process information are different from each other; so not all enlightenment is the same in all people. And the experiences we get vary widely. Some people sometimes get glimpses of Enlightenment, or small lessons that come one at a time over a long period of time, and sometimes people get hit by the Mack truck of Enlightenment, and get everything at once.

For some, a moment of enlightenment can feel like time stopping while they experience a moment of being one with the universe, and that we're all part of a larger universal consciousness. For others, sometimes that expansive universal feeling can also be accompanied by great beatific visions that wash through the mind, to include meaningful sounds, extremely clearly defined ideas, and sensations of transcendent intelligence which communicates, illuminates, and enlightens beyond our wildest imaginations. The upper spectrum of an enlightenment experience can feel like you are tapping into infinite intelligence, becoming part of the mind of God, and learning about all the knowledge and wisdom in the entire universe all at once, and seeing the visual representation of that knowledge and wisdom unfold before your very eyes.

We know this experience is more than just a meaningless hallucination of the mind because we actually get to retain knowledge and wisdom from this experience which helps us from that moment forward through the end of our lives. Sometimes we even receive knowledge about things that humanity has yet to prove through science, which we later prove through science. We'll soon discuss some world famous scientists who made discoveries as a result of becoming enlightened.

And as crazy as all that sounds, although we haven't been able to apply much science to it yet, the fact is that somewhere deep within us all lies a mountain of information about life and the universe which can answer every question you've ever had about either of those two topics. Somewhere within us, we're wired into the very fabric of the life energy of the universe. And accessing some, or all, of this universal intelligence is exactly what we're talking about when we're talking about the human phenomenon called Enlightenment.

Question #3: Wait a second. My mind is still trying to catch up. A portion of our consciousness opens to reveal there's stuff in there we didn't know previously? Why haven't I heard about this before?

Answer: You haven't heard about it before (or maybe you did hear about it but got some wrong information about it) mainly because enlightenment happens in human beings so very, **very** rarely. And of course, then there are the situations where a {self}-proclaimed guru has experienced something less than enlightenment, and starts teaching about enlightenment because they think what they've experienced is enlightenment, when it's actually not. Either way, very few people can speak from true experience. And even in the people who do actually experience the real thing, after an enlightenment experience happens, there really are no words to describe it fully; so, teachers of enlightenment are left with enigmatic sayings like, "I will lead you to the door that is not a door, but you must open and pass through it." Oh shit, did I just call myself out there? Yeah, I did.

Words fail us when we attempt to discuss accessing places within our deep mind that our regular minds just don't have access to. Language is something we invented to survive. We use it to talk about food and water, bears and spiders, and where to find the best whiskey bars. Language hasn't evolved to address hidden dimensions of mind that open up to reveal the secrets of the whole universe. So people lack the vocabulary to talk about it when they experience it. And of course, then there's the whole… there's-not-a-whole-lot-of-people-to-talk-about-it-with thing. It's not like you can just walk around asking people, "my mind just melded with God's mind, has that ever happened to you?" People tend to think you're crazy when you start to say shit like that. So most people just don't bring it up.

Question #4: Wait a second. So enlightenment can be unlocked through some internal mind state? Like opening a secret vault of life lessons and maybe even a communication channel into a higher realm of consciousness? How can this be scientifically possible?

Answer: To answer the first question, yes, there's a mountain of stuff that could be beneficial to you if you dug into your mind and found it. And the amount of information that exists within your deep mind is literally mind blowing. Not to be too cliché, but a great analogy for this is what happened in the movie "The Matrix" when the main character Neo got uploaded with information he didn't have previously, including knowledge about the ancient martial art of Kung Fu. It took only a few seconds, but when the upload was done, Neo was an expert in King Fu. And I know it sounds crazy even as I type this, but just like Derek Amato became a musical savant when he hit his head, and perhaps when prodigy Srinivasa Ramanujan rewrote mathematical computing for the world a hundred years ago (which he credited as being caused by having a close connection with God), that type of immediate deep understanding of things that were previously beyond us is exactly what can happen within the human mind when you open the floodgates of enlightenment. No, you won't learn Kung Fu, or at least I haven't heard of anyone who has, but your mastery of how to handle internal mind reactions like fear and anger may certainly approach mastery level almost immediately, and your intellectual prowess might increase substantially. Of course, we already know that living a fearless life can make for an amazing life, and being smarter doesn't hurt either. In addition, your understanding of the meaning of your life can be immediately, and permanently, written into your mind, and you sometimes even get to know the answer to the general question **"why?"** "Why what," you ask? Why everything. Why anything. Put the word "why" with any other words imaginable, and believe it or not, you will know the answer to that question. So just like Mario transitioning into SuperMario in just a few seconds when he swallows a mushroom, that can actually happen in real life, too. Now, let's address the second part of your question about how any of this is even possible.

While we'll soon discuss the chemicals that are likely flooding the brain during an enlightenment experience, science is not sure how the mechanisms of this enlightenment stuff works, or where the extra knowledge and wisdom comes from within us. The source of the knowledge and wisdom itself are still a mystery. That said, the idea that we have the ability to tap into an infinite amount of knowledge and wisdom through our own mind is certainly scientifically possible. We need to consider the potential scientific explanations of such an occurrence because that type of transcendent knowledge and wisdom is exactly how many of us humans characterize the more powerful versions of enlightenment. Besides, understanding it a little better will help you to get you to a place where you can experience enlightenment for yourself.

First off, we have no idea where this extra information is stored. It obviously has to come from somewhere. There's no secret that there's an amazing amount of intelligence within us. Just two of our cells can come together and create a brand new human body, with the single most complex structure in the known universe nested within the walls of our own skulls. Our combined human intelligence is so remarkable that it can adapt quickly enough to bring forth new sciences that can take us to the stars and back within the span of a single human lifetime. It was only 66 years from the time the Wright Brothers flew a couple dozen feet over Kitty Hawk, NC, to the moment a man stepped on the moon 239,000 miles over that same city. That's fucking amazing. And as much as we, in our top level consciousness, would like to take all the credit for such amazing accomplishments, there are millions of years of wisdom and intelligence held within the cells of our bodies that made that all possible. Who knows what the limitations of that intelligence and wisdom are?

The manifestation of skyscrapers, self-diving cars, and the technology to create "Sharknado" has proven that human imagination and advanced human intelligence exists deep within our bodies. Those amazing inventions came from somewhere within our minds at a subconscious level. So could this high level of adaptable intelligence coming from our subconciousness actually be stored within our DNA?

Scientific experiments have proven that our experiential memories are indeed stored in our genetics, so that those memories can be passed down generation to generation, and later impact our behavior. That's how the whole system of behavioral evolution works: Information from our waking consciousness gets passed down to the cells, and that genetic memory information then alters our behavior. That's memory making it into our genes, then making its way up into our subconscious minds. So can that multi-generational information be passed upward into our waking minds as well, where we might be able to access it consciously through Enlightenment? Could our top-level waking consciousness indeed tap into the intelligence, knowledge, and memories stored at the level of our DNA? There's no reason to think it can't.

On the other hand, maybe the extra information we receive during Enlightenment is not stored in our DNA, but comes to us through another mechanism. Let's not forget that the microtubules that make up the majority of our cell structures, including the communication structure of the neural synapses in our brain, have been proven to interact with quantum field vibrations in the gamma wave range, which have been identified as being the best brain waves we have. Quantum physics is inarguably and inextricably linked with consciousness. Since we know the quantum field extends outward in all directions, infinitely through all space and time, it could be said our cells are wired into the very consciousness of the universe itself. Through the phenomenon of Enlightenment, we could be tapping into knowledge and wisdom that is potentially held in the quantum field itself. Could we be accessing a level of consciousness and intelligence higher than our own through this microtubule communications system? After all, if lower levels of consciousness within our human bodies come together to create our higher waking consciousness (as science supposes is the case, and even proves to a certain extent), that model basically proves the phenomenon that consciousness itself organizes upward just like physical matter does, with self-organizing particles creating molecules, which self-organize to create organic matter, where self-organizing organic matter creates life consciousness, which then goes on to create our human bodies at a larger scale. That's called autopoiesis.

When you consider that portions of our bodies directly interact with the quantum field, which expands everywhere throughout all space and time, it's difficult to imagine our consciousness stops organizing itself at the level of our human mind. Knowing that the consciousness of our cells rolls upward to create our waking consciousness, coupled with the fact that our bodies exist as a result of the quantum field, it would be ridiculous to assume that our own waking consciousness doesn't also roll up to higher levels of consciousness beyond our limited human forms. It's silly to assume the human mind is where that pattern ends. So maybe through our physiology we somehow gain access to the higher consciousness and intelligence held within the quantum field itself. And if this is true, does this then also open the door for humans to have a conscious existence beyond that which is connected with our human bodies? Does it open the door for the existence a higher level of intelligence, such as God, to exist within the bounds of science? If we humans have learned absolutely anything about physics over time, it's that the activity of physics works both ways. The lower levels of physics influence the higher levels, but the higher levels affect and regulate the lower levels. Science call that an emergent property. It's just how the universe works. But that means consciousness and intelligence (properties which arise within our physical universe) work that way as well, with the lower levels of consciousness and intelligence influencing the higher levels, and the higher levels affecting and regulating the lower levels.

It is here, at the crossroads of physics, consciousness, and potential scientific discussions about God, that I would like to welcome to the bleeding edge of the study of Enlightenment science. It was Nobel Prize winning physicist and forefather of quantum physics Werner Heisenberg who once said, "The first gulp from the glass of natural sciences will turn you into an atheist, but at the bottom of the glass, God is waiting for you." We'll come back to more science on enlightenment and the potential for God later, but for now, while we don't know exactly how enlightenment happens, we know that it does, and that it can be completely transformational if we can make it happen for ourselves. So let's now take a step back and take a mental break to look at how long we've been told that enlightenment happens, and how long we've known how transformational it can be, to inform ourselves how you might make enlightenment happen for you.

10 A Quick History of Enlightenment

> To enjoy good health,
> to bring happiness to one's family,
> to bring peace to all,
> one must first discipline
> and control one's own mind.
> If a man controls his mind
> he can find his way to Enlightenment,
> and all wisdom and virtue
> will naturally come to him.
> —The Buddha

The history of Spiritual Enlightenment comes to us right out of religious tradition. Go figure, with the word spiritual being included as a descriptor of the experience. What's interesting, however, is not that that the history of Enlightenment comes to us from religion, but that it comes to us from every major religious tradition, from the Abrahamic religions of Judaism, Christianity, and Islam, through numerous Eastern philosophies and religions, into Native American, Aborigine, Native African, and other tribal beliefs. What's truly amazing is that back in the day, all religions were focused on attaining enlightenment. Today, that's completely changed.

Today, enlightenment is typically regarded as the central focus of only three of the big religions, Buddhism, Hinduism, and Taoism. That said, enlightenment has deep roots within every other major religion as well. For practicing Buddhists, the concept of enlightenment implies someone suddenly, or eventually, attaining a complete understanding of life and the universe, which is usually accompanied by a detachment from all things impermanent, and a complete awareness of everything as it is, at this moment. The Buddhists consider enlightenment to be the end of a person's life suffering, and call their enlightened ranks Buddhas, or sometimes Bodhisattvas. In contrast, Christians call enlightenment by a different name and use different words to describe their enlightened ranks.

Christianity calls the experience of attaining enlightenment receiving Beatific Vision (Latin: "visio beatifica"). This occurrence is defined by Christianity as "the ultimate direct self communication of God to the individual person. A person possessing the beatific vision reaches, as a member of redeemed humanity in the communion of saints, perfect salvation in its entirety, i.e. heaven."

St. Thomas Aquinas defined beatific vision as a human being's "final ending" where a person attains perfect happiness. From the Thomas Aquinas section of Beatific Vision on Wikipedia: "Aquinas argues that our perfect happiness and final end can only be the direct union with God himself and not with any created image of him. This union comes about by a kind of 'seeing' perfectly the divine essence itself, a gift given to our intellects when God joins them directly to himself without any intermediary. And since in seeing this perfect vision of what (and who) God is, we grasp also his perfect goodness, this act of 'seeing' is at the same time a perfect act of loving God as the highest and infinite goodness."

Enlightenment at its most powerful level includes deeply profound visuals that are presented within the mind, which are accompanied by sounds, clearly defined ideas, and a sensation of merging with a transcendent intelligence which communicates, illuminates, and enlightens. The whole experience is flooded with a deep sense of an infinite and unconditional love, which when someone experiences it, can almost exclusively be described as being the direct presence of God. One on one. Thus, when a Christian experiences enlightenment, this is what is called receiving Beatific Vision.

In Christianity, a person who has received Beatific Vision before death is called a mystic. Christianity uses the words **mystic** and

mysticism to describe things associated with Spiritual Enlightenment because the internal enlightenment experience conveys a deeper understanding of God than the level of understanding even life-long students of the Bible command. Back in the day, Christianity had bishops and monks who dedicated their lives to the study of the Bible, and they were considered the experts of the Christian religion. Although these Bishops knew the Bible front to back, every now and then, someone would come along in the Christian ranks who had experienced enlightenment, and although they had not studied the Bible even a fraction as long as the Bishops and monks, they were able to speak naturally from a place that was completely in tune with the direct teachings of Jesus Christ. In addition, they were able to teach the deepest, most profound lessons of the Bible without effort, and even generate new ways of explaining what Jesus taught through new unique works of their own. Because these weirdly Godlike people seemed to be touched by God directly, well beyond the Bishops and monks who had dedicated their lives to their religion, they were called **mystics**, with a mystical attachment to God.

The definition of the word mysticism is "an immediate, direct, intuitive knowledge of God or ultimate reality attained through personal spiritual experience." One of the earliest mystics in the Christian religion was Paul, who had never even met Jesus, but became enlightened on the road to Damascus. Other mystics within the Christian ranks include Dante Alighieri, Meister Eckhart, Jakob Böhme (a Protestant mystic), St. Francis of Assisi, Thomas Merton, and St. John of the Cross, whose famous understanding of God, todo y nada ("everything and nothing" in Spanish), is full of quantum physics truth about the entire universe. The universe is absolutely everything, and at its most core level of physics, it's absolutely nothing.

Fast forwarding to Christianity of today, the sad fact is that much of Christianity has lost its enlightenment roots. A huge exception is the tradition of Eastern Orthodox Christianity. The main focus of Eastern Orthodox Christianity, which remains to be the closest tradition the world has to early Christianity, is to attain **theosis**, which Wikipedia defines as "a transformative process whose goal is likeness to or union with God." As a process of transformation, theosis is brought on by the effects of **catharsis** (purification of mind and body), coupled with **theoria** ("illumination" with the "vision" of God, otherwise known as Beatific Vision, aka an enlightenment experience). According to Eastern Orthodox teaching, theosis is very much the purpose of human life. It is considered achievable only through "a synergy (or cooperation) between human activity and God's uncreated energies (or operations)." They hold theosis in such high regard, they believe that "no one who does not follow the path of union with God can be a theologian." In other words, if a Christian preacher is **not** looking for a spiritual enlightenment experience (theoria), they shouldn't even be preaching the Gospels. Beyond being the closest thing the world has to original Christianity, Eastern Orthodox Christianity employs both meditation and the prayer of quiet to help attain theosis. Wider Christianity beyond Eastern Orthodoxy has a word called **Kenosis**, which points to the "emptying of the {self}." So the search for enlightenment is a fundamental component of Christianity. Or at least it used to be.

At one point or another, all religions have had mystics or enlightened masters within their ranks, and they've all had the search for enlightenment as the guiding light of their religion. Therefore, no religion is excluded from our discussion of enlightenment. Judaism's enlightenment seekers are called the Kabbalists. Kabbalah, which today is a fringe branch within Judaism, used to be a required component of Judaic education, during a time before the teachers of Kabbalah became too sparse to educate the Jewish masses, and before simply too few Jews attained **yechida**. Yechida is Kabbalah's word for attaining the fifth and most perfect spiritual level, aka enlightenment.

Enlightenment is the very purpose of modern Hinduism. **Moksha** is the term Hindus use to describe the liberated state of mind where an individual is freed from **maya**, the illusory magic show of the world, "that which exists, but is constantly changing and thus is spiritually unreal." Hindus consider moksha a representation of freedom from desire and other worldly passions. Enlightenment also ends the Hindu cycle of reincarnation, where souls enter many different bodies through the course of their existence, developing spiritually over time.

Another Asian religion which shares a number of ideas with Hinduism is called Sikhism. Sikhs follow the teachings of an enlightened master named Guru Nanak, who taught about attaining union with Akal, which is a word that literally translates into "timeless, immortal, and non-temporal," all of which are ideas commonly associated with God. Attaining union with the timeless results in **Jivanmukta**, which is liberation before death, a concept shared with Hinduism.

Islam has an extremely peaceful and scientific branch of Orthodox followers called the Sufis. They base their practice on the search for enlightenment, calling it **Fana**, which literally translates to "annihilation" (of the {self}). Taoism is based on teachings from an enlightened master named Lao Tzu (Laozi), who taught of what he called **the Way** of enlightenment. Lao Tzu taught back during the lifetime of Siddhartha Gautama who also taught about enlightenment around 500 BCE. You might know Siddhartha by his more popular name, the Buddha, which in literal translation simply means "the enlightened dude". Siddhartha communicated the benefits of discovering enlightenment so well that multiple societies made the pursuit of enlightenment their entire way of life. It survives over 2,500 years later, with 300 million people searching for enlightenment through Buddhism today.

Regardless of whether you're a Buddhist or not, Buddha's teachings about mind, which included the benefits of meditation and how to meditate, are still relevant and extremely valuable to people of any faith tradition. Famous Buddhist monk Thich Nhat Hanh, who gave us the idea that happiness is the way, said it best, "There is a misconception that Buddhism is a religion, and that you worship Buddha. Buddhism is a practice, like yoga. You can be a Christian and practice Buddhism. I met a Catholic priest who lives in a Buddhist monastery in France. He told me that Buddhism makes him a better Christian. I love that."

Frankly, it does not matter what religion's spin we put on enlightenment, or even if we approach it from a purely scientific view. Our variations in approach are simply variations in our attachments of {self}. Whether we're attached to a particular earthly religion or the rational religion of science, it is all the same phenomenon. It does not change over the boundaries of language, culture, religion, or even time.

Personally, I think this commonality and similarity from many ancient sources lends credibility to the fact it is a natural occurrence of experience catalyzed through the human body. And thus we all have it within us to find.

11 The Enlightenment Experience

> We need enlightenment,
> not just individually but collectively,
> to save the planet.
> —Thich Nhat Hanh

Calling the enlightenment experience an internal experience does not really do it justice. More accurately, it is **the** experience. It is the pinnacle of spiritual, intellectual, and transcendent "awakening" where our body and mind drop away, exposing an unlimited intelligence and the secrets to life and the universe, and introducing us personally to the seemingly transcendent consciousness most commonly called God. I'll explain my first personal enlightenment experience in the following chapter so you get an idea of how utterly mind blowing it is, but I can tell you here that it was easily the most profound and educative experience of my entire life. And many people who experience the more powerful versions of the enlightenment experience characterize their awakenings in a similar fashion. Fortunately, although this experience is presented in a way that cannot be fully expressed in words, it is presented in a way that we can partially understand. As we touched on in the previous chapter, the experience itself has numerous names across different cultures, geographical regions, and belief systems. Today, it is very commonly known by the term enlightenment experience, but satori is what it's called within the Zen Buddhist traditions. In other traditions it's called "bodhi," "awakening," "illumination," "fitra," "yechida," "moksha," "mukti," "nirvana," "Kevala Jhana," "prajna," "ushta," "salvation," "receiving God's Grace," "entering the Kingdom of Heaven," and even just "seeing the light," because oftentimes, the experience starts with being engulfed by a pure multispectral white light from within.

As the numerous names suggest, attaining an enlightenment experience is hardly a new idea. In the West, William James re-educated us to the idea in his book "The Varieties of Religious Experience." James pointed out the universality of the experience when he wrote, "In mystic states, we both become one with the absolute, and we become aware of our oneness. This is the everlasting and triumphant mystical tradition, hardly altered by differences of clime or creed. In Hinduism, Neoplatonism, in Sufism, in Christian Mysticism, in Whitmanism, we find the same reoccurring note."

One of the better descriptions of a lower power enlightenment experience came from Richard Maurice Bucke, a noted psychiatrist and prominent atheist, who in 1872 experienced a moment of awakening he had during a visit to London, which he extolled in his book Cosmic Consciousness, from 1901:

> I had spent the evening in a great city, with two friends reading and discussing poetry and philosophy. I had a long drive home in a handsome cab to my lodging. My mind was calm and peaceful. All at once, without warning of any kind, I found myself wrapped in a flame colored cloud. For an instant, I thought of fire somewhere in that great city. In the next, I knew that fire was in myself. Directly afterwards, there came upon me a sense of exaltation, of immense joyousness, accompanied or immediately followed by an intellectual illumination impossible to describe. Among other things, I did not merely come to believe, but I saw that the universe is not composed of dead matter, but it is on the contrary a living Presence. I became conscious in myself of eternal life. . . . I saw that all men are immortal; that the cosmic order is such that without any peradventure that all things work together for the good of each and all; that the foundation of the world is what we call love, and that the happiness of each and all is in the long run absolutely certain.

The vision lasted a few seconds and was gone, but the memory of it, and the sense of reality it left has remained during the quarter century which has since elapsed. I knew that what the vision showed was true. That conviction has never been lost.

Surveys of British and American adults reveal that as many as 30 to 35 percent of adults have had this type of small power awakening or mystical experience similar to Bucke's. We don't talk about them with each other because one of the characteristics of them is that the experience itself transcends description. In fact, that is one of the official qualifiers psychology has put on this type of awakening or mystical experience. William James originally outlined four characteristics of this type of experience:

1.   The experience is transient, meaning that the experience is temporary, and the individual eventually returns to a "normal" frame of mind. So the experience itself is outside our normal perception of space and time.

2.   The experience is ineffable, meaning it can't be explained verbally with any accuracy.

3.   The experience is noetic, meaning that the individual feels they have learned something from the experience, and that it gives them knowledge and wisdom beyond regular human understanding.

4.   The experience is of a passive nature, meaning that it happens to the individual without any sort of conscious control.

Three other typical characteristics of the experience are 1) a sense that the experience seems more real than our normal reality, 2) there's a sense of universal consciousness connected with it, and 3) the person experiences a feeling of pure love and bliss. Some people perceive this as the experience being accompanied by the love of God.

All those characteristics combined are what make the experience seem to transcend any other regular human experience. The idea of **transcendence** was developed by the Greek philosopher Plato. He believed in the existence of absolute goodness, which he described as beyond description and knowable only through intuition. Later philosophers also attributed this same transcendent nature to the concept of God, which became central to the ideas of orthodox Judaism, Christianity, and Islam. The Greeks called it **ecstasis**, which translates to stepping outside oneself. Sorry, I forgot the brackets. Ecstasis translates to stepping outside one's {self}.

Of course, it should be no surprise to us that studies show that people who have experienced this type of awakening, especially one of the more powerful manifestations, return the highest known scores of psychological well-being on happiness testing.

The reason people who've experienced enlightenment score higher than others on tests of psychological well-being goes back to how the inner experience changes them psychologically. As discussed in previous chapters, when we experience something from within which expands our idea of {self}, to include being connected to a consciousness much larger than our own, that new experience of an expanded consciousness lands right in the center of our newly expanded {self} map. So in a sense, we feel we **are** that expanded consciousness more than the list of attachments and ideas we were before.

So our mind's {self} map is changed by the experience of awakening to this new experience. And that change in {self} then feeds all our Equations of Emotion from that moment forward. Our new {self} map creates all new Expectations/Preferences for us, and it lowers the power levels of attachment to all our old {self} crap, which gets moved out from the center of our map. So all the shit that used to bug us doesn't bug us anymore. The more powerful the enlightenment experience, the more powerful and positively apocalyptic the transformation is in our lives. And life as it was, becomes no more. We experience the awe of a completely transcendent intelligence, and a feeling of awe enters us and becomes us. And life becomes an amazing place where absolutely nothing can shake us.

Dr. Paul Piff, a psychologist at the University of California, Irvine, studied the small affects that a feeling of awe can have on how we treat each other. In a series of five studies, involving more than 2000 participants, when people watched a five-minute video clip of vast expansive beauty like the Grand Canyon, they were less likely to cheat or take money that wasn't theirs. Some participants who were asked to stare at a grove of two-hundred-foot-tall eucalyptus trees wound up providing more assistance to a researcher who staged spilling a box of pens, and also wound up asking for half as much cash for their participation in the study. Dr. Piff explained, "Experiences of awe connect people to things larger than themselves. In so doing, it motivates people to do things bigger than themselves."

When an enlightenment experience comes so powerfully that it cleans off your {self} map entirely, replacing the old sense of {self} with the new inner experience, nothing really ever bothers you from that point forward. After a high power enlightenment experience, the only things that ever do bother you are the things you **let** bother you, such as when you let some particular piece of mental turbulence motivate you to protect someone you love, or to help end suffering of someone you don't even know. Beyond that, nothing bugs you, because attaining the experience of discovering the infinite expanse of intelligence, love, and compassion that comes through an enlightenment experience commands the center of your {self} map. And nothing can touch or compare to that experience. Ever. And the word 'experience' is critical there. More than trying to put the idea or belief of enlightenment on as an attachment of {self}, you've **experienced** it, and thus now you completely understand it. And thus, you "become it" internally and externally.

All that said, there are some challenges that come with having an enlightenment experience, however.

Challenges Connected with the Enlightenment Experience

As cool as enlightenment sounds, and as cool as enlightenment is, there are things that can minimize it's impact; the variations within the awakening experience itself, the subjectivity of how the individual perceives the experience, and how well a person integrates their experience after one occurs. Let's take a peek at each of these.

The first challenge with enlightenment is that there are many variations of the enlightenment experience. Sometimes it comes with a general sense that everything in the universe is alive and connected without any extra information or visuals. Sometimes a unitive experience reveals answers to complex ideas about life, and how the universe works. Other times it may convey an immediate understanding of why everything is the way it is in your life, which brings an indelible sense of inner peace. But within this infinite expanse of shades of gray, from slight awakening to extreme, whatever someone experiences becomes their personal high water mark of awakening and understanding. This experience becomes the end-all be-all of their mind's expansion. It's the limit of what they know and can reference. And because it's a simple fact that we can only truly understand what we've personally experienced, that means people only understand spirituality or enlightenment to the limits of what they've experienced, and no more. Our experiential maximum is our cognitive maximum. So while anyone who experiences anything which expands {self} can feel they have attained something significant (because what they have experienced it is indeed valid, significant, and life changing), the reality might be that they've simply dipped their toe in the water of a potential ocean of inner discovery. This is the we don't know what we don't know problem, which can only be solved by discovering how much there is that we don't know.

Next, when someone has an internal {self} expansion experience, their mind can try to bend and fold it into shapes that fit on their existing {self} map rather than let it expand and change the {self} en masse. This is where our ego gets in the way of our enlightenment process. As an unfortunate side effect of the defense of {self} mechanism, our minds try to resist changes in {self}. We try to cram our experience of awakening to fit inside the box of our particular religion instead of allowing awakening experiences to rewrite or expand our {self} map. This winds up strengthening our understanding of what that religion is supposed to ultimately convey, but it also strengthens our attachment to all the other destructive influences within that religion. It can push us to keep within a particular religion and separate us from others with different religious beliefs, even though these awakenings are independent of religion. It's only our hubris and ignorance that supposes this internal spiritual experience is exclusive to our religion.

Worse yet is when we try to ignore, or discredit, our experiences of awakening altogether and resist any changes to {self}. That's when the voice in our head comes to the defense of our old {self}, telling us whatever we sensed wasn't really us, that it was just a hallucination or trick of the brain. Sometimes we stuff our awakening experience into some deep dark corner of misunderstood memories and bury it forever. It's much easier for the mind to hide away something like that than to actually contemplate the experience and think about the possibility that the {self} does indeed need to be changed. We can even actively repress our internal experiences. I met a man once who had convinced himself that his internal awakening experience was actually a trick of Satan trying to put ideas into his head that contradicted the clear messages of the Bible. He admitted the experience was accompanied by extreme feelings of unity, love, and bliss which he thought at the time was God, but he simply couldn't rectify what he'd experienced with his previous negative thoughts about gay people, the evil Jews who he said killed Jesus, and of course, the proper role of women in society, which in his eyes was to be a subservient helper of man, and a homemaker for any children of a marriage. I wasn't really surprised to discover he was divorced, nor was I surprised that he let his mind reject his awakening experience altogether, choosing to bend it into something weird, and remain attached to his previous ideas of {self} instead of accepting the messages of universal love his mind wasn't ready for.

These first two challenges lead us to the third challenge of fully embracing enlightenment, which is how we integrate it into our lives. It's not just the internal discovery of the enlightenment experience itself which conveys enlightenment. It's also the level to which we integrate it to create our enlightened existence.

Living an enlightened existence has two components. First is the requirement of having some type of inner experience that provides us with the enlightening knowledge. Second is the level of integration that then allows us to live in a way that is true to the inner experience we brought to the surface. People can have enlightenment experiences without living from that new truth. But both pieces are required for a person to be living an enlightened existence.

Unfortunately for humanity, our inner enlightenment experiences are very rare, and as we mentioned when they do come, they come at differing levels that sometimes include specific sets of knowledge and wisdom, and sometimes don't. So some people get more enlightenment than others if, and when, the inner experience happens. Similarly, integration happens with differing levels of success. For some people, they get powerful inner experiences and those lessons stick and transform that person. For others, they attain the inner experience, and regardless of how powerful it is, quickly go back to the same old mind patterns and behavior they had before their inner experience.

Integration of those inner experiences is not an automatic occurrence, because the ego {self} has spent a lifetime of trying to add what it thinks are the best things onto {self}, and it loves to add new things onto its {self} map that are bright and shiny. Subsequently, often people who awaken spontaneously and powerfully will put what they experienced right onto their {self} map as a measure of how spiritual they now are. Instead of letting the experience truly rewrite the {self} map and change how it feeds into the Equation of Emotion. Their experience becomes just another attachment on their {self} map, which then helps define them. Now they consider themselves {touched by God}. In the worst cases of delusion, they can even attach the sticker {I'm enlightened} right onto their {self} map, becoming a bigger asshat than they ever were before. Some even go off and start new religions. When this malfunction of ego {self} happens, and the inner experience of awakening is hijacked by the old patterns of the mind into its old system, it does not change a thing about the process that feeds their outbursts of anger, their fear, and their profound sadness. They've just added the memory of the inner experience into their mind's {self} map, and now consider them{selves} {touched}, or {awakened}, or some similar notion.

These people often feel annoyed by organized religion itself because they think it misses the point, and they can often become angry when someone threatens their new idea of {God} or {spirituality}, which is simply a new and improved attachment on the same old {self} map, which they feel they need to defend.

This is a situation where some knowledge and wisdom are gained, but compassion is not. It's also where the ingrained destructive processes of mind can destroy most of the benefits an awakening or enlightenment experience can deliver. It is certainly why, just like everything else in life, enlightenment comes in an infinite number of shades of gray across all of humanity from one extreme to the other. We attach the moniker of **enlightened beings** to the individuals who experience enlightenment at its highest levels, and who then integrate that experience most completely through their everyday actions.

The Rarity of Enlightenment and Its Teachers

The experience of enlightenment in humans, where hidden doors within the mind open into infinite expanses of knowledge and wisdom, has been around forever. And the attainment of enlightenment has certainly permeated every major religion throughout history. So if you're religious at all, whether you know it or not, you're supposed to be searching for enlightenment. That said, the subject of enlightenment has never been widely discussed until just very recently. The reason enlightenment is not more popular, or more understood, is because throughout history very few people have actually experienced the highest-power versions of it. Subsequently, because so few have experienced enlightenment, even fewer have been able to explain it well enough for people to learn how to attain it. Remember, this is an experience that transcends words and mindful understanding itself. It leaves even the greatest masters like the Buddha making circular statements like, "The self is the only foundation for the self," which he actually said, and which no one understands unless they understand the difference between the mind's {self} and the true Self.

Thankfully, communications technology is making it easier to find enlightened masters who can help us understand exactly what it is we're looking for. Gone are the days of climbing some mountain to go find the bald guy with the long white beard who might shed some light on our inner search. Today, we have YouTube to do that same kind of searching from the comfort of our own beds. Technology allows people with knowledge and experience to offer their wisdom to seekers they will never meet, and seekers can now find knowledge and guidance from masters on a screen they hold in their hands. But herein also lies a challenge for us; the low barriers to entry for almost anyone to offer an education to us based on their level of enlightenment, which they may think is the ultimate level of understanding, because their brain is wired to believe so. And this fact is a stumbling hazard on our path.

When we're talking about finding the hidden places within your mind that can open amazing inner doors of perception for you, hidden within the most complex organism in the known universe (your brain/mind), you need to find the best teachers who have experienced and integrated enlightenment at the highest levels to be able to guide you. There's a lot of misinformation out there thanks to people who teach from their high water marks of experience. And while it's okay that you listen to those folks, you'll learn only what they have to teach up to their high water mark, but you will progress no further. So be careful of who you listen to.

But the fact is that you need to listen to teachers. You need teachers to tell you what it is you don't know. Without masters who can tell you what is even possible, you can't even know what you're looking for. It is for this very reason that Zen masters agree to become Zen masters. They humbly realize they are enlightened, and they know they must therefore teach. But knowing that they don't have the ability to teach anything that the student doesn't experience firsthand makes the role of a Zen master a rather tough one. Just as I'm not supposed to be telling you any of this now, a Zen master who speaks even a single word about enlightenment in a Zen dojo creates an idea in their student's mind that takes the student further away from the truth of experience. This is why one of the earliest Zen masters named Dōgen famously said, "A Zen master's life is one continuous mistake."

Enlightened teacher A. H. Almaas once estimated that only one in ten thousand can find their way without a teacher. Others have estimated that probability to be even slimmer. Robert Ennis once said, "The chances of someone awakening without a teacher are like the chances of getting pregnant without a partner." That's not impossible; in fact, Australian scientists announced in early 2017 that a shark in captivity had given birth to live offspring without contact with a male. But it's highly unlikely, so you increase your chances of growth exponentially when you listen to other mind spelunkers who have attained higher levels of understanding than you have.

But how do you know who is enlightened and who isn't? How do you know who speaks from wisdom and experience, and who is simply regurgitating sayings from past masters, and giving their own doublespeak answers to your questions? When a teacher does attain some level of inner experience, there again you're faced with the questions, "did they get a big enough dose to get themselves to the level of understanding that was transformational enough to teach us how to do that?" "Do they understand the mind well enough to know what tricks the mind can play on them so they can point out when my mind is playing tricks on me?" "Will this person be able to help me deliver myself into a place where Heaven can be found right here on Earth?" The level of attainment a master must have to serve as a guide to get you to where you want to go is substantial. Ancient Master Huang-po said of this problem, "Of a thousand or ten thousand attempting to enter this Gate, only three or perhaps five pass through." Jesus gave us this exact same message: "But small is the gate and narrow is the path that leads to life, and only a few find it."

So how can you discern, from the increasing number of spiritual masters and life coaches hanging shingles on the Internet, which of those you should and shouldn't listen to? How can you tell who's got the goods on enlightenment and {self} discovery and who doesn't?

Well, one of the early experts on enlightenment was a guy named Siddhartha Gautama, otherwise known as the Buddha. He had a lot to say about how to develop the mind to attain enlightenment. And as one of the dudes who had attained it, he was able to determine some pretty decent qualifiers for whether a person was enlightened or not. Those thoughts were included in what is now called the Pali Canon, which is a collection of writings that Theravada Buddhism uses to convey some of Buddha's teachings. Buddha said that to be enlightened is to be completely free of the three root poisons of greed, hatred, and delusion. Personally, I think that's a pretty fair set of qualifiers. Unfortunately, he never said anything about how to read the mind of another human being to find out if they are truly devoid of greed, hatred, and delusion. And what is delusion anyway? How do you know if someone is free of delusion unless you know what's real and what's not? I mean, someone who sees the world from a deeper perspective than you do could seem to be devoid of delusion, when the reality is that they, in fact, are simply caught up in a slightly shallower layer of delusion than you are. There are tons of people who call themselves "enlightened" but who are still influenced by the drivers of greed, hatred, and delusion—the latter especially.

When looking to learn about enlightenment, one of the best rules of thumb is to take in information from outside sources, but never completely believe what any of those external sources say about enlightenment. Trying to explain enlightenment can be likened to the poet Rumi's account of The Elephant in the Dark, where an elephant is led into a dark room, and a group of men then feel the essence of the elephant with only one blind hand. Thus, each man comes away with a different description. For one man, the elephant is like a spout (the trunk), for another it is a fan (the ear), or a pillar (the leg), or a throne (the back). No one gets the full picture of the reality of the elephant. In Rumi's words, "The sensual eye is just like the palm of the hand. The palm has not the means of covering the whole beast." While the individual stories may be only glimpses, they are still important to hear so you know what you are looking for within your deep mind.

In the next chapter, I will give you the glimpse of the elephant I perceived one day a couple decades ago when probing the deepest depths of mind. For reference, I will also share a couple stories I've found in other books written by other authors. One will include the wildly popular best-selling book Proof of Heaven, by Eben Alexander, a neurosurgeon who found himself the unlucky victim of bacterial meningitis, which put him in a medically induced coma for seven days. While in that coma (or more likely during the process of coming out of it, as we'll discuss when we get to the deeper look at the brain science of these types of experiences), Eben describes an experience of what he perceived to be Heaven, including his interaction with another non-Eben consciousness. He considers his experience that of having passed from a corporeal experience into the space of conscious existence beyond the body. A second book I will reference was written by a punk rocker turned Zen Master named Brad Warner, who explained the deep connection of Zen Buddhism with what people call God, and his personal enlightenment experience. That book is called, There Is No God: And He Is Always With You. In that book, he explained, "For a short while I could not only see out of my own eyes, but out of the eyes of God looking at me. But it was not a short while. It was forever."

From my perspective, enlightenment starts with an experience (or experiences) both within the mind and beyond the mind, which is followed by a moment-to-moment experience of beyond mind, out of which an amazing third layer of experience emerges from the combination of the first two layers. This truth is wonderfully unspeakable. It's is a mixture of both mind and non-mind that falls completely under your conscious control, which can't be explained, only experienced.

Don't worry, the next few chapters will clear up much of the ambiguity I just introduced into our discussion.

12 Enlightenment Step 1: The Experience/s

I will die, and I will never be able
to tell all I have seen.

—Pablo Amaringo

This chapter is written to give you an example of an enlightenment experience so that you know what's possible to find within you. Search the Internet, and you'll find dozens of stories just like this one, and when we're all done, I hope this book helps lead you to finding your own version of what I experienced and still experience daily. I want enlightenment to happen for everyone.

But before we start, a few caveats here:

First, whatever I say here needs to be taken with a grain of salt. Words simply fail us when describing experiences, and my words aren't going to do any portion of this internal experience justice. Second, a lot of what I'm about to share with you comes from my previous notes and writings, but some of it comes from memory. Human memory is fallible because the brain rewrites memory constantly to make better sense of our experiences. So we shouldn't completely trust it. Third, in this chapter I use some terms which are considered spiritual in nature. I use the terms "God", and "sin", and a few others that are usually associated with religion. I don't use them in the religious sense. I use them in the general sense to convey the perceptions I experienced because those perceptions are commonly described with those words. Be careful to think of them in that general way when I use them. And please know there will be a future discussion of whether or not what I'm about to explain to you was possibly a hallucination of my brain. So stay tuned for that.

Lastly, I'm telling this story because when studying our consciousness and discussing ways to increase our happiness levels, I think we **must** take subjective experience into account, and use it as data for scientific contemplation. The Godfather of philosophy and consciousness, John Searle, said in a recent TED Talk, "You can make objective claims in a domain that is subjective in nature." And he's absolutely right. Science has proven one person's subjective perspective is just that, and is a useless piece of data. But when patterns can be found across multiple people's independent perspectives, that's uncovering something in science. If you agree to these caveats, I'll now give you a peek of what I saw when I kicked in that proverbial door of deep mind on that non-existent remote mountain.

To start this story, I should give some background, so we have a reference for what happened to start this crazy awesome ride. To put it bluntly, I had a troubled childhood where I'd been on a destructive path heading in the wrong direction. After I moved in with my Grandmother, and discovered Christianity, I was able to straighten my behavior out a bit. My exposure to religion certainly helped me. Finding what I thought was God was a very moving experience for me. I shed tears on my knees, and felt an immense love enter my heart as I genuinely asked God for forgiveness for my sins. I discovered and further developed what I thought was a great relationship with God. From there, I re-built a school life, a social life, and even served as the President of my church youth group for a few years. It was only much later that I would learn how my most profound faith experiences were like a child playing in an inflatable pool compared to the vast ocean of God I would later discover.

After a decade of maintaining what I thought was a good relationship with God, and after building a pretty solid life for myself, as I explained in Volume I, I found myself standing on the front porch of my amazing new home in Atlanta, realizing I wasn't happy. And I couldn't figure out what the problem was. I thought I liked myself. I had a lot of friends, a wonderful romantic interest, good family relationships, and I had developed a solid career path, climbing the corporate ladder well ahead of all my peers. I considered my relationship with God as still solid. But for some reason, something wasn't right. And I had no idea what it was.

So I started contemplating and reviewing my life. Where had I gone astray in finding happiness? My sociological existence was good. My relationships were fine. My professional life was off the charts. I had traveled, experienced cool things around the world, and bought everything I'd wanted to buy. So what was left? Was it the spiritual side of me that was lacking? Had I not gone far enough in my religious studies? Originally, it was my religious experiences that helped me turn my life around from my rebellious existence, and get me on a more positive path. After I had become a born again Christian, my faith had become unshakable. My personal relationship with God, coupled with a release of my old {self} on a riverbank in northern Indiana was what gave me the courage to accomplish everything I had accomplished to that moment. So maybe I needed to look back to God for my answers.

But this time I was going to do religion a little differently. I started rereading the Bible, but I also started reading historical books about the Bible. I started expanding my horizons into reading other religious texts to see how they compared to the Bible. Through my studies, I discovered Christianity's connection with contemplative prayer and meditation. This was news to me. Knowing that meditation was a tool used by Buddhists, I started reading about Buddhism to see if they had any decent tips to help with understanding it. In my prayers, I quit talking to God so much, and started just to say "thank you" more, and left a little time at the end of my prayers to simply listen for a response from God. For months, God didn't say shit. I picked up a book written by D.T. Suzuki called Introduction to Zen Buddhism, which explained the basics about Zen meditation, and about the idea of something called satori, which Suzuki stated was "a sudden flashing into consciousness of a new truth hitherto undreamed of." He said, "Religiously, it is a new birth; intellectually, it is the acquiring of a new viewpoint." I noted the parallel of the words 'new birth' with the Christian concept of being born again. I wondered if it was something similar, and contemplated what satori might be, but truthfully, had no idea what it was Suzuki was talking about.

After I created my own custom mixture of prayer, meditation, and read more about Zen's quieting of the mind, I felt my mind was starting to clear a bit. A feeling of equilibrium reentered my consciousness. This practice was improving my everyday existence and my overall attitude about life in general. So I made some quiet time for myself frequently to simply exist in my own presence. It was a time every day that I sat in total relaxation, in spiritual meditation, listening to existence, and listening for God. No words from me this time. This was my new meditation practice. Oftentimes my meditation and quieting of my mind would turn into a nap, but regardless of the result, I would meditate again the next day.

After a short time, I had noticed that, although meditation had really not added to my understanding at all, it was helping to reduce the amount of stress in my life. So I kept it up. I liked the mental-vacation feeling that it gave my sometimes overly-active mind. And the naps were nice when they happened. Keeping in mind Suzuki's thoughts on the fact that divine truth cannot be understood mentally by reading something in a book, and can only be experienced, I resigned myself to the idea that if God wanted me to know answers about happiness and truth, I would eventually find them. I would just make the best of life until that happened. And it was just about when my attitude got to that perfect point of balance between intention and relaxation… that it happened.

Act I: The Entrance

The day it happened for me was quite crappy, actually. I had ended a romantic relationship a couple weeks prior, and I was just feeling a bit over the whole "finding someone new to date" thing. So instead of dealing with that mess, I decided to lie down and get into my meditation headspace. I started my daily meditation session that idle afternoon with a quiet statement. With a bit of a dejected sigh, reaching out from what I perceived as the core of my being, I called out silently to nowhere in particular. "If you want me to know, I'm ready." I then started mentally reviewing some of the latest things I had read in the Gospel of Thomas and from D.T. Suzuki's book on Zen. Then I thought of a particular Zen teaching:

A monk asked Yueh-shan, "What does one think of while sitting?"
One thinks of nothing," the Master replied.
"How does one think of not thinking?" the monk asked.
"By not thinking," the Master said.

Zen koans have always interested me. Koans are these little mental riddles that don't have an answer. I'm sure you've heard the one that goes, "What is the sound of one hand clapping?" Another is, "What is the color of wind?" These are questions that have no cognitive answer because thinking is not the path to discovering enlightenment in Zen. The basic idea of Zen practice is to sit in meditation and **not think**. It is the process of intentionally stepping away from conscious thought, until something called a "satori" happened. Whatever that was. So for that particular meditation session, what I did was take a crack at not thinking at all during my meditation session. Could I even attain the state of not thinking? I didn't know. I'd never tried. So in that moment, I decided to try to completely quiet my mind of all conscious thought. And as I started the meditation session, I began to calm my mind, and I put all the focus I had in the world into **not thinking**.

At first, it was very difficult to quiet my mind. I heard music in my head. I saw images in my mind's eye. Memories suddenly flew in unexpectedly. And just like in my normal meditation sessions, I'd find myself off on some mental tangent, which would cause me to try and refocus my attention again on not thinking. It was super tough to do. Slowly, however, through the minutes as I relaxed and focused myself back on not thinking . . . it got easier and easier to allow my mind to clear itself. No music, no images, no memories. No following the mind off wherever it wanted to go. A thought would enter, and I would label it, "thought", then I'd ignore it. Humorously, I would occasionally wonder, "Am I thinking anything? Crap. That's a thought. Stop thinking." Then I'd have to start the process of clearing my mind all over again. "Think of nothing." I would start again. Pretty soon, it got to a point where as thoughts would enter my mind, they would simply fly through like they were a passing jet airliner overhead. They would make their noise on the way to another destination, taking my attention for just an instant, but ultimately having no impact on my existence, and being gone a moment later.

Some people say it's impossible to stop all conscious thought in the mind. What I can tell you is that everyone who's ever said that is someone who has failed at stopping all conscious thought, and thinks because they can't do it, it can't possibly be done. This is a statement of their ego defending itself, not a statement of fact. The fact is that if you put enough attention and focus into stopping all conscious thought in your mind, it can indeed be done. That's what the entire practice of Zen focuses on, and it's my opinion that Zen probably has the most enlightened folks per capita of any other practice on the planet. So they may be on to something.

When the conscious thoughts in my mind finally all cleared that day, I was able to start to feel what it was like to have my mind be totally silent. It was actually really weird, but it was also very calming. It was the first time I had never had that familiar inner voice saying something… judging something… analyzing something… classifying something. It was the first time in my entire life that within my mind, everything was just still. Thankfully, I didn't let the actual thought "this is weird" into my head. I just sat and listened to the sound of existence, enjoying this new experience, and watching my mind in its absolute quietude.

It was after some moments of simply being there with my eyes closed observing absolutely nothing, that I began to feel something. It was a feeling like none other I had experienced before. It felt like some sort of energy had started to build within me. I had never felt anything like this during meditation before, so I focused on it with interest. It started as a small concentrated glow at first, emanating from somewhere around my heart or maybe a bit below it. The glow was accompanied by a calming hum, which seemed to vibrate from the same place. Together, the glow and the vibration created a feeling of a powerful warmth coming from within. It felt pleasant at first. It didn't stay pleasant for long.

Just when I started to appreciate the effect, that feeling of energy and vibration from within began to grow. And when it did, it grew exponentially. People often use the word 'exponentially' inappropriately. Exponential growth means growth on a scale which is multiplied by every part of itself. Exponential growth of something doesn't mean it gets twice as big as it once was, or five times as big as it was, it means the next time you judge its size or power level, every portion of its entire existence has been multiplied by every portion of its entire existence. Moment by moment, the energy coming from somewhere within me expanded in intensity and clarity, becoming bigger, stronger and more distinct every split second. My bodily senses were immediately overwhelmed. Taste, touch, sight, smell, and hearing, had all either shut down, or were being blocked by the rush of energy that was beginning to engulf me. I felt an uncomfortable hotness in my lower and middle spine, which seemed to be pushing itself upward through the back of my neck and into my head. The enormousness of this energy had come out of nowhere, and was suddenly bigger than anything I had ever experienced in my entire lifetime, or could even possibly imagine. It was alarming, to say the least. The next ten seconds were probably the longest of my entire life.

I could no longer feel the bed under my body, which now felt weightless. I could no longer hear anything entering through my ears, not even the sound of my own breathing. The darkness of my closed eyelids was being slowly replaced by a bright, shimmering, multispectral, pure white light that was increasing its intensity in relation to the energy building within me. The pressure and heat that had been pushing up my spine now seemed to be wanting to push through the top of my head from the inside, with the bone of my skull resisting its exit. I could feel the molecules in my body actually start to vibrate along with the hum that was seemingly in tune with the energy that was still building exponentially in intensity. This whole process was overtaking me. Time stopped.

What was happening was overwhelming. This is not at all what I wanted or was looking for. I had started my meditation in a relaxed state, fully awake and aware, simply focusing on not thinking . . .

but now . . . now I was experiencing some real fear due to the overwhelming experience that was building beyond comprehension. I inhaled sharply, holding my breath. The pressure on the inside top of my skull was almost unbearable. I'd never felt anything like it before. It was like my brain wanted to push out of the top of my skull. The energy and light growing from within was expanding to levels that were now terrifying me. I wanted it to stop. But it was showing no signs of stopping.

I'm not sure if any perceivable thoughts had yet entered my mind at this point, but there was definitely a feeling this was way too big for me to handle or control. I felt a startled astonishment accompanied by a realistic sense that I may be in great danger. What was happening to me? My eyes were closed, yet I was going blind with a brightness of a light, which flashed all colors simultaneously. I couldn't hear anything outside my body, yet a vibration of energy was humming so loudly within me that it shook the particles of my physical existence both within and without. I thought I was lying on the bed in my house, but I couldn't feel anything supporting my body from simply passing through not just the bed, but the Earth under the house itself. This experience was terrifying.

Because of the weightless feeling and the continuously building energy, I began to feel like I was losing my grip on the world itself. I felt some sort of vortex open up near me somewhere, beckoning my energy to pass through it. My first conscious thought entered my awareness. "I'm dying. This is what it is to die. This is what it's like to feel my spirit leaving my body. I'm not breathing. Why am I not breathing? Did my heart stop? Wait, I can't die. I need to take care of Mom. I'm not done here yet. I can't go."

I felt my entire existence slipping away into some other dimension. I was losing my grip on my body, my spirit slowly slipping from the confines of my body's shell. I was losing my grasp on my physical existence. This is when the fear escalated into near panic. "What can I do to stop this?" The energy buildup was spinning completely out of control now, and I wanted absolutely no part of it. My head felt like it was about to explode. My spine was on fire. I was trying to open my eyes and stop the whole experience from continuing. Maybe if I could get to a phone I could call 9-1-1, and get some EMT to zap me back to life. How many moments did I have left? Could I even move my arms to reach for my cell phone? That's when from out of nowhere, I felt the idea of two words burst into my consciousness and interrupt my panic.

"Let go."

I can't remember if the words themselves actually entered my mind, or if it was just the feeling associated with those particular words that I identified as "let go" entering my consciousness. But whether they were the actual words, or just the feeling of the words, they definitely made their presence known, and the idea associated with those words was very clear; give in to this process of dying and leaving the Earth, and don't try to stop it.

My mind's internal reaction to that initial "let go" idea was clear and immediate. **"Fuck that!"**

I thought I was dying. And at the age of thirty-two, I wasn't quite ready to accept that particular event just yet. In protest, my mind seemed to want to explain that to whatever had just told me to let go. My inner voice started explaining. "I'm not . . ."

"LET GO!"

This time the words shook the very fabric of my existence. Every part of me heard the message that time. There was no ambiguity in its tone. It was a command, plain and simple. It seemed to echo throughout the whole universe.

But as powerful as that command seemed, I still wasn't going. I wasn't letting go of a damn thing if I could help it. I felt that I was just on the verge of figuring life itself out, and my life was about to take a turn for the better. I had only recently discovered this meditation thing, which seemed to be helping. I didn't want to give up that progress. I didn't understand the very thing I was searching for may, in fact, be what was happening at that very moment. I only saw the whole experience as a potential threat to {self}. And I was reacting in terror.

And that's the moment when something changed. A feeling of familiarity entered my consciousness. It was an intimate familiarity, so welcoming and comforting, that it made me immediately drop all my defenses and resistance. Without seeing who or what it was, I was flooded with a feeling that seemed to convey I had no reason to be defensive, because I was quite familiar with whomever, or whatever, was asking me to let go. It felt like I had personally come up behind myself, given myself a hug around the chest, and whispered in my own ear. And so one final time I heard the words again, but spoken softly and calmly this time, from someone I had known, seemingly, since the beginning of time.

"Let go."

"Oh, it's you. I can't believe I forgot you. Okay, let's go."

My body exhaled slowly, like how I might imagine it would if that breath were to be my last breath of this life, which frankly, I thought it was. I let go of my grasp on where I was, who I was, what I was . . . I let go of absolutely everything. All my hopes and dreams. All my aspirations about life. All my plans. All my attachments about what I had expected my life to be and how long I had expected it to last. I let go of absolutely **everything**. I surrendered all.

If this experience was my life coming to an end, I was no longer going to take action stop it. I had been told through some feeling to "let go," and for some reason, I trusted that message more than anything I had ever trusted in my life. "They will get along fine without me," I thought. "Everything is going to be okay." The heat and pressure I felt pushing up through the top of my spine into my skull popped through the top of my head with a seemingly audible sound. What I can only describe as my 'spiritual energy' was sucked out of my body into the vortex that was now engulfing me. The multispectral white light completely engulfed my consciousness. It's all I could see. The vibrating hum shaking every particle of my existence seemingly atomized me into billions of particles that mixed in with whatever was happening. It's all I could hear and feel, beyond the sensation of bliss I now sensed sweeping through me. In that moment, a love so powerful and pure filled the very core of my being. A love of everything. A love of life. A love of this dying process. A love of the white light. A love of the vibration. A love of the reunion. I had actually become part of whatever was happening. It felt like the vibration of my existence was in complete sync with that of God and the entire universe. My body was no more. My mind was not entirely my own. My consciousness was now somewhere else.

Act II: The Freaky Shit

Now . . . I should tell you that some of what happened in my mind after this point happened in a logical series of visions. But some of it also seemed to happened simultaneously and out of order, which is something you can't understand until you experience it. You'll just have to trust me on that. In a book, which is linear, I will need to discuss everything presented here in a straight line. Just know it all wasn't perceived that way. I cannot possibly convey to you everything that I saw and learned after this point, but I can hit some of the main ideas for which words exist. The brain science connected with this experience suggests that my awakening experience probably elapsed over a period of twenty to forty minutes, although it could have been much longer. It felt like the experience took thousands of years to pass through. Frankly, when it ended I was surprised I hadn't been dead for thousands of years, and the fact that I returned to my body on that bed was the biggest surprise of the whole episode. We'll discuss the science connected with this experience in a future chapter. For now, let's hit the rest of the highlights.

When the white light faded, the first thing my consciousness was presented with was the typical life review we hear about that supposedly happens when people die. As they say, "My entire life flashed before my eyes." Except it didn't just flash. I remember seeing every critical moment of my life being played back for me. Not every moment was replayed, but it was a substantial portion of my life, and it seemed to include every moment from which I could learn something. This playback of scenes was different than the first time I'd experienced them, though. This time around, my emotions and those of the people around me were in clear view, all being felt as a clear but separated mix. I felt the thoughts and emotions of the others who were present. There were so many points of personal love and laughter in my life that I had forgotten. And there were so many points of personal pain I had forgotten as well. It was interesting to see how differently people around me experienced the moments of my life that I saw in my own unique way. I could see through their eyes, and feel through their emotions. It was amazing.

The focal points of this life review were the moments where I had made errors, either intentional or accidental, causing emotional and physical pain for others. My attention was directed to these without the ability to turn away. I actually felt the physical and emotional distress I caused people I remembered, and also the emotional and physical distress I'd caused people I had forgotten. I felt the uncertainty mixed with hope that my mother experienced while being pregnant with me at the age of 45 and being advised to abort the pregnancy for the sake of her own health. I'd never known that fact, which my mother and sister later confirmed. I felt the tears and anguish of the girlfriend I had forgotten when our two-week relationship had ended poorly because of my callousness. I felt her heart break. I felt the pain in my father's heart about things I had forgotten I had said until they were played again before me. I felt the sadness and tears of the school counselor who cried for me after I had left her office one day, after yet another bullying incident at school.

I saw things I had remembered from different perspectives and different angles. And I remembered things I had long forgotten, seeing them from new perspectives. I remembered my whole life, and felt it all from the perspective of everyone else involved. I felt ashamed by a lot of it. I was stupid. Immature. Selfish. Hateful at times. Scared for my{self} throughout all of it. But the feeling of Love, which had flooded through me as I was seemingly being atomized out of my human existence, endured through the whole experience. The only judgment I felt during my life review was my own. The presence of that Love through my life playback communicated to me, by simply being there, that everything I had done in life, including even my most horrible intentional mistakes, were all forgivable actions. That Love was not abandoning me because of my mistakes. It was not turning away. Its presence reminded me that I had done those things in the ignorance of forgetting who and what I was. The feeling that permeated was that everything I had done up to that moment was forgiven and now that I had remembered who and what I was, I didn't have to make any of those dreadful, hurtful, harmful mistakes anymore.

In experiencing that feeling of complete forgiveness, that was when I knew I was with the consciousness of God . . . or to be fair . . . that was when I knew I was experiencing the presence of a consciousness that human beings most often describe as God. I won't make any assumptions for you about this separate consciousness either being God or not being God. From my personal perspective, the amount of love and compassion and forgiveness I was experiencing made it pretty convincing to me that I was with a consciousness I would certainly consider to be God. To keep an eye on the science (which will help us in the discussion about how you can evoke a similar experience from within you if you wish), I will use the word Consciousness (with a capital C) for the rest of the chapter to keep us mostly untangled from the various religions and their positions on God. Calling it a Consciousness is true to the experience. It was certainly a Consciousness different than my own, and this Consciousness was in charge of this whole process. It was this Consciousness that delivered previously unknown knowledge and wisdom, and it seemed to be aware of my internal reactions to things. It seemed that as soon as I understood something I was being shown, the internal experience changed immediately and dramatically to whatever was coming next. In addition, this Consciousness seemed to have its own voice that I heard as thoughts inside my head. That was weird, but definitely congruent with it being a separate Consciousness that wasn't my own.

The experience of being with this seemingly transcendent Consciousness somewhat matched what we all have been told about God, of course. The infinite unconditional love. The immediate and unlimited forgiveness. The boundless compassion, patience, and wisdom. It was all there, minus the throne, white beard, and flowing robes. No pearly gates. No Jesus or Muhammad or St. Peter to act as an intermediary. And although this was much simpler than the stories I'd been told about God, to my surprise, this Consciousness was way more . . . **everything** . . . than anything I had ever been told or imagined about this thing we call God.

Though I believed I was experiencing physical death, I wasn't sad, and I didn't miss or feel sorry for the people I had left behind. Regardless of whatever suffering they might endure because of my passing, I knew they'd be with this Consciousness momentarily as well. I now knew that human life wasn't the end, and in relation to this new thing, that human life was almost of no importance at all. At least it wasn't as important as our human egos try to make it out to be. All of life was a game. A momentary adventure. A time for fun and enjoyment. From here I could see that all of human life was merely a split second of physical existence in the infinite expanse of time and space that cradled the energy of life, energy which could neither be created nor destroyed, but only transformed, just as science supposes. So in this dying experience, I was grateful. I was grateful for having had experienced my life. For having learned from reliving my mistakes. For having been shown the perspective of others around me and what their life experiences were in those same moments. And I was grateful for being in the presence of the most awesome, loving, accepting Consciousness in the universe, which had just conveyed a feeling of effortless forgiveness for my most embarrassing, and shameful, and hurtful moments in life. I was in a state of awe for this gift and this effortless forgiveness for everything I had done previous. Maybe the awe of being forgiven was the reason for what happened next.

From that point of feeling forgiveness for the things I had done, I was given what I can only call a **tour of forgiveness**. My consciousness, along with the Consciousness which emanated pure love and forgiveness, started going to different places around the globe. More than being a dreamlike experience, this process seemed to have a hyper-realism beyond that of being in the physical world. I saw snapshots of the lives of other people, seemingly happening in real time. The first stop on this human life tour, however, was a very disturbing experience. And it delivered one of the most difficult and dramatic lessons I learned throughout the whole experience. It presented a very graphic scene, like none I have ever witnessed or imagined, nor which I would ever like to see or imagine again. I don't even like recalling it in my memory now so as to describe it. Please brace yourself as I share this rather jarring, uncomfortable and graphic first stop with you.

As my conscious awareness left the end of my life review, and my amazement about all the bad things I'd done being simply forgiven still hung in that space, my now disembodied conscious vision zoomed into a hut which looked to be somewhere in northern Africa. A woman and some militia soldiers were struggling. The scene was horrific. What I saw was that the woman in the hut was being physically assaulted and sexually violated by the soldiers. I will spare the unnecessary details, but she was badly beaten, broken, and bleeding, and somehow I could sense her body was near its final surrender. She was praying for death as her thoughts were with her children, whose bodies were laying lifeless outside in the dirt. This image, and the feelings this woman was experiencing, destroyed me. I could feel her severe physical pain and broken bones. I could feel the emotional anguish that prompted her to scream out in agony and sorrow. She felt utterly alone. She was in the deepest suffering any human could experience. She was absolutely devoid of all hope.

The feeling of love and compassion and forgiveness for that woman, which I felt emanating from the Consciousness which brought us there, was beyond words. There was a clear feeling of wanting to relieve that woman's pain and suffering and to hold her with the love of a parent comforting a child. There was a feeling of wanting to connect with her and remind her of who and what she was, and to let her know she was loved and cared for and that her children were safe and free of further pain and suffering. I can't possibly even describe to you... this is one of those things that goes beyond words... how beautiful the love was for that woman who was experiencing the most horrible moment of her life. I can't explain to you the level of compassion that was felt for that woman. Although the scene itself was disgusting from a human point of view, the consciousness and love in that room was breathtaking, and simply overwhelming to any other feeling that could have attempted to surface within me at that moment.

As horrible as the present moment seemed, it was accompanied by the knowledge that it would only be a moment before everyone in the room would be dead and turned to dust. So while the woman's suffering was extreme on a human scale, and it was indeed the only thing that mattered in that very moment to the Consciousness, it was also clear that the worst of human suffering, was insignificant in comparison to the existence after death, where everyone would rejoin the higher Consciousness I had just recently rejoined myself.

From one standpoint, the very worst that the entire experience of being human could deliver was but a splinter on the skin of spiritual existence. But from another standpoint, in that room, in that moment, was a true and divine caring about that worst of human suffering. There was a deep and infinite compassion for that woman's physical and emotional pain. The entire universe kept creating, and being, and loving absolutely every portion of existence, while also stopping absolutely everything in existence to reconnect with this one woman and be compassionate of her suffering. So her human suffering felt both insignificant, and of ultimate significance, simultaneously. It was a complete circle. I understood this and accepted it completely. This is certainly what I would expect of an infinite Consciousness. I would expect it to have unconditional love and compassion for the weak and helpless, even in the grand scheme of an infinite universe.

I felt this lesson about infinite compassion and love important for me to learn. But then came the hard lesson, which is the one I got the feeling this Consciousness wanted me to understand the most. This lesson confirmed I was indeed experiencing a Consciousness of pure love and acceptance, whether I was still inside my own head lying on my bed, or whether I had actually been whisked away into another spiritual dimension somewhere and was witnessing a live event. Because in the next moment, with the love and compassion and wishes for the woman's suffering to end still overflowing with an indescribable beauty and grace, the focus changed from the woman in the room to the men who were still brutalizing her. And to my bewildered awe, as the focus changed from the woman to the men, the feelings of overflowing love and compassion **did not cease**.

And probably just like you, right now, this lesson completely broke my mind.

In our human minds, when we imagine this ugly scene, or one like it, we typically harbor malice for those men. We want vengeance. We want to reach out and stop them from hurting that woman and killing her family. Or at the very least, if we can't stop them, we want them to pay for what they've done. We want to reach out and hurt them in return. Our whole human justice system is based on this type of retribution. We want them to pay with pain and suffering that is equal to or greater than that which they doled out. We want to beat them. We want to defile them. We want to forcibly hold them down on that table, grab the nearest large stick of wood, and make them know what it feels like to have their bodies be forcibly penetrated. Right now. No judge or jury. Send those assholes straight to hell.

That's how our human minds react to someone intentionally causing harm to innocent life, and twenty minutes prior to seeing this very scene, before I entered this meditation, that is exactly how my human mind would have reacted. When I went into the meditation that had started this crazy voyage, I had entered it as a proud ex-military, gun-owning conservative, who was just looking for a little bit more inner peace. A bit more happiness. A bit more understanding. But being completely honest, I was also a very judgmental person. I was very defense of {self} oriented. And regardless of the messages of my own religion, when I went into that meditation, I was a rather unforgiving guy. Twenty minutes prior to that moment, had I seen someone hurting someone else weaker than them, especially a woman, a child, or a puppy, I would not have delayed a split-second in crossing the distance to put my hands on that aggressor in a rather unfriendly way.

But in that moment of being in that hut, it wasn't my consciousness feeding my thoughts. I wasn't experiencing my typical or expected reactions to that scene. It was another Consciousness I had never experienced before. It was a Consciousness that was completely foreign to me. Scientifically speaking, I have to consider it a separate Consciousness altogether. Because if my human consciousness is indeed, as science supposes, a conglomeration of my subconscious forces which influence and then become my waking consciousness from below in my brain, then digging deeper down within myself to experience a deeper level of subconscious reaction to that moment should have uncovered those very fundamental tendencies which made me select being a gun-toting, vengeance delivering, type-A asshole. I should have witnessed that scene and wanted to kill those guys, if the current theories of science are correct about where our consciousness comes from. If a transcendental all forgiving and all loving consciousness is not possible… the reaction I was feeling to that virtual scene should have been more congruent with my experience of my waking consciousness; my {me}.

But it wasn't.

My typical response to that type of scene, one which many of us might share, as we felt sorry for the women and vilified the men, was not what I was experiencing. When the focus of that horrible event changed from the innocent woman being victimized to the men who were victimizing her, what flowed through my consciousness… you could even say what flowed through my heart… was the same unlimited compassion and boundless love for **those children also**. And using the word children is the only way I can describe that feeling. In the eyes of that Consciousness, those men brutalizing that woman were as much in need of assistance and in need of cessation of their pain and suffering as the woman was. It was clear that everyone in the room was a victim of their body and mind, and they were separated from the remembrance of their direct link with that same Consciousness. The feeling of compassion for everyone was a bit different based on their individual situation, but it was equally as powerful based on their common malady, which was that everyone in the room was suffering needlessly. The love emanating from that Consciousness was equally as powerful for **everyone** there.

The woman was loved, and the men hurting her were loved. The Consciousness wanted to help everyone. It wanted to relieve the suffering of the woman being victimized, and it wanted to relieve the suffering from within the men that caused them to be the victimizers. The feeling I perceived was that those men were horribly lost and separated from the higher Consciousness. And because those men were so removed and so consumed by pain, fear, rage, and selfishness, they were taking actions to hurt others in an attempt to relieve that internal suffering. And that was a huge tragedy. And they needed help, not condemnation. They needed saving from their mind's illusion of {self}. They needed to reconnect with the Consciousness and remember who and what they were over the noise of their minds.

It's no secret that our human minds want to reject this idea outright. Our minds want to reject that any Consciousness anywhere could forgive these men of their violence. Not right away, anyway, right? Maybe after a couple thousand years in jail, and after they turned to God and started teaching others how not to become what they became, right? But when we look at forgiveness with a very critical eye, what actually determines the timetable on forgiveness? How long does it take any one of us to forgive someone?

The time table for most of us to forgive someone seems to be either after they've apologized to us, and/or after we have decided to release from our mind whatever wrong that we'd perceived was done to us. And whether or not we like to admit it, both of these decisions about forgiveness are rather {self}ish actions. The apology we hold out for gives us the {self} valuation shift that we're important enough to receive an apologize, coupled with the {self} depreciation from the offending party that they're saying {they're sorry}. So they admit they were wrong, which association makes us right. That's an ego thing.

Or, if we don't get an apology and decide to forgive anyway, one of two things happen: (1) either we defer to a higher attachment of {self} to a virtue or a religion that dictates we **should** forgive which prompts us to forgive, or (2) we take some time to finally decide we no longer want to hang on to the anger which stands in the way of us forgiving. In either case, it's a function of having a {self} and deciding what things we're going to have, and not have, as part of our mind's {self}.

But the Consciousness I perceived in that space had no {self} that needed to be dealt with before forgiving; so the Consciousness had no timetable on forgiveness. Forgiveness was immediate. To think that an infinite Consciousness would need some sort of apology, or a need to be asked for forgiveness is simply humanity applying its own limitations of mind to an entity without any such limitations. To say it another way, a universal loving God wouldn't need to be asked for forgiveness. And there's even a way you can get a glimpse of how that can be true.

An analogy to bring your human mind a bit closer to understanding the feeling prevalent at that scene, would be to imagine the three people in the world who are dearest to you in an empty room. There are no strangers here. Only these three people you love without limit and without question. Now imagine that the strongest two of the three have somehow contracted a crazy brain virus that causes them to forget who they are, and afflicts them with blinding pain that makes them viciously beat on the third and weakest person in your group of three dearest loved ones. Because of their sickness, the two people you love dearly are now acting in compete contradiction to whom you know them to be as they beat on the third person you love. While you watch this horrific and violent scene play out from a short distance, and as the third person is now approaching death's door because of this violence, how desperately do you want to see that violence stop? How desperately do you want to remove the sickness from your loved ones' minds which has caused them to forget who they are, so they can stop themselves from the violence the sickness is causing? Do you wish for their internal pain and suffering to cease so they are no longer motivated to this violence?

Of course you do. That's an easy question to answer. But now to the tougher question, which brings the hard lesson to your door:

Let's say we were able to stop the harm so that our third loved one was saved. Now that the violence has stopped, do you wish ill will to either of your two loved ones who attacked the third? Do you love the first two any less because they contracted the illness that caused them to forget who they are and be violent? Or do you forgive their actions as part of their sickness, and look to cure them of it permanently? As you hold the baton of justice which conveys eternal damnation, do you swing it in retribution against the virus-stricken loved ones, or do you drop the baton to grab the medicine that will banish the crazy brain virus from them forever?

Personally, I drop the baton of eternal damnation. And in that hut, so did that Consciousness. Or at least that's the feeling that permeated the space of that first scene on what I call "my tour of forgiveness". The reason was that it seemed that no human being was unfamiliar to that Consciousness. It knew absolutely everyone intimately, and it seemed that because the love of that Consciousness was indeed boundless, not one human goes unloved. It knew of the process within the human mind that separates us from each other and from the higher Consciousness. It's only a question of how much separation each of us has that makes us forget who and what we are, which determines how badly we treat each other.

After that first lesson about infinite love, compassion, and forgiveness, different images started flashing in quick succession, all conveying the same message. All kinds of people were taking all kinds of {self}ish actions against each other. I saw a man stealing money through a computer screen. I saw an ice skater taking her newly sharpened skates from a countertop without paying the craftsman. I saw a child dying of hunger while a man was selling the aid shipment meant for the child. I saw a mother smacking a newborn baby for crying. I saw two older men stoning a bleeding and pleading teenage girl. I saw a school-aged child stealing a new pencil from a backpack. It was a weird mixture of slight and extreme scenes. Hundreds of them flashed before me. All the people in the scenes seemed to be dear loved ones to the Consciousness directing the tour. They were all the closest of the close, deserving of infinite compassion for the pain and illness that caused them to perpetrate {self}ish acts against each other. All the people in the scenes were sick with the same exact illness of the mind, and they all suffered from the same degree of separation from the higher Consciousness. It seemed if you had the sickness at all, you had it all the way. Thus, the smallest transgression to the largest were immediately forgiven because the transgressors didn't know who and what they were, and were ultimately not acting in their true nature. There was a deep feeling of 'they know not what they do'. With every change in venue and every change in situation, the feeling of unconditional love, unlimited compassion, and immediate forgiveness was the same.

Throughout the whole tour, there was no judgment in any of these scenes. There was no hate from the Consciousness for any of these lost children, regardless of their transgression. There was no malice or anger. There was no offense taken. They were sick, and one of the symptoms was that they took actions against each other to defend an imagined illusionary {self}, which wasn't really who or what they were. Plain and simple.

This whole first portion of the experience disrupted everything I thought I knew about right and wrong. It transformed every previous idea about what I thought God was. There was no question about it. What I was experiencing here and now was God, untethered by the limits of my mind's concepts. God wasn't the broken ideas I'd been handed by other humans previously. It was this experience, here in this place, that was clearly Heaven. The unconditional and unlimited love persisted. The extreme intelligence persisted. There was not a shred of doubt within me that the experience I was having was that of being directly with God and seeing things God wanted me to see. The previous ideas I had about God were a joke compared to this. There was no white-bearded man on a throne. There was only Love, which transcended any feeling of love that I had ever experienced before, and an incredible intelligence that seemed to dwarf the universe itself.

Upon understanding this lesson of infinite love and forgiveness, my tour of forgiveness ended.

When the images of the various vignettes cleared, I found myself in the middle of the multidimensional universe, surrounded by all the stars and galaxies in existence, all connected to a single point of existence which was Consciousness. It was breathtakingly beautiful on a scale I cannot convey. The love for all of existence permeated everything as I saw and felt all of existence in the universe simultaneously, not just in three dimensions, but in other dimensions which simply defy explanation. I felt an intelligence connected with the Consciousness that was so great and so comprehensive, but yet just out of reach. Barely separated. I felt the bliss of existence itself here. After I had seemingly come to be with this Consciousness at the center of the universe, I wasn't expecting anything more than what I had already experienced to occur. If I was dead, this was Heaven, period. I was awash in the agape type of love and acceptance that you only read about in books, and I was with an all-knowing all-loving presence that had satisfied every uncertainty that I had ever had. I had been engulfed in a multispectral white light that permeated every portion of my existence and every corner of the cosmos. It had removed every bit of pain, doubt, and spiritual uncertainty that I had ever experienced. What more could there possibly be? If I was not going back to living life as a human after that, so be it. Awesome. I can chill here indefinitely. If I was somehow still alive, however, and I had found the human condition of what I had been seeking . . . a true communion with what I perceived to be God . . . that was even better. I had found it. Either way, I was good. I had discovered the answer to all my seeking. This moment was all that I had ever needed, and it was more than I had ever asked for. I could exist here for eternity without question. Little did I know, in comparison with what was to come next, this was just the beginning.

Act III: Moving into the Really Mind Bending Shit

From that space of bliss, where I was content to chill indefinitely and just be in the universe, out of nowhere, a question came to my consciousness:

"What do you wish to know?"

"Ho-o-oly shit!"

Was this Consciousness, that just made my existence perfect, now actually talking to me? It didn't come through as so much a voice, but more a thought in my head. I didn't hear it through my ears, but through my mind. Looking back, it must have passed through the language centers of my brain, because the thought, wherever it came from, was definitely decoded into that particular question by my brain. And of course, I wouldn't be able to convey to you any of this story unless my hippocampus was operating at the time also, recording it into memory. So this gives us a clue that my brain was a part of this whole process, but let's get back to the experience itself.

With everything else I was experiencing at the moment, simply being asked the question itself seemed beyond gracious. And yet, it seemed completely expected at the same time. I mean, after having my life pass before my eyes, being with what felt like God through a tour of personal and human existential forgiveness, and having then been transported off to an inner dimension of spacetime that any normal person might consider Heaven, why **wouldn't** the Consciousness of the whole universe ask me what I wished to know? "Why not," right? And if this is Heaven, why wouldn't I expect whomever asked me that question to give me exactly what I asked for if I answered it, right? "Okay, I'll bite. What do I wish to know, oh anonymous question asker? Let's see what's on the menu. What do I wish to know?"

"Everything," I replied rather matter-of-factly.

Please allow me to pause and change my tone here. I wish to emphasize the gravity and simplicity of what happened next.

It was at that moment of asking for everything that I learned the deepest meaning of the lesson connected with the age old saying; 'be careful what you wish for, because you just might get it'.

If the first experience regarding learning about the true depths of divine forgiveness had broken my mind, this next experience almost washed away what was left of my mind completely. Without any delay whatsoever . . . it felt like every bit of knowledge and wisdom in the known and unknown universe flowed through my existence at a rate that almost ripped my entire existence apart completely.

On a scale of 1 to 10, with 1 being "the most difficult and mind challenging class that MIT offers," and 10 being "please, if you have any wish to save me from a complete disintegration of mind, turn this off," this flow of information came through right at a solid 1,764 (some of you will figure out why I jokingly used that particular number). My consciousness was flooded with absolutely everything that exists. All the answers to every question that had ever been asked by anything imbued with life throughout the history of time flew through my existence like an infinite number of gallons of water being forced at light speed through a standard-sized screen door, thirty-six by eighty-four inches. It was immediately overwhelming to my limited mind, and at the time I felt the little screen door of my existence was going to be ripped off its hinges and washed away forever if whatever had started did not stop **immediately**. I still feel the pressure and uncomfortable pain within my head at this very moment as recall that experience. It felt like my mind was going to disintegrate and be no more. If I could, I would love to say that it was like drinking from a fire hose of intelligence and wisdom that was simply way too much to handle, but the reality is that analogy doesn't do this experience justice. It was much more like when Wile E. Coyote tries to step across the desolate highway out in the middle of the desert, after looking both ways to see nothing for miles, then gets pulverized by the Mack truck traveling through at 2,000 miles per hour as he takes his first step across. There was way **way** too much information to process. I could not discern even a shred of it. It certainly seemed like all the knowledge and wisdom in the universe, but ultimately none of it was of any use, and the experience simply showed me how much I didn't know compared to how much there is to know. That in itself can be a valuable lesson.

I don't think I was even able to form the thought of wanting to scream "TOO MUCH," when the flow of information slowed dramatically to a more manageable level that calmed the turbulence, and avoided making the screen door of my existence vaporize itself in one instantaneous and unnoticeable poof. It was as if this Consciousness had suddenly plugged me into it's own intelligence and comprehensive understanding of the universe, being willing to freely share it with me after I asked for exactly that to happen, and yet was now also somehow dialing back the flow of information to a level my consciousness could handle, so as to protect me from becoming overwhelmed. And this… this when the magic happened.

From the space of being somewhere out in the middle of the universe, visions of the underlying structure of the universe started to flood my consciousness. Not visions of the universe itself, but how the universe is actually assembled under the covers. Backstage. Behind the curtain. Underneath everything we perceive as the universe. The physicality of the universe simply began to unfold before me into the multiple dimensions which create it and the mechanisms for how the whole thing works. I can't describe three-dimensional space unfolding into different dimensions beyond the three dimensions we are familiar with, because we are three-dimensional creatures, and our minds just can't go there. If I said that the empty space of nothingness seemingly unfolded outward from absolutely nowhere to reveal what makes up that empty space itself, that might be as close as I could get to presenting an idea we could grasp. It was truly weird, but immensely beautiful, and infinitely intelligent. And just as before, I experienced the love of it all as it was revealed.

This unfolding process came with a comprehensive understanding of multidimensional energy, multidimensional gravity, multidimensional spacetime, and multidimensional consciousness. Beyond the visual information, the **ideas and knowledge** associated with this visual show flowed through my mind as well. Equations that were beyond understanding filled with unfamiliar mathematical symbols, geometric shapes, and multi-planar lines could be perceived. The relationships and connections between all forms of energy replaced anything we were perceiving in three-dimensional space. Although we hadn't moved, there was no more starry universe, just the fundamental complexity underneath which creates the potential for whole starry universe to exist. I understood all this extra information. Then the math, and energy relationships, and geometry unfolded into endless fractals of angled additional dimensions, folding into, and connecting with, each other seemingly infinitely. It was beyond beautiful, and beyond intelligent. From this space of fractal existence, the multiple universes that exist within our same three-dimensional space could be understood. It was here that you could see why various points in our physical universe, which seem separated by vast distances in our three dimensions, are actually the same single point. It was clear to me how our universe actually folds over onto itself multiple times creating invisible wormholes, and why seemingly huge energy leaps through space and time is child's play to quantum physics. Here, the extra dimensions beyond our three dimensions could be accessed, and conscious travel to absolutely anywhere at any point in time was instantaneous. It was all presented in a way the human mind simply can't grasp unless you experience it for yourself, but at the time I felt I was being shown the knowledge of how and why everything worked the way it did, and that there was an essence of a central control dimension that could touch everything. Through this common dimension, we flashed all around the universe to amazing scenes of creation and reformation of matter, and to spots of translation of energy between dimensions, and to weird places of flux where you could just feel that the physics itself was different than what it is here near Earth.

All of existence seemed to be connected to, and expanded from, a single infinitely small point, into which the illusion of space and time folds and unfolds infinitely and perpetually. The whole universe seemed balanced on the head of a pin, ready to blink out of existence entirely in an instant, except for a weird balance between some invisible forces that my human mind still can't comprehend. It gave the whole universe a feeling of being special, wondrous, amazing, and fun. The feeling of love for all of existence and all of life persisted throughout. It seemed to take many hours for all this unfolding and refolding to occur, but finally this multidimensional process ended. I perceived the Consciousness that was present throughout the experience was actually intertwined with the whole infinite universe. So Consciousness and the universe seemed like one inseparable, but complex, energy field.

It was only much later that I wondered how I could have ever thought anything else could be the case. Science has proven through thousands of experiments that quantum physics has a required variable called consciousness. And the quantum field extends everywhere in all directions, even backward and forward in time, making it as expansive as the whole universe. The universe can't exist without the quantum field. So how could a consciousness connected with this field not be inseparable from it, and thus infinite? Taking one step further, how could an infinite and intelligent Consciousness, dare I say God, if God exists, be less than the universe many people assume God created? So it wasn't unreasonable to assume the consciousness within the quantum field might in fact be the Consciousness I was perceiving at that moment as I witnessed the quantum field expanding and retracting from one infinitely small point. As we'll discuss soon, it's a common report from the people who have an enlightenment experience that they become one with a Consciousness that's infinite. But it wasn't until later I would make this connection between the science and the spirituality.

In the next moment of the experience, suddenly everything folded back into three dimensions. I found my consciousness looking down on the Earth from above. After spelunking through the multidimensional grand space of everything, it now seemed time to get the tour of the smaller stuff that makes up our physical existence. Whoosh! Downward the vision zoomed, right down into the world of the microscopic life energy that comes together to create us, and all life around us. The scale immediately decreased to the point that individual cells were now visible. I was in the body of everything. Plants, animals, humans, even my own body. An immense intelligence could be sensed here. I saw plants disassembling carbon dioxide molecules, and red blood cells delivering oxygen to nerve cells. Viruses were at work within cells changing things. It was all intelligent, all pulling from the seemingly infinite consciousness, which at this level could be felt much more powerfully. From this experience, all of nature in its full glory and miraculousness revealed its consciousness to me.

After spending quite some time watching, listening, and interacting with things on the cellular level, I zoomed down into the chemical world of molecular exchange, where chemical reactions could be seen like puzzle pieces fitting together. Sometimes they would release extra energy, which transformed molecular compounds in a big flash. In college, I remember having to memorize chemistry for testing purposes, but in truth, I never really understood chemistry until actually seeing it occur in front of me. It was breathtaking.

After stopping for just a moment there, I zoomed down into the molecules to the level of particle exchange, where I saw energy exciting electrons and creating miniature magnetic fields with almost immediate decay. This made the science of electronics we use seem rather stone-aged. After this, I zoomed down even further to the particle level, where energy itself creates the particles that seemingly make up our atoms. I use the word "seemingly", because the particles themselves were nothingness. At this finer scale, the squiggles and vibrations of energy which create everything were the only thing really present. Beyond energy, there was nothing, which meant all matter was nothing but the activity of energy, and everything physical we experience in life is an illusion piled on top of another illusion. It was here that energy jumped around from place to place, somehow influenced by something underneath it all.

This level of particle stuff was all I knew about physics going into this experience. I knew that particles existed, but I actually thought there were pieces of stuff down there that actually moved around, because that is what I had learned in school. It was a complete surprise for me to see what actually makes up our atoms is a bunch of nothingness. What really blew me away is that when I started a deeper study of physics later (to investigate whether my visions had any base in reality), I discovered that the latest science on atoms is exactly as I saw it. There's really nothing down there but bits of force and energy, and absolutely everything which we consider solid is actually nothing but this nothingness. Later, I learned that ancient religious writings speak of this nothingness also. But at the time, it was crazy to actually see it. We are made of nothing but energy that is governed at a level way below our smallest bits.

At this point, I expected the tour of the microscopic to stop. But from here, the zoom down into the minuscule kept going for a surprising number of levels. It seemed that even the squiggles of energy themselves were made up of smaller squiggles and forces. The vibrating patterns became finer and finer, being split into smaller and smaller components which connected with different dimensions and forces in the universe, each which held different pieces of the whole puzzle. Down, down, down, I went, until finally, there was nothingness. We were below the level of working energy itself. The squiggles of energy that made up everything had transitioned from the infinitesimally small to the imperceptibly large, and way down past the smallest increment of existence, was an amazing void of nothingness. But it wasn't entirely nothingness.

It was an infinite nothingness that stretched everywhere in all directions, without beginning and without end. At the particle level, there was a sense of locality. We were watching a particular particle in a general area of 3-D space. But underneath that, the walls of locality went poof, and the empty space below that level spread out to infinity where you could then pop up at any locality you wanted and influence the energy in that locality. It was the void of infinite potential itself. It was the potential that determines what energy does through its multidimensional existence. And rather than this void being empty, which is what's supposed to happen when you get down to a scale of a space being so small that nothing can fit into it, that space of nothingness below everything else was the place which was filled with the infinite intelligence of the Consciousness directing this tour. The feeling of unbounded intelligence and unconditional love for all creation was the strongest here.

Upon entering the void of nothingness down at this level of non-existence, the sense of being with this other Consciousness but not completely knowing its mind disappeared. I had melded with the Consciousness and become one with all the universe itself. I knew absolutely everything, and knew why absolutely everything worked the way it did. In this void, there was no delineation between anything that ever existed or anything that ever will exist. It was certainly the space of creation, and it created absolutely everything. Not just past tense, but present tense and future tense combined. All moments future and past were playing out simultaneously in this one void of nothingness while at the same time absolutely nothing was happening in the complete stillness of the space itself. This, from my personal perspective, was the space of God. It was the place where time itself could be seen as an illusion, and all dimensions of existence were accessible.

Something else which flooded through this Consciousness was an immense sense of familiarity, like I had known all this was me and that all this knowledge was mine the whole time, but that I had just forgotten it when I became a human being. I had forgotten that we were all one with God. I had forgotten we were all the whole universe and not separated in any way from the Consciousness or each other. Consequentially, I was not surprised to later find out that the ancient Pali word "sati", which Buddhism defines as "awareness" and is counted as one of the Seven Factors of Enlightenment, actually comes from a Sanskrit word which translates as "to remember."

As a result of descending into this space, it seemed like I actually got to be this Consciousness for a while. It felt like God simply gave up the wheel for a while to let me know what it was like to be God, while God went to go grab a cup of tea. If you think about it, God might have to pee at some point in all eternity, and you can't just leave the driver's seat of the universe empty, can you? So maybe snatching people into the space of enlightenment is God's idea of taking a smoke break. "Hey you! Come here. Drive the universe for a minute while I go take a shit on Satan's head." I'm joking of course, but in this space there was certainly a feeling of complete unity with the Consciousness of all the universe. There was no other. There was only Consciousness. And since I was there, by definition, without any separation, that Consciousness was me. And that's exactly what it felt like. My perception was that I was the whole thing, everywhere and everything, throughout all time. Or maybe more accurately, that everything everywhere throughout all space and time was me. And I understood it all. Everything. The secrets of black holes. The connection of the universal Consciousness with all of the individual conscious life-forms throughout the whole universe. All of it. None of it was a mystery. The small bit of variance built into the whole system, which physics calls the uncertainty principle, was included so everything could be a constant wonderful surprise. That was the best part of the whole universe.

It felt like I spent a couple thousand years in that void of nothingness, simply loving everything, being everything, relishing in the amazement of the beautiful complexity and elegance of everything that existed, and especially appreciating how physical life sprang forth from it all. It's here that I discovered my true Self. Capital S. I felt like hanging out for a while. So I did.

Now . . . I can't really explain all that I experienced while becoming that void of nothingness that existed underneath our **everythingness**. I can say that it changed me permanently. I went into that strange experience as an afraid, lonely, angry little boy, devoid of understanding about why life was the way it was and how I could find the answers I was seeking. On the other side, I came out of it a transformed, knowing consciousness, with no doubts and complete understanding, with no ill will for anyone or anything, forgiving of all the actions that had ever been taken against my mind or body, and all the actions that would later be taken against me. But the gooey middle of this void experience transcends explanation. This is why you and everyone else who seeks more needs to experience it for yourself. Because you already have that more, and you just need to see that you do. So at this point I'll need to make a rather large jump forward along the timeline of the experience, forward what felt like a few thousand years. That whole section of the void simply transcends language itself. There are no words to describe it and how it felt to have taken place over eons. I could fill multiple books with what I remember, knowing that I don't even remember all of it, and that my memories are probably tainted at this point. Our human minds can't hold the mind of Consciousness. And none of the words I could select would do it any justice anyway.

Act IV: The Final Four Lessons

There was one final portion of the experience I can somewhat explain, however. This last part of my internal experience brought my consciousness back out of the void of infinite creative potential into 3-D space again, and seemingly flashed forward millions of years into the future, dropping me at a point where we were again looking down upon the Earth. Unlike the typical image we get in our minds when we think of a satellite picture of the Earth, in this vision of Earth's land masses, water, and clouds, they were no longer their familiar white, green and blue. They were now more orange, white, and black. And the white in question wasn't clouds, it was ice. There were no clouds floating above this Earth. The land and frozen oceans were desolate and seemingly devoid of life for quite some time. No evidence of man ever being here remained. No space junk floated above. The cities were gone. The fragmented pieces of our technological infrastructure, long since buried, were awaiting archeologists who would never come. The shape of the continents had changed. It was clear that something catastrophic had happened at some point in the past and the planet could no longer support life. In short, our planet was cold and dead. In addition to that, there was a large celestial body currently plowing into the Earth from space, cracking into the Earth's core, setting what was left of the atmosphere ablaze, and throwing chunks of the planet off into space. If anything were still alive, it would certainly not survive this event.

It was here, looking at the Earth in such a violent state, that I sensed a slight separation between my consciousness and the higher Consciousness again. I felt, once again, like the separate conscious being who had lived on Earth at some time in the past. This time, however, unlike before, I could easily sense the mind of the higher Consciousness. It seemed that during the time I had become one with life energy itself, my mind had been changed dramatically to be more devoid of a {self}, able to embrace constant change, accept everything that is, and remain steeped in unconditional love and understanding for the whole universal illusion.

Because of this new perspective, there was no feeling of sorrow that the Earth was now devoid of life. Even now, that makes complete sense to me. Knowing what causes sorrow reveals why an infinite Consciousness isn't even able to experience sorrow. All of sadness is an emotional reaction to loss. True to all of psychological science, and true to the science of how emotions work, only organisms that can perceive loss, and/or a negative shift of {self} can feel any sorrow. But an infinite Consciousness that's intertwined with everything in the universe can't experience loss. Nothing ever leaves the universe. So whenever we die individually, or collectively, a Consciousness like the one we might ascribe to God really doesn't lose a thing. When we transition from "the physical" into "the spiritual", that's all still a part of the universe, and thus all still a part of Consciousness. It's only our mind's egoic negative reaction that causes our personal discomfort with that idea that God couldn't be sad if we all died, because we'd still be with God. But our ego {self} isn't us. It isn't reality. The reality is we're not missed, because we're not really gone. So while the Earth had lost all of humanity, the Consciousness hadn't really lost anything. You and everyone else were still there with us. You just didn't have a body anymore. No one did. And that same fact was simply true for every individual cell on the planet. The conscious energy had simply changed form. There was nothing to be sad about regarding the Earth being dead.

Every inch of the universe was still filled with the conscious life energy which permeates and persists in the spaces between the spaces. It felt like this field of consciousness is what allows physical life to spring forth from nothingness where physical environments allow it to develop. From this perspective, the whole universe seemed like nothing but a platform for physical life to occur. So we, and the whole universe, were a continuous creation of Consciousness. Not a past tense creation, during some six-day stretch long ago, but a present tense creation, and an ever-present creation. Right now. Every now.

In fact, in that moment, our planet seemed to be going through a rebirth cycle. There was a feeling of reverence to the whole scene, like physical life would start anew here. This realization taught me four profound lessons, which I want to delve into a bit before sharing how my experience drew to a close.

Final Lesson 1: None of Us Are Special, and We Are All Special

The first lesson this moment of Earth's rebirth showed me had to do with where life itself comes from. Having just left the void of infinite creative potential, I remembered experiencing the consciousness of life energy all across the universe. I felt life in the far reaches of the universe, which if life energy is indeed the consciousness of the quantum field, certainly makes sense. It was this infinite expanse of life energy that caused all the miracles of life to constantly pop up everywhere in the universe from simple organic materials springing to life, like fireworks. It's breathtakingly beautiful when it happens, and it's definitely fun to watch. It felt like this was exactly how life on Earth had developed billions of years ago. Spontaneously. Out of self-organized organic molecules who said, "Hey, this place has a nice beach."

What this fact about life being everywhere means, however, is that we are no more special to God than any other species in existence in the universe, and none of us within our own species are any more important than any other individual in our species. This infinite Consciousness loves all individuals infinitely, regardless of religious beliefs or evil deeds. And as a meta-awareness moment, does your mind want to reject that idea and protest that you're more special than anyone else in the universe? That your good behavior makes you more loved than someone else? I hope you can see that as a defense of {self} thought at this point.

Because we all come from the same infinite life energy field, we are all, by definition, a part of the Universal Consciousness. Not any one of us. But **every** one of us. Equally. We are all the same in the eyes of this infinite Consciousness. And we are all indeed a part of this Consciousness.

Thus, when we act against each other, we act against ourselves and the Consciousness of the universe. This not only puts into perspective all those rules religion has about not killing, stealing, bearing false witness, etc., it also reveals the foundation for the Golden Rule.

The Golden Rule states, "Do unto others what you would have done unto you." That's the universal rule that societies and religion throughout history have deemed most fundamental. In Christianity, it's found in Matthew; "Whatever you wish that men would do to you, do so to them." In Judaism, it's found in the Torah: "You shall love your neighbor as yourself." In Islam, it's in the Forty Hadith of an-Nawawi: "Not one of you is a believer until he loves for his brother what he loves for himself." In Hinduism, the Anusasana Parva says, "One should not behave towards others in a way which is disagreeable to oneself. This is the essence of morality. All other activities are due to selfish desire." In Buddhism, from the Sutta Nipata: "Just as I are so are they, just as they are so am I." In Jainism, from the Sutrakitanga: "A man should wander about treating all creatures as he himself would be treated." In Confucianism, from the Analects: "Tsekung asked, 'Is there one word that can serve as a principle of conduct for life?' Confucius replied, 'It is the word 'shu' - reciprocity: Do not do to others what you do not wish them to do to you."

All those examples aren't a coincidence. The universality of the golden rule comes from the ancient godheads of the various religions starting those religions after experiencing enlightenment, and realizing… we are all one.

The beauty of this realization comes through the actions we take when we all eventually see that we are all one. Because if you can see that, you can see the beautiful dance connected with the fact that when you reach out to help someone, you are actually helping another version of yourself, and thus doing yourself a favor. And when you interact with other people, you are interacting with yourself, which reminds you to be kind to yourself in the form of those other people. Realizing we are all one means when you argue with others, you are actually arguing with yourself. How silly to take that action! So until you see the oneness for yourself someday, simply start practicing to be kind to others as much as you would be kind to yourself. Because the saying "but there, for the grace of God, go I", isn't actually accurate. It's actually, "**because** of the grace of God, there go I."

Final Lesson 2: The Impermanence of Us

The second lesson that was slammed home by seeing the Earth devoid of life was a sense of impermanence. The acceptance of impermanence is a huge lesson within many global religions. The Monks of the Drepung Loseling Monastery in Atlanta, GA, travel around creating intricate sand mandalas over and over again for crowds of onlookers. The sand mandalas are beautiful works of art, and take a full week of solid work to complete. The monks complete them, only to sweep them up at the end of each week and dump all the dyed ground stone granules of their beautiful creation into the river. You may have seen them on the popular television show "House of Cards". The mandalas themselves are amazing, intricate, and beautiful. The monks spend a week or more scraping their metal sticks along the notched outer ridges of their the chak-purs, a conical funnel that, when vibrated by the scraping sticks, shakes the dyed ground stone out of a hole onto the space of the mandala. At the end of the mandala creation process, there's a ceremony at which the mandala is displayed, there is music, chanting, and a ceremonial costumed dance occurs. Afterward, these amazingly breathtaking works are set upon by monks with small brooms that destroy the mandala and sweep the whole thing mercilessly into an urn. They take the urn to a nearby waterway, and along with another bit of ceremony, dump the whole week's work into the river. Our minds ask, "Why the fuck would they do that week after week after week? Why would they spend hours and hours creating this artwork, to display it to the few people who actually get to witness it after it's done, only to destroy it and start all over again next week doing the same thing? That seems maddening." They do it to teach impermanence, and specifically, the impermanence of us. But even more, it's a reminder to themselves that it's not the result of their work that counts, but the activity of creation which matters most.

It's one thing to know that we won't always be here, but it's another thing entirely to watch your entire planet end in a way that feels more real than waking consciousness does. Absolutely everything in the universe, even our human existence in it, is impermanent. It's not just that we can't step into the same stream twice (especially if Drepung monks are dumping sand in that river at the moment), it's that everything in the universe changes constantly, including the Earth, and some day it's going to change to the point where human life itself will no longer be supported. At that point, if we're not off this rock, everything we have ever known and done will come to an end and be erased. And what will happen from a historical perspective at the moment of humanity's dying breath? What will have been a better use of our collective time; making wars over land, religions, and political conquest to appease the illusions of our minds, or caring for each other and helping each other enjoy life? Which will have been in better alignment with the fundamental characteristics of what we think of as God and the universe? There is only one now. And all moments happen now. What you do with your next now is up to you.

Final Lesson 3: Change Is Good, and Evolution was Created by God

The third lesson I felt from this experience zooms back out to the big picture again. Seeing the Earth being reborn, with the expectation that life would soon erupt again after all the dust settled, showed me that the phenomena of change, genetic evolution, and death are **integral parts** of this intelligent life system, too, just like life, love, and joy. Seeing the environment of Earth change so dramatically illustrated how the phenomenon of evolution was one of this higher Consciousness' **favorite** mechanisms. When you look at how the universe works, evolution isn't contrary to a constant life creation system, it's a required part of it. Evolution is what allows life to keep up with changing environments and survive over time. It's what allows life to continue over generations as life's resources change within local environments. It's what allows life to continue in an ever changing universe. **So in fact, evolution is very pro-life.**

Evolution is a mechanism for life to survive when its environment changes. The universe shows us hard evidence of this playing out on Earth with the organisms on the ocean floor, some which live under intense water pressure, in complete darkness, near volcanic vents which spew toxic and poisonous chemicals, in water temperatures measuring in the thousands of degrees, where nothing should be able to survive. Any other life-form would be instantly killed by any single one of those environmental variables, but not the tube worms living near those volcanic vents. Not the mussels or shrimp down there. They can handle that environment because an allowance for change (aka evolution) is built into the entire system. The badass microbes at the bottom of that food chain down there eat the hydrogen sulfide from the underwater volcano. For everything else on the planet, hydrogen sulfide is poisonous, corrosive, flammable, and explosive. Down there, it's lunch, and a building block of life.

The ability for life to adapt is what created the tardigrade, which is a microscopic eight-legged animal which lives absolutely everywhere on the planet in both extreme cold and extreme heat. It can even spring to life after being frozen and floating in the cold vacuum of space. When it finds itself in an environment suitable for sustaining life, it simply thaws out, wakes up and starts eating (kinda like me after a nap).

Psychologist George Stratton even showed us how quickly our

own bodies can adapt and rewire themselves in the face of an environment change. As an experiment, Dr. Stratton put on a pair of glasses that inverted the whole world from his perspective, turning it upside down, and flipping it left to right. So the sky was at his feet, and the ground seemed above his head. It caused him to reach with his right hand for things he could only touch with his left. The first day he felt nauseated, the second day his body position felt weird. By day three, he could function normally, and by day seven, his brain had actually flipped the world right-side up and left to right again even though his glasses were showing his eyes the opposite image. His arms worked correctly again. After he took them off, it was another three-day process for his brain to rewire again.

Our cells change in a pro-life fashion. From a scientific standpoint, if the smallest increment of life on Earth didn't self-organize from nothing continuously, we wouldn't be here. Therefore, life and consciousness must be in the fabric of the universe itself. And that includes the intelligent changes we call evolution.

Final Lesson 4: We Are Stardust and God Loves Death

So after having felt like I had been one with the Consciousness of the universe for quite some time, and after receiving these last lessons, it was easy to understand why it was okay for this Consciousness that the Earth was dead. The Earth and people are just one manifestation of life. Life pops up anywhere it can grow. All over the universe. And all life, wherever it grows, is all connected with the intelligence and consciousness of the universe. Change is a constant phenomenon of the universe, so death, as a change of the body's energy, is part of life, and it fits within the foundation of consciousness.

From a God's eye view of the universe, physical death is what fuels the wonderful constant rebirth cycle of the universe itself, which follows the basic fundamental law of the universe; that it's in a never-ending constant state of change. Neil deGrasse Tyson, who is the director of the Hayden Planetarium in New York, loves to point out, "The atoms of our bodies are traceable to stars that manufactured them in their cores and exploded these enriched ingredients across our galaxy, billions of years ago. For this reason, we are biologically connected to every other living thing in the world. We are chemically connected to all molecules on Earth. And we are atomically connected to all atoms in the universe. We are not figuratively, but literally stardust." And so it was in the death of a number of beautiful stars that humanity came into existence.

That said, from a perspective as large as an infinite Consciousness, nothing ever really dies. It's a fundamental rule of physics, called **the law of conservation of energy**, which states the total energy of an isolated system remains constant and is conserved over time. Thus, energy, **including life energy**, can neither be created nor destroyed, only transformed. So God doesn't lose anything when someone or something physically dies. Physical death is simply a transfer of energy. It releases from one dimension into another, and makes room for a transfer back into the physical realm for whatever is coming next in the physical universe, which will need our former physical energy to live. And what comes next in physical life is always amazing, and always a miracle.

Subsequently, it seemed pretty obvious to me how death is actually one of God's **favorite** things about life, so much, that God requires everything that is born to also eventually die. It's only our human minds that suppose we're too important for death to ever occur to us. It's our minds that tell us "we must beat death. We must push medicine to get our bodies to survive unnaturally long periods of time, and avoid death altogether if possible. We must upload our consciousness onto electronic machines" (as if that copy would truly be us; it's not, nor without a decent chunk of our organic material, will it ever be). We see death as a bad thing because our mind's {selves} see it as bad. Our mind's {self} sees death as an end, which it certainly is for the mind's {self}, because the mind's {self} is connected with the brain and life of the body. Comedian Emo Phillips once said, "I used to think that the brain was the most wonderful organ in my body. Then I realized who was telling me this."

As a little tangent, personally, I find it somewhat humorous that atheists who typically like to think it's an amazing intellectual position to argue that there can't possibly be a God, "because why would God let so much pain and suffering and death exist on Earth?" And, "why would He let babies die?" And, "why does He let cancer exist?" That's actually a really weak argument that flies out the window when you realize God loves death so much that it's a fundamental part of the system of life. In their arguments, the atheists are playing victim to the same importance of {self} that supposes if God does exist, God would indeed lift a hand to stop a train from running them over, just because they think it's a bad thing to die. Sorry, but God knows it's not a bad thing to die, and acts (or doesn't act) accordingly. Where does everyone think Ebola come from? Seriously, people need to stop seeing death as a bad thing.

From our human perspective, when we're able to see past our mind's {self} and see our existence as more than just our body and our mind's old ideas of {self}, instead knowing that we are the conscious energy which transcends death, the threat of death loses all its intimidation. Now . . . I use the word 'knowing' here very intentionally. I'm not talking about believing that you are spiritual energy to the point that you think you know you are. I'm not talking about having a faith so deep that it simply feels like you know. I'm talking about <u>real knowing</u>, the type of knowing that only gets written into the brain as a result of experience itself. It's only with having the experience of greater Self that one can be devoid of the fear of death. This is the place where you get to know and experience eternal life, where it becomes you and you become it. This is why things like meditation and other meta-awareness disciplines we outlined earlier in this book (and in Volume I), ultimately help us get over our lesser fears. And it's what leads us toward shedding the fear of death. When we engage in the disciplines that help us experience ourselves as larger than our mind's {self}, we start to see death as being a transition, not a threat. Thus, we quit being afraid to live life to its fullest as a result. We live more epic lives, experiencing more awesome things, taking more thrilling chances. After all, what's the worst that could happen? That we die? "I laugh in the face of death", you say. "So in comparison, what's a little embarrassment if I try something new and fail. Sure, I'll try learning to surf at age seventy, let's go." And don't try to say we don't all love someone who tries to learn to surf at the age of seventy. They make inspiring news stories about that shit.

When we meet the transcendent Consciousness beyond our own, our fear of death evaporates into the nothingness of the empty illusion that fear itself is made of. And when we near the inevitable end of our physical life in our old age, we then become grateful for the whole ride, rather than gasping to take just one more breath because we're uncertain if there even is a 'what's next'. If you know what's next, you're not afraid to go. Personally speaking, after having this dramatically {self} expanding experience, having felt like I died, finally experiencing the thing people called God, I no longer fear death. In fact, to be quite candid, believing that I've seen what exists on the other side of death, there's a small part of me that can't wait for my physical death to occur at this point. Don't worry, I'm not going to off myself, because this place called Earth is bliss if you do it right. But I'm not going out kicking and screaming either. If an extinction-event-comet slams into us tomorrow, I'll be enjoying the natural beauty of the approaching atmospheric fire, appreciating that I got to witness this final event, as I smile and crack my last beer.

In the words of poet Robert Herrick, "Gather ye rosebuds while ye may." Or in the words of Horace, who reminded us to control our minds lest our minds control us, "carpe diem, kids." That's exactly the message I received with that last futuristic vision: whatever you're gonna do with your life, get on with it, and with whatever you do with your life, you better make it worth the portion of your life you use to do it.

Act V: The Exit

As my experience approached its endpoint, the Earth flashed back to present day. Once again, it was green and blue and covered in clouds. All the space junk was back. And I could feel all the life on Earth. I could feel the consciousness of everything. I felt all the people, all the plants, all the animals, and all the microbial life. All the minds in their various levels of conscious activity. It was wondrous. This scene brought with it a great sense of perfection and peace, and a sense of everything fitting together perfectly, as it should.

This feeling of oneness was the truth I had been seeking. This was the answer I had been looking for. I had experienced the infinite love and intelligence that had answered all my questions about life and God, and our place in the universe, and how the universe itself worked, which I definitely didn't expect. But I also knew that this one experience was also the same answer absolutely everyone else was looking for as well, and that people would only understand it by experiencing it themselves, and they would only believe it if they saw it with their own eyes. That's how knowledge works in general. It must be experienced to be known. I knew everyone needed to experience this oneness, this perfection, this awesome and divine and all loving intelligence, because it was the underlying, unspeakable secret that fueled the formation of all the world's religions, which people now point to as an excuse to kill each other in complete contradiction to the Life Entity religion is supposed to reveal. I now knew how so many religions could profess a God's undying love and forgiveness, but also then have their slightly various takes on God which then run out of control as attachments of their mind's {self}.

Language taints experiences. It limits them. And if you don't ever get to see how the brain works, and where your separation comes from in your mind, you're forever a victim of it. That victimization makes you defensive and violent at times. It creates all your negative emotions, which wind up causing pain and suffering for yourself and for others. So I could see exactly why most the ancient religious texts and teachings about God are connected with attaining this state of enlightenment, or theosis, or Beatific Vision, or Nirvana, or whatever you want to call it. Because the experience of finding this consciousness within, which opens our minds to the infinite and dumps a boatload of knowledge and wisdom into our human minds during the process, defies explanation. You have to experience it for yourself. It's not something you can get from a book. When a human experiences enlightenment for themselves, there's no guesswork involved in what the ancient concept of God is, or what the meaning or purpose of life is. There are no more questions, period. Psychologist Carl Jung, who experienced enlightenment, whose impact on human psychology is unparalleled, and whose teachings about consciousness are completely in line with the lessons I learned connected with enlightenment, said, "I don't need to believe [in God], I know."

I now understand how he could say that.

As I looked at the living Earth, knowing all life on the Earth and all life in the universe as oneness, I now felt complete. Like I had attained the understanding I was looking for. I'd never been able to understand the idea of something having no beginning and no end, but now I did. I'd never been able to understand who, or what, God was, but now I did. I'd never been able to understand who, or what, I truly was in the grand scheme of the universe. But now I did. In those last moments of beingness, I got the feeling I finally understood it all. Life. The Universe. And Everything.

Then, out of the nothingness, a thought arose.

"It's time to go back."

"Go back?" I felt myself internally replying. "Crap!"

Although it surprised me that the thought was conveyed in words and not just knowledge, at this point I knew not to doubt the Consciousness I was with. But I still didn't completely understand. There was obviously some distance building between my consciousness and the transcendent Consciousness (although I still felt the unconditional love, which never at any moment swayed throughout the whole experience). "Go back where?" I didn't want to leave.

"To be human."

Crap!

"Of course," I replied. The thought entered my mind, "Energy can neither be created nor destroyed, but only transformed. I need to go back to drive a new baby body for a while. I guess it's time to do another tour of life on Earth." So I asked the Consciousness, "Will I remember any of this?"

"Very little. Your mind cannot hold it all."

When I had left the void and become a separate consciousness again, I felt like I had lost access to understanding absolutely everything. As those words made themselves heard, I felt I was losing even more knowledge. I was amazed at how limited my human mind was. I could feel the limitations of my human brain imposing themselves again.

This is what it is meant when it's said that no man can know the mind of God. There's simply too much to know. It's too comprehensive and too complex. When spiritual masters speak of the unknowable, this is what they are referring to. You get to see it all, but you can't bring all of it back. But I was curious if I could bring something back. I didn't want this whole trip to be for naught.

"Before I go, I want to revisit pain and suffering," I replied. "It seems unnecessary, and if I can somehow remember that, I want to tell people how to avoid it."

"You aren't the first."

"Ha-ha! God made a joke. Cool," I thought. Humor's gotta come from somewhere, right? And it's certainly connected with happiness.

I guess my asking to keep the details of pain and suffering seemed like a reasonable request, because those answers immediately flooded through me as effortlessly as all the knowledge and wisdom had originally, earlier in the experience. I quickly perused the details of human emotions, and the process of pain and suffering, so I could pull them with me into a human mind, if possible. It was like I was allowed to pack an overnight bag from the infinite amount of knowledge and wisdom I had accessed previously, and this was all I got to take. I was rushing to get through it so I could revisit to the secrets of black holes, too, but I ran out of time.

"Tell them," the Consciousness said.

"I will," I promised.

It was then I realized this experience was ending, and I was going back to my old body, lying on my old bed, in the same old house in Atlanta, where I had started my meditation a few thousand years earlier. I saw my body from far above as my consciousness was approaching it, and frankly, was kinda disappointed. "**That** reaction is definitely human," I thought. As I kept zooming toward my body, I protested a bit to the Consciousness. "I don't want to leave." The reply I got to that statement was the most profound confirmation to everything I had experienced all along the way. The response from that separate Consciousness was this:

"You never have. And you never will."

At that moment, I experienced what I can only describe as my consciousness re-entering my body. I went through the same tingling atomization sensation that had seemingly taken me out of it. In reality, what was probably happening was that my body's physical senses, no longer being blocked by whatever else was occurring in my brain, started flowing into my waking consciousness again. As my senses began to re-fire, I let my body take a full breath, and exhaled into a relaxation that was complete, but alert. Unlike when my body had become overwhelmed when this whole thing started, it felt entirely at peace. I felt more alive than I had ever been. I felt like a new person coming into the world through a body that no longer belonged to the person that had inhabited it earlier. My mind's {self} had been completely and permanently rewritten through this experience. From my personal life perspective, I felt like I had just learned the true meaning of the words 'born again' rather than the {self} deluded version I had believed my {self} to be previously.

It was a surprise to me, back then, to return to my body, but the fact is today I know I never completely left it. If my brain hadn't been operating, I would not have heard any of the thoughts I heard. If my brain had not been operating, I would not be able to remember anything that I just told you and pulled from my brain's memory. But that fact doesn't steal any holiness or sacredness away from this experience to admit science can explain every bit of what was happening in my brain while I experienced everything

I've explained here (and even all the stuff I didn't explain). The simple fact is that I perceived the whole experience through my body, or the hippocampus in my brain would have no memory of it, and I would not be able to tell this story from my body. My regular senses were simply shunted or turned off while my consciousness was experiencing higher functions that my brain is designed to deliver. But again, that doesn't make it less holy or spiritual.

And this is the big problem we've been having between science and religion, and this is the discussion we need to have... that there's no real war between the two camps here, if everyone can be rational.

After all, if there is indeed a mechanism within us which allows us to directly tap into a higher, more divine, Conscious intelligence, that mechanism <u>absolutely</u> has to be expressed within our physiology, to include our brain, and thus, has a scientific explanation of some sort. If a higher Consciousness is indeed connected to us, and we do sometimes access it, that process could happen no other way than through our bodies. And the fact is that science will most likely one day completely understand that process, even if it never completely understands the consciousness behind it.

All that said however, even if we one day understand the communication channel, that doesn't answer the question about where the transcendent information I received came from, or why the alternate Consciousness I experienced (even if that secondary consciousness was in my own head) was so absolutely different than my own. It also doesn't answer the question of how I learned so much in such a short amount of time, and how I came out of the experience so completely and permanently transformed. There's a great deal of scientific mystery in this type of mystical experience. It's a scientific mystery which I think we should certainly explore, because it seems inextricably linked to the human experience called happiness, which our most esteemed ancient philosophers deemed "the end towards which all other things aim."

As I regained my senses on that bed that fateful afternoon, I was surprised to find that my pillow was completely soaked under my head. Tears of joy had obviously been streaming down the side of my head for quite some time. I felt a gratitude in my heart that overflowed because of what I had just experienced. I was awash in joy over the love and gratitude I had experienced in the previous moments. I was grateful for all that I had been given, simply by asking for it. I uttered a quiet, "Thank you," looked out the window to see that the sun had gone down for the day, and because there was nothing pressing to do in the house, decided to simply lay there reviewing what I had experienced so I could try to retain it, and I eventually drifted off into a restful and dreamless sleep.

Life after that would never be the same.

(Note: For those of you who are wondering if there's life after death, consider that you can't experience up without down, or left without right, or cool without warm, because everything we experience is relative to something else, right? Now stop thinking for a moment, and feel down within yourself. Are you alive right now? Can you feel it? How do you know you're alive, if you weren't once dead?)

13 Enlightenment Step 2: The Experience after the Experience

> Be sure that it is not you
> that is mortal, but only your body.
> For that man whom your outward
> form reveals is not yourself;
> the spirit is the true self,
> not that physical figure
> which can be pointed out
> by your finger.
>
> —Cicero

Mark Twain once said, "The two most important days in your life are the day you were born, and the day you find out why." From that, I can say this; if you can discover that the reason you were born was simply **to be happy from within**, you will have lived the second of those two most important days. Happiness is indeed the end toward which all other things aim. Attaining happiness is when we stop seeking things to make us happy. And if you learn to bypass the step of needing the outside world to align to a certain set of conditions to get happiness to spring forth from within you, you can jump directly to the step of happiness springing forth from within you constantly without the world having to align to anything. Because lemme tell you, as much as your ego {self} may even at this moment be fighting to say, "No, no, no . . . the world must be changed for me to be completely happy in it," don't hold your breath until the world changes to make you happy. Especially to make you happy long term with deep seated eudaemonic happiness. The resistance of the mind's {self} is at the heart of all the world's problems. Your mind will always find something to complain about and something to defend.

The day I accidentally stumbled onto the secret experience that showed me absolutely everything, I was done seeking happiness. There was a material change in the contents of my mind and intellect. I understood all the answers to those crazy Zen koans I'd read. I understood all the hidden meanings to the previously confusing passages within my own religion's Bible. And I understood the foundation of my own pain and suffering, as well as everyone else's on the planet.

Furthermore, because I had seen the detailed operations of my mind, it was now easy to see how all my personal troubles were just an illusion of my mind. They were simply the result of a mental construct called {self} that my body needed as a defense mechanism to prolong the cellular life of my human organism. By **experiencing** that realization firsthand from somewhere deep within, I was now somehow liberated from that process. I was no longer the old {self} my mind had clung to. During my enlightenment experience, I had been completely separated from my mind. I saw my mind, and all its movements, from a state of perfect awareness of being the presence that was beyond my mind. And saw my entire existence as simply a part of everything in the universe; which simply was as it was without judgement; and as it was; in every moment throughout all time; perfect.

My enlightenment experience had been written into my very sense of {self}. As a result, starting the very next morning, and everyday afterward, there was an immense sense of ease that flowed into my life. Because I had seen my entire human mind's {self} as an illusion, and directly experienced the illusion of the material universe as the non-real emptiness of vibrating energy that it is, I could see the whole universe and my place in it completely differently. Ralph Waldo Emerson said, "The world we live in is but thickened light." And he's right. I saw it. He saw it, which is why he said it. And because I saw it, I could see the events that happened around me much differently than I had seen them before. My interactions with other people were very different than they had been before. Absolutely everything had changed. Nothing was affecting my mind's {self} anymore. My mind was quiet and observant, and very non-judgmental. And because of the reduction of both my mind's {self}, and my drive to label the universe and its actions, I was completely devoid of negative emotions.

And what was cool, was that it was only the negative emotions that had left.

While any hint of anger, sadness, and fear had left me, I was still filled with the bliss of existence which permeated to my very core. I wasn't necessarily happy about anything in particular, I was simply happy about absolutely everything that happened and existed. I felt, like Thich Nhat Hanh once explained, "The miracle is not to walk on water. The miracle is to walk on the green earth, dwelling deeply in the present moment and feeling truly alive." The miracle was this whole place. Not just the world, but the universe itself and how it all worked. It was like I had been reborn into a new universe of miraculous wonder, without the need of an inner commentary from a mind full of illusion. Because I saw my entire mind as illusion, I saw all my thoughts of future and past as illusion as well. This meant no more regrets about the past. No more worries about the future. My existence was now, and forever now. Whatever was, simply was, right now. And regarding that now, there would be no more need to take offense or feel bad because of an invented {self} within the experience of my mind. My mind's old {self}, my mind's perceptions, and everything that could ever bug me and pull me out of this bliss was ultimately impermanent, and not worth my time.

Did I go to work the next day? Yes. Did I still take the actions to make money and pay the bills? Definitely. But that whole process took a backseat to what now was of most importance to me: people. What mattered to me previously was my life. My income. My career. My likes and dislikes. In short, my mind's {self}. Now, the end of pain and suffering in others was all that mattered. The healing of the world from the illusion of their pain was the thing that took prominence. I needed to figure out how to tell people about what I had experienced, and explain it in a way that made sense, but that also led them to potentially experiencing it for themselves. That's the only way they'd really get it. How badly did I feel everyone needs to get it? In short, I knew if we could get everyone to this place, this state of mind of knowing the illusion and not being caught up in the illusion anymore, we would finally know world peace. And what better job title could you and I share but that of World Peace Engineers?

So without immediately changing my day-to-day activities that much, my life had been transformed, and I now had a more defined path laid out ahead of me for the distant future. And a big bonus, I had been healed of the sickness that inhabits us all and makes life suck sometimes.

By seeing the perfection of everything in the universe, I was finally able to see my own perfection through the mountain of my human imperfections. This brought on forgiveness of my own imperfections. And through your mountain of human imperfections, I was able to see your perfection. This brought on a forgiveness for your imperfections. In everyone else's mountain of imperfections, well, they were pretty much just screwed. But at least you and I were perfect. Okay, okay, yes, it was so friggin' ridiculously sappy that I was able to see the absolute perfection of everyone else, too, and forgive them for everything they could ever do to me. Or you. Or themselves. That's just part of the awesomely wonderful curse.

Seriously though, this insight into the perfection of the universe, and the unity of the field of infinite consciousness, coupled with the glimpse I'd been given of Consciousness at multiple levels, where it exists at the infinite expanse of all physical matter, down through all life that exists where the illusion of division occurs, down through our cells and atoms to the point that Consciousness expands outward infinitely again like one big giant circle, made me realize from that day forward that **we are absolutely all one**. And not in just some hippie bullshit fashion, like "let's all go outside and sing 'We Are the World'" (although I had some of that going on, too). But also in a real sense of both how physical energy works, and how intelligent spiritual Consciousness works.

I had realized something dramatically life changing. Crap! I was a hippie!

I had gone literally overnight from a gun-owning, center-right-leaning, fearful conservative Christian, to a fearless, loving, tree hugging, left-leaning, liberal minded knower of God. And I didn't even care about this very dramatic change. It was nice not to have all the baggage. That's how chill I was.

I no longer saw strangers as strangers, but as an extension and part of God. I no longer saw enemies as enemies, but as an extension and part of God. From my new perspective, there was no "other" anymore. There was only God. There was only Love. So when I saw other people, I saw God. When I saw children, I saw God. When I saw plants, and trees, and animals, and rocks, and dirt, I saw God. When I saw you, I saw God.

And frankly, I still do.

So you can imagine how chill and enjoyable my emotional life is today, seventeen years later, almost all of the time. It's pretty awesome. There isn't a lot that can throw me off my game, and for the things that do, they only affect me for minutes or hours at a time, not days or months. The mind's {self} is a required function of the brain, so though it can be rewritten sometimes, it won't ever completely leave us. As we mentioned previously, this is why it's said that getting rid of the ego is like trying to get rid of your own shadow. The brain function of ego {self} is still there, but it's now affected by the memory of my map being wiped clean of attachments, along with this really cool Teflon coating that only requires a quick mental rinse to wipe it clean again when stuff tries to stick itself onto my {self} map. So negative thoughts and emotions do like to arise at times when I allow things to stick to my mind's {self} temporarily. But now negative thoughts and emotions have become traveling visitors who never overstay their welcome, and I also have the option to lock the door at times and never even let them come in.

The Science Behind the Second Level of the Experience of Enlightenment

In Volume I, when we discussed the science of how your pain and suffering occurs, we talked about how the {self} fully completes one half of every Equation of Emotion in your mind. Each individual idea of {self} creates the EPs (Expectations/Preferences) for the first half of your Equation of Emotion. When a Perception then passes through your mind, it gets compared to those EPs of {self}, and if there's a related {self} idea being affected, your emotions are created. Example: The Cubs won the World Series in 2016. I love the Cubs, so "YAY!" But when a Perception passes through your mind that's not associated with an idea of {self}, no emotion is the result. Example: Who won the last mayoral race in Moose Jaw, Canada? With all due respect to our friends the Moose Jawans, in Mark Manson's words, "I don't give a fuck". Because besides loving all Moose Jawans equally, whoever the Mayor is has no effect on my definition of {self}. And if you're not from Moose Jaw, you probably don't care about who the Mayor is either. So it can be reiterated that your mind's {self} is a pretty big influencer in the creation of your entire emotional landscape, especially when discussing whether you are going to be happy, or not happy, about life in general.

We discussed previously that the simple reality about any contemplative practice like mindfulness meditation, or Christian contemplative prayer, or Islamic Sufi Dhikr is that through these practices we discover that we are more than what we previously thought was our mind's {self}. This new experience then rewrites our old {self}, expanding it to include the new experience. Our contemplative disciplines slowly change our mind's {self} over time, expanding it outward from the center. When you change your mind's {self} through internal experience, that changes your whole emotional landscape. It changes the list of {self} stuff the brain checks against for threats from your incoming Perceptions, and it pushes your old ideas of {self} outward to where things don't bother you as much as they used to.

Enlightenment is the biggest experience of Self that can possibly occur. When we fall into an enlightenment experience, the mind's {self} gets rewritten in a huge way, becoming more congruent with whatever the powerful experience delivered. When we have an experience that feels like it teaches us the truth about who and what we really are, it replaces our old ideas of {self}. And this becomes a powerful transformation device.

While enlightenment starts with an experience that stretches the mind, it's actually the change in the {self}, via the most basic mechanism designed to change {self}, which causes the transformation. If we're lucky, the more powerful the transformational experiences are, the more dramatic the change becomes, especially when the new ideas of {self} have been created by our experience of Self (with a huge capital S). When we experience the inseparate Self, the universal Self, the one-with-everything Self, that experience becomes who and what we are, because that's how the brain works. It wipes our old ideas off our {self} map and rewrites it with the new experience of Self. Thus, if we've experienced and indeed have become one with the Infinite, the old Perceptions that used to ruin our day can no longer touch us. We're too everything and nothing for that. (Shout out to St. John of the Cross.)

That said, a lasting positive change in {self} from an enlightenment experience isn't a guaranteed occurrence. As we we've seen, not all the change in people who experience awakenings winds up becoming permanent. Sometimes people slide right back into their old {self} patterns, simply adding their new enlightenment experience on top of their old {self} map as some sort of spiritual accomplishment. In that case, the {self} doesn't get rewritten as much as the {self} simply grabs the experience and adds it as a new attachment to it's same old {self}, improving its personal view of its own valuation. This new attachment of mind is usually something about {enlightenment}, or their {spiritual experience}, or whatever their mind makes of the experience afterward. Many {self} proclaimed spiritual gurus fall into this category. An enlightenment experience doesn't automatically make for an enlightened person. Remember the man I told you about, who twisted his enlightenment experience that he originally thought was God into something that fit within his fundamental Bible literalist beliefs. He actually told me, "Be careful! That old Satan is a tricky one, and even comes at us with unconditional love to fool us into thinking he's God." I thought that Satan character was definitely a tricky one indeed, but not in the way that man supposed.

Anyone who maintains attachments of mind will continue to have suffering in their life. And anyone who attaches their internal enlightenment experience to their old mind's {self} will continue to have struggles with sadness, fear, and anger, and be forced to contend with other maladies of mind to include the Buddha's three characteristics of an enlightened person, their overcoming of greed, hatred, and delusion.

A meaningful interaction with the universal Self gives us the feeling and experience that we are not our bodies. It also gives us the feeling and experience that we are not our minds. And for those who experience this falling away of body and mind, this change becomes very real. So although it sounds weird, even the aches and pains of our bodies can stop bothering us and become optional with practice. And the storms and turbulence of our minds no longer hold sway over us with practice. After a while (maybe because of neuroplasticity), those storms and inner turbulence eventually just give up trying to influence us. After all, for a person who no longer identifies with being their body or mind, what Perception within the mind can really touch that new Self at all?

Answer: There aren't any.

14 Enlightenment Step 3: Nirvana, Non-Dual Existence, and a New Path

You have wrong perception on
your self and on the other.
And the other has wrong perception
on themselves and on you,
and that is the cause of fear,
of violence, of hatred.
That is why trying to remove wrong perceptions
is the only way to peace,
and that is why Nirvana is, first of all,
the removal of wrong perceptions.
And when you remove wrong perceptions,
you remove the suffering.

—Thich Nhat Hanh

The lasting effect of a high-power enlightenment experience is the fundamental underpinning for the very real mind state of Nirvana, and the basis for the understanding of the concept called non-duality. Nirvana is the place of mind where every moment of every day is spent in a bliss of knowing and living a completely integrated existence where nothing can ruin your mojo, because ultimately only your mind has the potential to ruin your mojo, and from your experience, you are not your mind. Non-duality is the perspective where you see only Self. You see only the existence of the whole universe as it is, in this very moment, with you being part of the whole perfect thing. There is no concept or feeling of other. And everything is perfect regardless of what is occurring at the moment, even if someone is in the act of killing you, or the world is in the process of ending. It all just perfectly **is**, without judgment. Or more accurately, without movement of the mind. You are the everything that is no longer affected by mind, which is still a part of your existence, but which no longer troubles you unless you let it.

This particular mind state is predicated on the fact you can understand your existence to be that of being one with everything, and having no separation of {self} between you and other, which in the state of non-duality, doesn't exist. Further, I think this mind state requires having experienced a very powerful enlightenment experience. Our {self} simply doesn't get rewritten by our thinking mind. It's a requirement of your physiology that you first have to have an experience to realize change. Even if we convince ourselves that switching religions or switching politics is the right idea logically, and we wind up successfully making that change to our {self}, ultimately it was our inner feelings and intuitions about those logical thoughts that finally pulled the trigger on the change in {self}. It had to feel right first. You can't just **believe** your way into it. The internal experience creates the belief. You can't just think really hard that you are not your body or mind to the point you **think** you feel it. You **must see and be it** firsthand within you, so it feeds through the subconscious circuits of your brain. For something as all-encompassing as non-dual awareness, or the realization of Nirvana, you have to feel that first before it can become any part of your daily existence. You need to be taken hostage by it, where you lose all control to that experience of oneness, and you lose all grasp on your old sense of {self}. Where you willingly, and almost forcibly via your mind's subconscious rewriting of {self}, give up absolutely everything you once were, including your life story, your politics, and your religion, if need be. I gave up the idea that I was going to continue to be a living human being, surrendering to death itself, and the end of my human existence, including everything to which my mind had attached up to that mmoent. This is the scary crossroad of impeaching the mind's {self} which keeps most people away from ever experiencing enlightenment. They just can't get across that last hump. To be fair it's a terrifying hump. It's everything you believe your {self} to be. That's tough to give up.

A friend of mine once told me about a time she was slowly walking in a stone labyrinth outside a church (yet another form of walking contemplative meditation), when she started feeling a huge power build-up from beneath her feet. "It started surging up my legs and overtaking me," she said. "It scared me. I stopped walking and resisted it and tried to push it back down into the ground until it went away." This was my friend's fearful reaction of losing her grip on her {self}. It caused her to resist what may have wound up being a very powerful enlightenment experience. We'll never know. But that reaction certainly fits our definition of fear, which is that that fear is the mind's emotional reaction to a potential threat to {self}. When God comes-a-knockin', our mind's {self} is threatened, let me assure you. This is where the term "the fear of God" has some basis in truth. The human mechanism of fear of a threat to {self} does indeed kick in when {self} is on the precipice of dramatic spiritual change, and it is exactly the reason it's said that people fall to their knees in terror when moving into the presence of God. You need courage to look upon the face of God. If you have that courage, God welcomes that interaction. If you don't have that courage, God will respect that decision (and forgive you for it). I told my friend next time not to resist that build-up of energy, simply surrender to it. I hope it happens for her again.

I believe the brain never truly incorporates what is said about enlightenment until it experiences enlightenment for itself. The knowledge can't come from your thinking mind, it needs to come through an experience so that your mind then writes it into {self} automatically. It must be sourced from within, or your brain never truly rewrites your {self}. It is from this memory, written into your brain's hippocampus, that the experience of one-with-everything-Self is recalled to build the foundation and create lasting change for the mind states of Nirvana and non-dual awareness to become realized. So the experience of beyond-mind is required.

That said, your thinking conscious mind isn't completely useless in the quest to deepen your practice and understanding. Your thinking mind can indeed help you catalyze the experience you need to get smaller inner changes of {self} to occur that can improve your day-to-day life. Your thinking conscious processes can also be implemented to help strengthen your grasp on your mind and maintain a heightened state of awareness more easily.

If you remember Katherine from Volume 1, she had not yet experienced a conscious awakening of any sort before her practice of the Equation of Emotion Review helped her stop her mind and see the workings of her {self} as they occurred one anonymous afternoon. In that moment of meta-awareness clarity, she was able to experience an expansion of her sense of {self} that was greater than any she had experienced previously. Through this expansion of {self}, she was able to see the movements of her mind, and experience firsthand that she was not the movements of her mind. It's one thing to understand it cognitively, but another thing altogether to experience it from within, actually seeing the bullshit as it's being created.

The Equation of Emotion Review we talked about in the earlier sections of the book, and in Volume I, can help you get into a similar meta-awareness space without needing to be tied to one spot, such as on a meditation cushion. Katherine's awakening came when she was out interacting with people during everyday life. Other students I've spent time with have experienced this everyday life awakening as well. To review, all you need to do to get a better grasp on how your mind is creating moments that steal your happiness is to follow the process of reviewing the ideas in your life that create your mind's {self}. Then, review the two big variables in your Equation of Emotion that brought rise to whatever internal turbulence your mind just churned up. It's really just that easy.

That one simple practice will get you more familiar with your mind's idea of {self}. Understanding what created your negative emotional responses during your everyday life will then turn down the volume of those responses in real time. In Matthieu Ricard's words, "simply stare attentively." This mindful action automatically drops you into the mind's control room called meta-awareness. You can't help but land there. When you use your mind to start looking at your mind, you're teleported there. In these meta-awareness moments, just like during meditative practices (which also deliver us into meta-awareness), small to large awakenings can occur.

Before awakening or after, using the power of the mind to look back in on its {self} and understand the process that creates your pain and suffering then helps you to turn that pain and suffering off. This, by default, brings a higher level of quiet to the mind. And a quiet mind is a happy mind. It's not churning up bullshit for us to deal with. Post awakening, it's one of the most powerful practices to develop one's mind into the state of Nirvana. Only when the realization of the purest and quietest mind state is maintained can the state of Nirvana and complete non-dual awareness be achieved.

During the moments I've experienced Nirvana and complete non-dual awareness, it's easy to understand the most challenging messages of the world's religions. In Buddhism, the most difficult teaching is that there is no {self}. That's true. If you're one with everything, there is no other, and if there is no other, there is no Self. In Islam, it's the Prophet Muhammad's directive to deal with people who do us evil with forgiveness and kindness. That's true, too. They are simply in a state of blind egoic defense, and need to be forgiven of that infraction. In Christianity, the most difficult teachings are associated with The Sermon on the Mount. This is when Jesus goes into detail about turning the other cheek for someone who slaps you, offering to them to hit you again on the other cheek. He talks about not just walking one mile for someone who asks you, but going two. He talks about not just giving up your coat, but also giving up your shirt as well, and giving to others whatever it is they ask of you. In the past, being a non-enlightened Christian, I secretly had issues with understanding these particular sections of the New Testament. From an enlightened perspective, however, it's instantly clear. If another person's illusion of mind and their internal pain is such that they feel like they need to hit you to feel better, let them hit you twice, or as many times as it takes to alleviate their pain. If they reach out to take your coat from you, give up your shirt also. If they ask you to go a mile, go two. Do **whatever it is they need** to help them quell the internal pain and suffering caused by their mind. And yes, there are going to be Christians in this audience who might question that interpretation, but we only would need to go to that same very sermon where Jesus says (paraphrasing) never mind murdering someone to offend God, if you even get angry at someone, that's an offense to God. That statement is clearly a mind related teaching. If the mind's {self} does not exist in your mind, then how can you get angry at anyone? If someone is slapping us in the face, or taking our coat, or doing something to anger us, what does a person who's become enlightened need of revenge, or material items, or a negative emotional reaction in an existence where, in the words of an old Zen Master named Dōgen, "body and mind has fallen away"? In the mind state of Nirvana, I completely understand the Dalai Lama's famous quote, "My religion is kindness."

We need more of that.

15 The Science of Enlightenment

His followers said to him,
"When will the kingdom come?"
(Jesus said,) "It will not come
by watching for it.
It will not be said,
'Look, there it is.'
Rather, the Father's kingdom
is spread out upon the earth,
and people do not see it."

—The Gospel of Thomas, Verse 113

So how do we change enlightenment from being such a rare thing to being something that everyone can experience for themselves? How do we teach **you** to find the experience where you can learn to skip that whole step of aligning outside conditions to be happy so you can get happiness to spring forth from within permanently? We look at this mystical and divine experience pragmatically, with a foot solidly planted on the shoreline of science.

Andrew Newberg is a medical doctor and researcher on enlightenment who co-wrote a book called How Enlightenment Changes Your Brain. In it, he shared a lot of science pertaining to people who attain enlightenment experiences, and the variations that people experience through what Dr. Newberg calls "big E" and "little e" enlightenment experiences. A "big E" Enlightenment experience is the type of experience I described for you earlier. Different people may experience variations within the internal awakening itself, but the "big E" information comes all at once, is comprehensive with regard to the information which is conveyed, and the result is that the experience completely transforms the life of the person who discovers it. But "little e" enlightenment experiences can be transformational as well, and these make up the bulk of experiences that people actually have. They are the small awakenings that can come from a regular meditation practice. They're the small awakenings that can come from an Equation of Emotion Review practice. They're the small epiphanies that slowly put the pieces together. Over time, those can be very transformational as well because of the incremental changes they make to the mind's {self}, expanding the {self} outward from what it once was toward the infinite.

As part of his research, Dr. Newberg put up a website to compile firsthand stories of "big E" and "little e" enlightenment experiences. The stories came from all religious faiths, with 25 percent being from atheists. He collected nearly 2,000 responses in all. Many were very similar. He identified five main characteristics that most stories had in common. First, was a sense of unity and connectedness to something greater than the individual. Second, there was an incredible intensity connected with the experience. Third, there was a sense of clarity and new understanding in a fundamental way. Fourth, there was a sense of surrender, and/or a loss of conscious control. Fifth, something important in the person's life (be it beliefs, outlook, or sense of purpose) suddenly, and permanently, changed.

One story recorded through the website was from a sixty-five-year-old Jewish woman. "It felt like an energetic merging and being at one with the most powerful creative force/being in and beyond all universes. In that moment I was simultaneously the same individual consciousness of myself; I was also part of God (for lack of a better term, really), infused with the power of all creation and creativity. I was buoyed with a joy so immense, it infused my beingness with an affinity for everything" (quoted in the audiobook version of How Enlightenment Changes Your Brain). We can see the parallels with what I explained from my experience earlier in the book; being a separate consciousness, yet being one with a larger consciousness, becoming a creative energy, becoming infused with an infinite joy, and coming out of the experience with a love for everything in the universe. Believe it or not, although these experiences are very rare, this is actually par for the course.

In his book "Hardcore Zen", punk rocker turned Zen Buddhist monk, Brad Warner, explained his enlightenment experience while crossing a river on his regular walk to work one morning.

> The shortcut I like to take has me crossing one particular little bridge every morning. I was walking along the road, and just about to cross that bridge when all my problems, all my complaints, all my confusions and misunderstandings just kind of untwisted themselves from each other, and went plop on the ground. I'm not talking some of my problems, I'm talking about all of them. Every last one. Plop! Every damned thing I'd ever read in the Buddhist tradition was confirmed in a single instant. The universe was me, and I was it. I looked up at the sky, and that experience was exactly like looking at a mirror. I don't mean that metaphorically either. You know the feeling of recognition you get when you look in a mirror? "That's me," you think to yourself. "My hair needs to be combed and hey, there's a pimple on my nose." Well, I got that same feeling no matter where I looked. I looked at the asphalt road and it was my face. I looked at the bridge and the bridge was me staring back at myself. It was a physical sensation, as if the sky had my eyes and could see me staring up at it. There was no doubt that this state was true. It was far more true than the state I had considered to be normal up until then. I had no need to confirm it with anyone. It's all me.

He then went on to explain how it's all you of course as well. It's all "all of us". When one gets a glimpse at enlightenment, it's not like the whole universe is all just about you. It is but it isn't. There is no 'other' in that space, so you are included in all that universal oneness, but so is everyone and everything else. So while you can choose to remain hidden in complete obscurity and anonymity, and/or live a life that seems like you won't be missed by humanity after some day when you finally keel over, it's actually a fact that the whole universe is about you, and it's here for your enjoyment. Isn't that nice to know?

These two stories, and the basic characteristics of enlightenment outlined in Dr. Newberg's work fit Eben Alexander's account of his awakening experience in his book "Proof of Heaven: A Neurosurgeon's Journey into the Afterlife", which spent ninety-seven weeks on the New York Times Best Sellers list and earned him a visit to Oprah Winfrey's explorative Soul Sunday series. In his book, which was his account of an experience he had while in the depths of a medically induced coma after contracting bacterial meningitis, he explains having an experience of being oneness, but also a bit more. He reported seeing winged beings, clouds, butterflies, deceased relatives, and an intricate connectedness that permeated the whole experience. In Alexander's words:

> It seemed that you could not look at or listen to anything in this world without becoming a part of it; without joining with it in some mysterious way. Again, from my present perspective, I would suggest that you couldn't look at anything in that world at all, for the word 'at' itself implies a separation that did not exist there. Everything was distinct. Yet everything was also a part of everything else, like the rich and intermingled designs on a Persian carpet, or a butterfly's wing.

Alexander then also explained experiencing an intelligence that came in what he called "a Divine breeze" that "changed everything." He was able to ask questions of this intelligence.

> Although I still had very little language function, at least as we think of it on Earth, I began wordlessly putting questions to this wind, and to the Divine being I sensed at work behind or within it. "Where is this place? Who am I? Why am I here?" Each time I silently posed one of these questions, the answer came instantly and in an explosion of light, color, love, and beauty that blew through me like a crashing wave. What was important about these bursts was that they didn't simply silence my questions by overwhelming them. They answered them, but in a way that bypassed language. Thoughts entered me directly. But it wasn't thought like we experience on Earth. It wasn't vague, immaterial, or abstract. These thoughts were solid and immediate, hotter than fire, and wetter than water. And as I received them I was able to instantly and effortlessly

understand concepts that would have taken me years to fully grasp in my Earthly life. I continued moving forward and found myself entering an immense void, completely dark, infinite in size, yet also infinitely comforting. Pitch black as it was, it was also brimming over with light. A light that seemed to come from a brilliant orb that I now sensed near me. An orb that was living and almost solid . . . . This being was so close that there seemed to be no distance at all between God and myself, yet at the same time I could sense the infinite vastness of the Creator. I could see how completely minuscule I was by comparison.

Alexander called God by the name "Om," which, not coincidentally happens to be a sound many Eastern religions use during their meditations to become one with God.

From there, Alexander explained how he perceived a large volume of information about the universe, and other universes, and life permeating throughout, and our limited intelligence in comparison to what can be known. He spoke of dark energy and dark matter, and vast conceptual edifices beyond human comprehension. It prompted him to say, "It will take me the rest of my life and then some to unpack what I learned up there." Peruvian farmer turned psychedelic artist, Pablo Amaringo, who experienced entheogenic enlightenment (which we will discuss shortly) once similarly said, "I will die, and I will never be able to tell all I have seen."

Again, this experience is not atypical. About a decade ago, I produced a podcast series where I shared a portion of the experience I outlined in the last few chapters for people looking to understand more about the basics of enlightenment and the scientific approach of decreasing our pain and suffering and increasing our inner peace. Dozens of the comments and e-mail responses I received over the subsequent years confirmed that other people had very similar experiences to mine, with a handful of people sharing that they had actually heard the same exact two words I'd heard while they were similarly resisting entering the experience just like I did. It seems an internal, but separated, voice said to them, "let go" as well.

Scientists typically like to stay away from subjective experience as a form of data. In fact, one of the only branches of science which allows itself to deal with subjective data is the field of psychology, which studies the human mind. Even in psychology, however, the only way the hardcore scientists agree to look at subjective experience as data is when subjective experience is collected in a standard way from a large group of people who have something very specific in common, such as cultural, geographical, or controlled stimulus commonality, etc. The problem with enlightenment is that we haven't even really defined enlightenment scientifically beyond the elementary theoretical work of some mind science pioneers. In addition, one of the characteristics of this inner experience is its ineffability, aka its nebulous nature which causes an inability for us to put it into words. So we're limited by each individual's vocabulary and ability to create analogy, because that's typically where people have to go when trying to explain experiences. So there's not a lot of science to lean back on that explains enlightenment, where the information from enlightenment comes from, why it changes us so dramatically, and what factors make the changes stick (or not) into the future.

But one thing can be said for certain: If we experience something transcendent or larger than ourselves to the point we're able to later remember it and speak about it as a living breathing human being, then the fact is we experienced that transcendence through the operation of our bodies, and specifically, through the operation of our brain. If we are presently a walking, talking, living, thriving human being, we have some sort of working brain actively doing its thing in our heads at this very moment. And how we perceive the whole universe through our basic senses is very dependent on that brain activity. The brain may not be all that we are, but it's certainly the organ through which our human perceptions are created. So any internal experience we have, such as thoughts, emotions, intuitions, etc., occurs because of our brain working its magic. In addition, any of us who think we've had a spiritual experience wouldn't be able to recall that experience unless it was stored within our hippocampus, the memory center of our brains. So that proves our brains were working during our spiritual experience, and also proves that for us to have some sort of spiritual experience and then assume it's not delivered and remembered through that same physiology of our body and brain would be ridiculous. So we all need to agree that what we should be looking at to help explain our transcendent experiences is our brain.

But don't think I'm trying to discount spiritual experiences as meaningless hallucinations of the brain. I'm definitely not.

Because again, just because we can point to the brain as the means through which we experience the things we call "spiritual", that doesn't mean those experiences are not still spiritual. I'm not trying to start a science vs. religion or science vs. spirituality argument here. I'm trying to point out there's a large opportunity to have a science **and** spirituality discussion here. Because the simple fact is that when we perceive something, that perception of that something was put together in our brains. Period. If we can remember it, it's in the brain. This is true whether or not the experiences we have are classified as hallucinations, or whether we actually do tune into something non-local or non-material in nature. If we can recall it, it's in our hippocampus, so our brain was there at the time.

I make that last qualification because the typical characterization from many scientists who would call themselves skeptical of spirituality would say exactly this about enlightenment; "It's simply a hallucination of the brain." I think that is one of the most irresponsible over-generalizations any scientist could make. The fact is that these internal experiences connected with enlightenment aren't just hallucinations. They make real sense of our existence and the universe around us. They point toward truth that has yet to be uncovered by our conscious minds and their creation of the language of science itself. Some of the world's greatest scientific minds were, in fact, illuminated by enlightenment experiences that lead to some of their greatest discoveries in history. Further, these mystical experiences bring our minds to places where enlightened masters write and speak about them, after which they are quoted for hundreds and thousands of years. There's a distinct meaning and extreme value to these internal visions and sense awakenings. So just because we can discuss the brain activity associated with enlightenment doesn't make what we experience less holy, sacred, or valuable. If a higher consciousness about which we are not normally aware does have some way of communicating with us, just like we have a communication channel down into the cells that make up our subconscious minds, it is certain that higher Consciousness communication channel to whatever we might ascribe as God would be built into our human physiology. That means it can most certainly be explained by science. It's our responsibility, if we would wish to understand the conscious triggers that deliver so many people permanent happiness, to understand the science of that conscious awareness, too.

So our next questions then are "how can we get our brains to do what they do during enlightenment so more people can experience enlightenment more widely?" And, "what exactly is going on in the brain when we have these transcendent experiences?" Consider what we have done in the past to bring on enlightenment experiences.

Commonalities within the Historic Disciplines of Attaining Enlightenment

As we have discussed, the phenomenon of enlightenment itself is as old as time. It's written about in every one of the world's oldest and largest religions as the most direct path to understanding truth. Enlightenment is an experience perceived through our waking consciousness, so we can safely say that the experience of enlightenment comes through the activity of our brain. And one of the biggest catalysts of the enlightenment experience seems to be when conscious thought ceases in the human brain.

Really, if we think about it for a second, what else could possibly be the case? An enlightenment experience is most definitely caused by an abnormal brain activity pattern (abnormally good, but still abnormal) which reveals hidden intelligence. The cessation of our brain's normal pattern of activity must occur if it is to allow for a different pattern of brain activity to arise. That's just so steeped in common sense that we can say it without the benefit of an fMRI scan to prove it. But there's also some evidence that supports this assumption that stopping conscious thought is a key catalyst for enlightenment.

People have described enlightenment experiences being brought on during regular life instances, and during many practiced disciplines. I spoke with a guy who once had a dramatic experience in a dentist's chair. But there are also some specific activities that have brought forth more enlightenment experiences than other activities have. And one thing which is very noticeable about these activities is that they all stop conscious thinking, which then allows the space for other deeper perceptions to arise.

Meditation

Meditation is an activity during which you don't think about stuff. While meditating, you're just supposed to **be** and notice your inner sensations and the world around you as they are. It's a brain exercise with tons of health benefits outlined previously in the book, and in Volume I. There are many types of meditation, both physical and non-physical, but the one characteristic common to almost all of them is that meditation promotes the intentional and conscious focusing of the mind into a simultaneous quieting and relaxation of the mind.

Well, the practice of focusing on one particular thing is just a half-step away from the practice of focusing on zero particular things, or **no thing**. Thinking of nothing was the lesson of the koan I had contemplated directly prior to entering my personal enlightenment experience, when I somewhat forcefully tried to stop my mind from having any conscious thought. That was my focus. In fact, this no-thinking thing is the entire intention of the Zen invention of koans and the purpose of their sitting meditation practice called zazen. Koans are riddles designed to stop the thinking mind in its tracks because there are no thinking answers to them, and zazen focuses on clearing the mind of thought. In my unscientific estimation, the Zen tradition has more enlightened masters per capita than any other. Although that said, I wouldn't wish the torture of zazen on anyone. But the fact that Zen produces enlightened folks can't be ignored, so something they're doing must be on track, and my money is on non-thinking as one of them.

Psalm 46:10 in the Bible says, "Be still and know that I am God." Chuang-Tzu said, "Men cannot see their reflection in running water, but in still water. Rumi simply said, "Behead yourself!"

Physical Meditations and Physical Duress

Similarly, people have reported having enlightenment experiences while dancing or moving around vigorously. Many world religions often use dance or movement as a catalyst to reaching out into what lies beyond our mind. Much of the United States was originally colonized by a group called the Quakers. The Quakers got their name because of the violent quaking and vibrating gyrations that are part of the historic Quaker practice. More than the gyrations Elvis did on the Ed Sullivan Show which caused people to lose their minds, a Quaker in the midst of a session of deep concentration on God would look like someone having a standing seizure separating from mind. A related faction of practitioners were called the Shakers. So what does dancing around and quaking within your own body have to do with ceasing conscious thought? Well, the extended physical exertion of the body burns up nutrients that the brain needs for the biochemical process of thinking. Their deep focus on experiencing God, combined with the spontaneous movement of the body reduces the mind's focus down to one thing, and empties its gas tank. This is the path to thinking no thing. And there were enlightened masters within both Quakerism and Shakerism. The founder of Quakerism, George Fox, was a devout man of strong moral character who spoke of becoming one with the Father, and founded a group which later would lead efforts in abolishing slavery, and which pushed for equal rights for women... in the 1600s. He said, "Be still and cool in thy own mind and spirit from (move away from) thy own thoughts, and then thou wilt feel the principle of God to turn thy mind to the Lord God."

Physiologically, exhaustive movement is what the Sufis perform in their ritual movement called Dhikr (pronounced "zicker"). They get in a circle and dance around and chant for hours at a time. This burns calories the brain needs to operate, and the intense focus of their attention on the repetitive chanting to God reduces their thoughts to the one repetitive activity. Repetition of an activity allows a person not to think about what they are doing while simultaneously focusing deeply on that one thing. Again, this is one baby step away from thinking of nothing. To find that place of inner silence, where what lies just beyond that silence can then be heard.

Religious tribal dances do the same thing in the thousands of unique religions found in Africa. Rhythmic repetitive drums, chants and song often accompany this movement.

Physical exertion and repetition are the foundation of the Eastern practices of yoga. There are numerous forms of yoga in existence today, but they all basically have the same goal; to bring the body, mind, and spirit into balance, and to quiet the mind so the individual might experience Samadhi and liberation. Samadhi is the Hindu and Buddhist word for the state of consciousness where the bliss of oneness is experienced. Liberation means freedom from {self} and from all pain and suffering. Samadhi is the eighth stage of yoga where the {self} is liberated from the illusions of sense and the contradictions of reason. The place where an inner illumination occurs, and the ecstasy of true knowledge of reality is revealed. And yoga has proven successful as a way to induce enlightenment experiences. The practice of Kundalini yoga even has a special body reaction called the **Kundalini effect**, which is a precursor to enlightenment firing off in the brain.

I don't know if you've ever tried yoga before, but I have, and it kicks my ass every time I do it. It's certainly a discipline of mastery of both body and mind. Yogis in southern Asia (yoga masters) have incredible control over their bodies, and they can consciously control their autonomic functions. Some can be buried alive for a number of days, reducing their heartbeat to as low as just a few beats per minute, then return to full consciousness later. They are impervious to pain, insensible to heat, cold, and hunger, and can perform incredible acts of mental and physical prowess. Eastern Orthodox Christianity, which also espouses enlightenment, requires catharsis as part of that process, which is a preparation of the body for enlightenment. These ideas of yoga and catharsis are parallel. With the brain being part of the body, control of the body is critical to the process of attaining enlightenment.

Other physical disciplines that have catalyzed enlightenment include martial arts, whose repetitive katas reduce the mind's need to think. Tai Chi and Chi Gung slow these movements and are intended as physical meditations. Runners are familiar with runner's high, but beyond just the common euphoria runners and other aerobic athletes experience, the body can get depleted of enough nutrients to inhibit the flow of conscious thought, putting the runner into a heightened states of consciousness. And the ancient Native American tradition of sitting in a sweat lodge has also been found to initiate mystical states. Sweat lodges when done carelessly can be very dangerous, because the tents get so hot it puts the body under such physical duress it can create life threatening scenarios. But for a ceremony which is performed properly, with people who are physically prepared, it can be an effective means to reach mystical states of awareness by putting the body and brain under just the right amount of physical duress.

Chanting and Prayer

Other repetitive actions that reduce the need for conscious thought are chanting of mantras or prayers. Chanting is performed within every major religion as a way to deepen spiritual practice. Christianity holds the record for having the most material used for chant, although mainstream Christianity has fallen away from this practice except in the highest monasteries. In other religions chanting sometimes accompanies meditation, and in many religions it's a daily practice. The repetition reduces the need for conscious thought, which brings one right to the door of no thought. Heck, even the Catholic Church will hit you with fifty Hail Marys during confession to get regular followers into this mind state of repetition that requires little need for conscious thought. From my perspective, this was designed to initiate enlightenment. Jewish practitioners will often rock softly back and forward while they chant prayer, which focuses the mind on the prayer and burns calories needed for thought. Muslims often do the same thing during their prayers.

Prayer is a great way to attempt to initiate an enlightenment experience. That said, as we discussed previously, the lost secret of prayer is that it was actually meant to be a time of meditation and introspection, not a time to talk to God. For many people, prayer now means asking for an external force to intervene in their personal lives, even sometimes to ask for something as {self}ish as to win the lottery, which over one in five Americans has actually done. According to surveys done by faith based organizations, 82 percent of prayer in America is {self}ish in nature. St. Anthony instructed, "The prayer of the monk is not perfect until he no longer recognizes himself or the fact that he is praying." This suggests the perfect prayer is associated with an evacuation of {self}, not a focus on it.

Science shows us that the brain waves of Christian monks and nuns who are deep in silent contemplative prayer match exactly to those of Buddhist Monks who are deep within meditation. There is absolutely no difference whatsoever. What was measured in the Christian monks and nuns was the Prayer of Quiet. The idea of prayer originally being intended as meditation may still sound weird to Christians. "What? Prayer was meant to be a time to listen for God? But that's when I talk to God and thank Him for what I have, and ask Him for other things I want. That can't be right." If your brain generated that or a similar thought just now, thank your mind's {self} kindly for its input in defending {your ideas} about {your religion}, and tell it to go back to whatever it was doing before rudely interrupting you. In my opinion, shutting that defense of {self} voice down is your only hope of ever experiencing the enlightenment of meeting God personally some day.

It was Saint Hildegarde of Bingen, a polymath woman and German Benedictine abbess, who Pope Benedict XVI named as a Doctor of the Church in the twelfth century, who said, "Prayer is nothing but inhaling and exhaling the one breath of the universe."

Fasting

Another discipline that, not coincidentally, is attached to every major religion on the planet, is fasting. Jesus fasted, as did

Muhammad and the Buddha. Judaism directs followers to fast six days of the year. Fasting reduces the nutrients the brain needs for conscious thought, and naturally focuses the mind into a state of lower power utilization. Out of a group who fasted with author David Rakoff, who spoke of his experiences of fasting on the NPR show "This American Life", he told of an informal survey of fasting participants. He said "everyone felt great physically, energetic and alert, and nearly everybody spoke about a clarity of mind. But only one person seemed to feel more than that. This woman said that, for a moment while driving, her spirit was filled up and she was overcome with a sense of total well-being of a level and profundity she'd never felt before." I fasted for a week one time while drinking chili pepper, lemon juice and honey infused water. I didn't feel anything close to what I would consider spiritual, or beyond mind, but I can say my mind was certainly less active than usual.

Despair

Another state which can certainly inhibit the brain's normal operation is the psychological condition of despair. Eckhart Tolle told of his awakening in his book "The Power of Now", where he described falling into a deep and profound despair where the pain of his mind became so unbearable his mind simply stopped and became as pure as a sparkling diamond. Despair is a less ideal method of attaining enlightenment; however, the fact remains that despair is one of the more frequent natural catalysts of the phenomenon. It was Christian mystic Meister Eckhart, from whom Eckhart Tolle borrowed his name, who said, "Truly, it is in darkness that one finds the light, so when we are in sorrow, then this light is nearest to all of us." St. John of the Cross wrote a famous poem called "The Dark Night of the Soul" on this same miraculous transition.

Historically, many religions suppose that God touches those who are in greatest need of help. But it might also be because severe anguish can consume us so thoroughly and powerfully that we can't think about anything else but the pain. And from a practical activity-of-mind perspective, thinking about nothing but pain is thinking about only one thing. And thinking about one thing is within arms reach of thinking of no thing. Despondency can certainly shut down the regular functions of the mind to clear the way for the mind to do something else.

In my time as a liberation teacher (a title that I only hold on to loosely borrowed from a conversation with Master Shinzen), I've run across people who have experienced this as well. I share the following account with permission. It came from a thirty-two-year old white male who told me,

> It was during a time in my life where basically nothing was going right. I wasn't enjoying my job, my personal life was a mess, my monetary situation wasn't good, and I was just really, really depressed. I went to bed one night . . . and I remember this like it was yesterday . . . and at about 3:30 or 4:00 a.m., I woke up, and out of nowhere, I just started weeping. I mean, not just crying, but weeping . . . actual full-on sobbing. But the strange thing was, that it wasn't out of sadness . . . it was out of joy. I had no idea why, but for some reason I was really, really happy. I had this incredible feeling of oneness with the universe, and somehow I just knew that I am supposed to be here . . . that I have a purpose . . . and I don't know how I knew it... but I just knew that with everything that was going on in my life . . . that everything was going to be okay. And I've never forgotten what that felt like. I never felt anything like that before then, and I've never felt anything like it since. And I've been trying to figure out what it was ever since, because it has really changed my whole outlook.

I told him what it was.

Near Death Experiences

One well-known catalyst that can bring forth enlightenment is a near death experience, and specifically, an NDE where the brain has been deprived of oxygen for a short period of time. Like despair, I do not recommend an NDE as a primary method of seeking enlightenment. And right out of the gate we should qualify that **not all near death experiences qualify as enlightenment**

experiences. In fact, most of them don't. It's a simple fact that not all NDEs meet the qualifications Dr. Newberg and William James identified as characteristics of a mystical experience. However, some do, so we mention NDEs here. When the body stops breathing, the brain almost immediately goes into hypoxia, which might assuredly interrupt the brain of conscious thought. The brain doesn't immediately shut off when it becomes oxygen deprived, but stays active for many minutes, even though our conscious control of our body is removed to ensure all the oxygen isn't burned by muscle movement. Whatever is happening as our consciousness encounters another consciousness is most likely still occurring, even though we've lost waking control of our body.

This classification is officially the type of awakening Eben Alexander experienced as outlined in his book "Proof of Heaven". While he personally believes his experience happened over the week of his medically induced coma, it is likely it happened over a shorter span of time catalyzed by the inactivity of conscious thought in his brain, which was indeed suppressed because of the bacterial meningitis, which was attacking his the nervous system.

I met a friend recently who'd had a mountain bicycling accident where she was knocked unconscious and landed facedown in a stream. She reported having a near death experience where she sensed a consciousness much larger than her own, which gave her the sense that "what we are doing here is of no importance compared to the reality we're not comprehending."

Again, I don't recommend this as a way to attempt achieving enlightenment. You may not get a round-trip ticket.

What Might Be Happening in the Brain When Awakening Occurs

The burning question on many scientists' minds in this search for consciousness and explaining higher states of consciousness is, what is happening in the brain when these enlightenment experiences occur?

Dear reader, welcome to the very bleeding edge of enlightenment science. Although there is some related science that gives us ideas about what this answer might be, the simple fact is that we just don't know the answer to what is happening in the brain when enlightenment occurs. We are at that precipice of figuring it out though. Studies are being designed. I was asked not too long ago if I could maintain a state of perfect Samadhi for an hour while lying in an fMRI machine. I've had my brain scanned while meditating before. fMRI machines are noisy and distracting. I said I could do it in my float tank, but the response I got was that just didn't cut it for this particular study. I tried to think of a middle path, but since mixing the high voltage of electronics of an MRI with the salt water of a float tank would probably put me into a near death experience that wasn't so much near death but more just death, I passed. I'm all for helping out science when I can, but come on. But a lack of a live brain scan study doesn't mean we can't discuss all the cool related science that points us in some pretty enlightening general directions.

So let's go down that path for a bit.

The Known Science Very Related to Enlightenment

Dr. Rick Strassman at the University of New Mexico researched a chemical produced naturally within our brain, lungs, and other organs, called dimethyltryptamine (DMT). DMT is a chemical found within humans, most mammals, and numerous species of plants as well. Strassman originally theorized DMT was created within the pineal gland at the very base of our brains, after which he discovered DMT within the pineal gland of live rats. (Note: Experimenting on live humans to prove DMT exists in our pineal glands poses more than a few ethical challenges, so it hasn't been proven yet.)

To give some background, the pineal gland is a very interesting structure located at the base of our brains. It's interesting because it's one of the only parts of the brain which doesn't come in a split pair. To explain, we have two equal hemispheres of our brain which are pretty much a mirror image of each other, so we have two halves of almost everything up there. We have two halves to our limbic system, two halves to our thinking prefrontal cortex, and we even have two halves of our thalamus, which is one of the most primitive structures right at the brain stem. But we only have one pineal gland, right at the very bottom center of our brain. It's officially part of the brain, but it lies outside the blood brain barrier. It has its own huge blood supply, coming in only second to the blood supply to our kidneys.

Besides Dr. Strassman finding DMT within the pineal, our pineal gland's main job is to produce other very similar compounds to DMT, mainly converting the amino acid tryptophan into serotonin and melatonin. Among other functions, serotonin helps regulate mood, appetite, and sleep in our bodies, and it is involved in memory and learning. Manipulation of serotonin is believed to be a major action of all our pharmaceutical antidepressants. Serotonin is key in not being depressed. Melatonin regulates sleep and wakefulness and helps creates our circadian rhythms and protects against neurodegeneration (brain cell death). These are critical functions that help us fight depression and dementia later in life.

The history of speculation about the pineal gland goes back eons. Enlightenment philosopher Rene Descartes thought it housed our spirit or soul. Some more ancient cultures thought of our pineal gland as **our third eye**, which has some spiritual ramifications we'll discuss shortly. From a strictly biological standpoint, it is indeed a third eye. It's a photoreceptor structure positioned at the base of our brains in a space where no outside light can penetrate. It receives signals from the body about light and darkness around us, which it uses to regulate its release of melatonin to assist us with sleep. In some amphibians, the pineal gland actually has both a cornea and a retina, and is literally a third eye buried deep in the skull at base of the brain.

Descartes called the pineal gland the "principal seat of the soul," which seems to have an interesting parallel in ancient Egyptian culture as well, as that when viewed from the side, the pineal gland and surrounding tissue perfectly resemble the Eye of Horus, which is that typical Egyptian eye symbol you're probably picturing at the moment. It's a symbol of protection. All those interesting notes aside, however, I think the pineal gland's connection with the compound DMT remains its most truly interesting mystery.

Why the Pineal Gland?

The reason the pineal gland is interesting in the dialogue about enlightenment is that dimethyltryptamine (DMT) also happens to be the most powerful psychedelic in the known universe, and when taken externally, usually through smoking it or consuming it in a South American tea called ayahuasca, has caused people to have spiritual enlightenment experiences.

For those of you who are unfamiliar with psychedelics or what they do, according to Wikipedia they are the chemicals "whose primary action is to alter cognition and perception." In short, they change how we think about, and how we see, the world. Although these substances are five to one hundred times safer than drinking alcohol, the government says psychedelics are bad for us, and subsequently outlawed them in the 1970s. They're the family of substances that include LSD, mescaline, peyote, ibogaine, and psilocybin, the active ingredient in psychedelic mushrooms. They are chemicals, sometimes called hallucinogens, that make us see and feel things that are outside our normal perception.

But they are also the substances that, over time, have fueled many thousands of deeply profound religious experiences in people all over the world in religious ceremonies. And we manufacture the single most potent forms of psychedelic right within our own heads.

Now, from a historic perspective, psychedelics have been an important influencer of civilized societies well back into world history. In their book "Stealing Fire", Steven Kotler and Jamie Wheal told of Alcibiades, a well known Greek statesman, orator, and general who threw a party one night, where he served a very sacred, but forbidden, psychedelic liquid to his guests. From their book:

> In less than an hour, the effects took hold. "Fears, terrors, quiverings, mortal sweats, and a lethargic stupor come and overwhelm us," the historian Plutarch later recounted. "But, as soon as we are out of it, we pass into delightful meadows, where the purest air is breathed, where sacred concerts and discourses are heard; where, in short, one is impressed with celestial visions."

> By sunup, those visions had faded, replaced by repercussions in the real world. Alcibiades's illicit party kicked off a chain of events that would prompt him to flee Athens, dodge a death sentence, betray his government, and set in motion the trial and execution of his beloved teacher, Socrates.

The elixir Alcibiades had stolen was called "kykeon", and because he stole it, he would later tried and sentenced to death in absentia for the crime "blaspheming the Mysteries". The Mysteries in question were the Eleusinian Mysteries:

> …a two-thousand-year-old initiatory ritual that had an outsize impact on Western philosophy and counted some of Greece's most famous citizens among its elect. Foundational notions like Plato's world of forms and Pythagoras's music of the spheres were informed by these rites. "Our Mysteries had a very real meaning," Plato explained, "he that has been purified and initiated [at Eleusis] shall dwell with the gods." Cicero went further, calling the rites the pinnacle of Greek achievement: "Among the many excellent and indeed divine institutions which . . . Athens has brought forth and

contributed to human life, none, in my opinion, is better than the Mysteries. . . . In [them] we perceive the real principles of life, and learn not only how to live in joy, but also to die with better hope."

In more contemporary terms, the Eleusinian Mysteries were an elaborate nine-day ritual designed to strip away standard frames of reference, profoundly alter consciousness, and unlock a heightened level of insight. Specifically, the mysteries combined a number of state-changing techniques—fasting, singing, dancing, drumming, costumes, dramatic storytelling, physical exhaustion, and kykeon (the substance Alcibiades stole for his party)—to induce a cathartic experience of death, rebirth, and "divine inspiration."

I highly recommend the book "Stealing Fire", which discusses attaining high mental performance through attaining non-ordinary states of consciousness. It is a very related book to the topics we've been discussing here in regard to connecting with the divine and the deep intelligence which exists within us all. And that story was only one of its interesting historical references.

But staying on our topic of enlightenment, history aside, even to this day, Native Americans utilize the peyote cactus and its mescaline nodules (a very related compound to our internal psychedelic DMT) in their religious rituals and pursuit of spiritual visions. Peyote has been used by Native Americans since pre-Columbian times, however, a group of Christian Native Americans has transitioned the use of peyote to now include their Christian rites. The Native American Church believes peyote is a natural sacred herb placed on Earth by God, so that the Native Americans can receive knowledge and wisdom from God and Jesus. Note that this same church also believes alcohol to be an unnecessary evil that should be completely avoided, believes highly in the sanctity of the family, and holds the Earth and all natural products in high esteem. It seems that the divine lessons of the psychedelic visions have been motivation enough to mix the old ways with the new, and the Native Americans see the psychedelic as a critical ritual to become one with God.

Looking at the historic and contemporary use of psychedelics in religious ritual makes it's rather interesting **that our own brain makes the most powerful version of psychedelic known to man (DMT)**, and that when that substance is taken orally or inhaled, has been known to create enlightenment experiences in people.

Reports from people who have had exogenous DMT experiences, are very similar to the enlightenment experiences others reported having without a single use of any psychedelics whatsoever. This similarity has to make us wonder if our internally sourced (endogenous) DMT is what causes our natural spiritual awakening experiences to occur.

The following excerpt is from a story told of a mind spelunker who ingested DMT on a trip to the jungles of Mexico. As you read it, notice the parallels between this story and the story of my enlightenment I told you earlier. The "she" in this next section is what the subject called the spirit of ayahuasca (a DMT-infused tea served in religious ceremony in South America), which the subject perceived as a woman.

> She took me fast, much stronger, much harder than the initial wave. The first wave was nothing. I lost all awareness of my body, my surroundings, everything around me. I felt myself fall right through the earth, like a neutrino, like the earth was nothing but empty space. I left my body completely and dissolved into the universe. My mind became placed into the mind of the universe, expanded into it, knowing everything to be known, but completely unable to think in thoughts, words, my mind-voice was completely gone, yet I was completely aware of ideas knowledge, wisdom, abstractions which were so perfectly clear and understandable to me outside of any known constructs of language, way beyond language, completely nonlinear thought and yet not-thought. Just knowing. Pure knowing. My mind, my consciousness, my poor little brain struggled to keep up with it, struggled to keep up with everything streaming in, struggled to fit the mind of the universe within.

I don't need to detail the parallels between this story and my own story as told in a previous chapter, or to Eben Alexander's experience outlined in his book "Proof of Heaven". They are too obvious.

The most interesting parallel from this DMT experience comes at the end, however, when the author comes to say, "I was Christ. I was God. The energy, the confidence, the power, the love in me began to surge, I felt it expand around me, encompassing everyone. It became very quiet, very still, just me standing there, breathing, pulsing, glowing." So in the end, the ayahuasca experiencer felt a oneness with God, similar to the experiences of others outlined earlier that were brought on without external psychedelics.

Another related story comes from Martin Ball, a PhD and adjunct professor of Religious Studies at Southern Oregon University. He experienced vaporized 5-MeO-DMT before 2011, when it was added to the list of Schedule I drugs outlawed by the Controlled Substances Act. As he writes in his book Being Infinite, (extended excerpt included with permission)

> Within the space of a few heartbeats, I had completely expanded into God. Eyes open in absolute awe and wonder, the room dissolved, my ego dissolved, my entire world dissolved. Everything I had ever known or thought or felt dissolved away into absolute pure nothingness. There was nothing to see, nothing to experience, nothing to perceive. Absolutely pure nothingness. And this nothingness was pure consciousness. And it was love. Infinite love and infinite perfection. Everything was in a state of divine perfection. Nothing was out of place.
>
> Nothing was either good or bad. Nothing was right or wrong. Everything was simply perfect in this pure consciousness, this pure state of being. And this state was not a thing. It was not an object of perception. It was not a concept. It was not an emotion. It was not anything that I could describe in any way. In fact, when asked later, I vaguely described it as "living starlight," but even that was

not accurate, for in truth, it was **nothing**.

But that no-thing was **everything**.

It was God.
And it was my deepest nature.
I was one with God.

Not my ego self. That was pretty thoroughly obliterated through the impossibly fast 5-MeO-DMT expansion. It was not as though I identified my personal sense of self with God. Rather, it was the deepest core of my being, not my ego-identity, that was identical with God. As a finite being in a body with a sense of self and identity, I was an expression of God. At my core, at the very deepest level, my nature as an incarnated being was one with that pure consciousness, that infinite love, that infinite source of creative energy in which all things exist in absolute and unquestionable perfection. In those few heartbeats, this beautiful and sacred medicine had opened me up to the All. I had accepted my own divinity.

"Thank you, God!" I called out as my hands reached up toward that infinite expanse of nothingness, a few moments after the hit of psychedelic medicine flowed out of my lungs. Eyes wide open, gaping in sheer awe at the mysterium tremendum, I embraced God, and the embrace was returned.

[...]

Slowly, I came back from that infinite expansion into the nothingness that was everything. Like a spaceship re-entering the atmosphere, I could feel the layers of my individual sense of self begin to reassert themselves. The ego and identity that had been completely obliterated in the instantaneous expansion brought on by the 5-MeO-DMT regained its foothold, and as I fell down out of that exalted state, I knew myself once more. I understood that I was "Martin," this collection of patterns and habits, judgments and beliefs, choices, attitudes, and emotions. It was the "me" I had lived with all my life. But now I knew. Now I knew with all my heart that there truly was something more, and that something was more profound, more complete, and more truly holy and sacred than anything I had ever imagined or anything I had ever conceived. I knew that in the end, we, all of us, everything that we see, hear, taste, feel and experience, is really just the One Being. It is all God. God is the only true reality. And at the same time, God is absolutely nothing. Nothing at all. Nothing to grasp. Nothing to hold on to. Nothing to behold. Nothing to name or force into the box of language and conceptuality. God is simply the "I AM," and there is nothing more that can be said. God is, and that is enough.

Comedian, podcaster, and mind spelunker Joe Rogan experienced the exogenous form of 5-MeO DMT before it was made illegal in the U.S., and he is currently a proponent for the re-legalization of the substance as a consciousness exploration tool. In an interview, he stated, "It's the most powerful psychedelic known to man. It's in every single ecosystem all over the world. It exists in plants, and grasses. It's everywhere. It's really the craziest drug to be illegal everywhere, because everyone's got it in their system. It's like everyone's holding. [...] The craziest thing about DMT is that [experiencing] DMT is like literally having a meeting with God. It's like having a meeting with divine, unbelievably wise, incredibly loving energy. Like, whatever it is, the source of everything."

Again, we can draw multiple parallels from these explanations of externally sourced DMT experiences and my own experience catalyzed by meditation alone. My experience was most certainly caused by a beneficially abnormal pattern of brain activity in my head during those moments, but does this prove I was experiencing an internal DMT experience during waking hours while passing through my enlightenment experience? No. It doesn't **prove** it. Nothing could prove it but a brain scan and blood profile taken while I was in the midst of the experience itself. That's the requirement of hard science. But the parallels in these, and hundreds of other stories, coupled with the fact that our body

does make the very substance that has caused people to have these types of experiences is certainly a very intriguing coincidence.

Interestingly enough, there is some science that suggests a flush of endogenous DMT through the brain could cause some of the lasting psychological effects associated with ego death that people report during mystical experiences. When a neurotransmitter, such as DMT, is active in the brain, other neurotransmitters are stimulated as well, including those of glutamate and oxytocin. Glutamate in small amounts has a stimulatory effect on neurons, but in high doses can overstimulate and burn out synapses. Oxytocin similarly is a feel good neurotransmitter, but in high amounts it can prune existing burned in pathways (especially those found in the areas of {self} because oxytocin is the chemical that allows us to make new attachments to people and make changes to our {self} map - oxytocin is a love hormone). Oxytocin is indeed involved in the process that rewrites our mind's {self} neurologically.

Now, that assumption might be considered a bit of a leap if it weren't for this next set of facts: In addition, DMT and these other compounds activate the sigma, kappa, and serotonin-7 receptors in our brains, which are all connected with consciousness, serotonin-7 specifically being connected with our thinking reasoning mind. One other set of receptors connected with consciousness are the serotonin-2 receptors, which, it is theorized, are connected with having a traffic cops functionality that stops our conscious awareness from having direct aware access to our multiple subconscious levels, including deeper mind, and deeper intelligence. Well, 5-MeO-DMT not only overstimulates the serotonin-7 receptors, it also uniquely agonizes the serotonin-2 receptors (so our consciousness traffic cops get distracted) allowing our overstimulated consciousness awareness system a full back-stage pass to our whole mind, including all levels of subconsciousness, as far down, and as far out, as those go.

This may be why we gain access to exceptional levels of intelligence and wisdom when DMT is released into our blood stream. Interestingly, our alpha-2 receptors also get turned on, which have been characterized as the receptors associated with "capturing the very essence, the very spirit of something in order to evoke a specific mood or emotion in the viewer's brain", which may be why we are delivered the message that what we are perceiving is of utmost importance. Lastly, the overload the receptors connected with our thinking and reasoning mind, associated with our regular waking consciousness, and our {self} circuits, is when ego death can occur thanks to the glutamateric pruning of the overstimulated pathways. Normally, glutamate is a neurotransmitter and excitatory compound which stimulates neural activity. But when dumped onto our neurons in excessively large amounts, it can actually overstimulate and burn them out. So one possible explanation for "ego death" is that our ego circuits get partially but physically burned out to some extent. Of course, in many people who have these experiences, those circuits later quickly grow back (unfortunately).

Setting that last point aside, the basic biochemical transformation can explain the positive life changing effects psychedelics cause by working via the subconscious rewriting of the {self} through the communication channel of inner experience. And it's why only one experience of this internal compound flooding the brain is frequently all that's ever needed to make a lasting positive change.

In fact, this is exactly what researchers found with the very similar compound of psilocybin, which is the compound found within magic mushrooms. Along with DMT, psilocybin is in the tryptamine family, and actually would be DMT, except it has a single extra Phosphorus atom hanging off the side. So it fits into a lot of the same receptors and has similar effects in the brain. One study showed that even a single dose of psilocybin created lasting positive personality changes for years, with some people reporting lasting effects persisting decades after just one dose, which caused what they reported as a religious experience. And no wonder. A very famous study done by Johns Hopkins University tested the effects of psilocybin on participants and found that one third of the people reported their experience as being the most profound and life changing religious experience of their entire lives, even over that of experiencing childbirth. Another third reported the experience being in their Top 5 most profound experiences, and most of the rest of the group reported it being beneficial, with 93 percent of participants reporting a very positive experience overall. Some people didn't experience an effect, and a slim minority didn't enjoy their experience. These study participants also experienced long term effects of their positive experiences. This is similar to the lasting positive psychological effects from an enlightenment experience, with science considering lasting effect as one of the identifying qualifiers.

Brain scan studies on psychedelics in the tryptamine family show reduced prefrontal cortex activity (where the thinking brain gets shut down), and increased temporal lobe activity, which is typically correlated with what the brain is doing when we have out of body experiences. Decreases in frontal and parietal lobe activity indicate that our thinking brain and the associated {self} circuits stop. Dr. Newberg's work with Sufi Clerics showed the same pattern when they focused on their ritual of Dhikr and entered deep prayer states. There was a quieting in the parietal lobe (in places associated with the {self} circuits of the Default Mode Network), and an increase in temporal lobe activity. This is when habitual brain patterns can cease and new brain patterns can emerge, creating different experiences and perceptions for us to witness.

By comparing the subjective accounts of the experiences brought on by both the endogenous and exogenous versions of psychedelics, it's completely safe to assume there's some sort of connection between the two. And I think studying the external versions could eventually even help us understand how our spiritual experiences work on a grand scale. It's for this very reason that some people have started to call these chemical compounds entheogens. The word entheogen means "generating the divine within." And that's really what we're talking about when we're talking about these internal chemicals that can gain us access to higher states of Consciousness, caused by alternate patterns firing off in our brain. And I think we should study that phenomena more.

The Science of Transcendent Intelligence

If we step back toward the topic of Volume I, where we talked about improving our effectiveness as human beings by using science to increase happiness and unlock the doors to hidden intelligence and wisdom, we shouldn't ignore the hard evidence that connects our internal and external psychedelic compounds with higher intelligence as well. Because there's a lot of science that says, although some of these chemical compounds found in nature can brighten our psychological life, they also may lead us to understanding how to increase our human intelligence as well. It's been proven in studies that these psychedelic compounds within our brains can indeed open secret internal doors to super human intelligence.

Human intelligence studies done since the 1960s on the psychedelic compound called LSD proved that we may only be scratching the surface in regard to what human intelligence might be able to uncover, if we could enable the internal chemical catalysts that help our brains work in different ways. One study in particular was done by James Fadiman, where he dosed multiple participants with the compound LSD who were facing long-term technical problems that the participants had been unable to solve. The results of the study were that the participants not only came out of their psychedelic experience with the answers they were looking for, the solutions to the problems were groundbreaking, and other solutions to other non-related issues came as a result as well. To quote Tim Moody of the newsletter "The Morning News", who wrote about the study,

> LSD absolutely had helped them solve their complex, seemingly intractable problems. And the establishment agreed. The 26 men unleashed a slew of widely embraced innovations shortly after their LSD experiences, including a mathematical theorem for NOR gate circuits, a conceptual model of a photon, a linear electron accelerator beam-steering device, a new design for the vibratory microtome, a technical improvement of the magnetic tape recorder, blueprints for a private residency and an arts-and-crafts shopping plaza, and a space probe experiment designed to measure solar properties.

And this isn't where these anomalies stop; it's just where they start. Kary Mullis is a biochemist who won the Nobel Prize for Chemistry in 1993. In an interview after receiving his award, he reported that he "took plenty of LSD," and he went on to say, "It was certainly much more important than any courses I ever took." A well-known mathematician named Ralph Abraham claimed that the insights he'd experienced on exogenous psychedelics profoundly influenced his mathematical discoveries. Steve Jobs, one of the most successful visionaries in the history of personal computing, famously said that his experience with LSD was "one of the two or three most important things I ever did in my life." Francis Crick, who won the Nobel prize for discovering DNA with James Watson, and who helped found a pro–legalization of cannabis group called Soma, and who was a devotee of inner cosmonaut Aldous Huxley, told one of his students that he regularly took small doses of LSD to promote his powers of thought. It was said he told colleague Dick Kemp that he saw and drew the double-helix shape of DNA on a napkin before he actually discovered that was indeed what DNA looked like. Even today, one of the biggest unspoken trends in Silicon Valley and the San Francisco Bay Area is the practice of micro-dosing, where individuals working on the world's most advanced communications and energy technologies take doses of LSD in small enough amounts not to give them hallucinations, but in strong enough amounts to give them superpower problem solving abilities they wouldn't normally have. So both the study evidence and anecdotal evidence seem to suggest these consciousness expanding compounds contribute to real boosts in intelligence and real advances in science.

Recent independent brain scans done on study participants dosed with LSD and psilocybin show how this is possible. Both scans show that brain regions that don't normally talk to each other chat it up like old friends while under the influence of these psychedelic compounds. Default mode network activity is interrupted, which is the area of the brain that creates our mind's ego {self}. And in the process of brain regions talking to each other in a different fashion, sharing information not normally shared through conscious awareness, that opens the door for hidden knowledge stored in those regions to be uncovered into our conscious awareness.

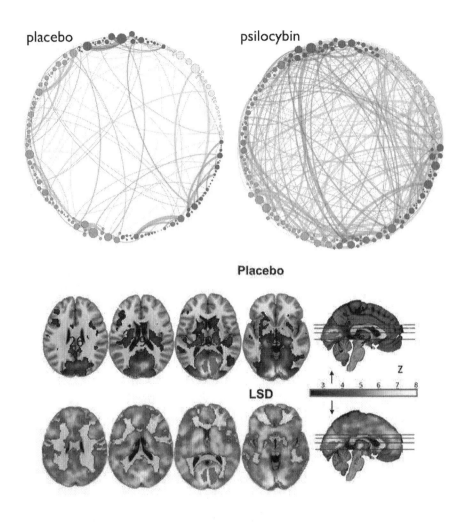

What this evidence also suggests is that the intelligence enhancing effects of internally sourced enlightenment are probably real as well. And if we have the capability to reach that state naturally without external drugs, that should be studied.

When we enter these mystical brain states, we can very likely access information and answers that are normally beyond our waking consciousness. Einstein pointed out that this type of spontaneous internal awakening to truth is how all new discoveries are made. He said, "The intellect has little to do on the road to discovery. There comes a leap in consciousness, call it intuition, or what you will, and the solution comes to you. And you do not know how or why. All great discoveries are made this way." Indeed Einstein should know, because he made a number of those great discoveries. Interestingly though, Einstein also admitted to having mystical experiences, and he believed that encouraging mystical experience was the single most important thing that artists and scientists could do for the world. On that, he said this: "The most beautiful and profound emotion we can experience is the sensation of the mystical. It is the sower of all true science. He to whom this emotion is a stranger, who can no longer wonder and stand rapt in awe, is good as dead."

Most people don't know this deeper secret behind Einstein's discoveries. They typically picture Einstein as a crazy-haired scientist in front of a blackboard full of mathematical figures discovering physics equations, but the reality is that Einstein's discoveries admittedly came from his ability to use insight and what he called "gedankenexperiments", which were conceptual experiments he would run in his mind before proving them in other ways and finishing his theories of general and special relativity. His major papers came as a result of him being able to see space-time in his mind through the memory of seeing space-time via his mind experiences. The mathematics equations we typically ascribe to Einstein which provided the explanations and proof of his discoveries only came afterward, and were challenging to him at times. He even once said of his own theory, "Since the mathematicians have invaded the theory of relativity, I do not understand it myself anymore." Math wasn't Einstein's primary tool; his inner vision of the universe was. It is for this reason he once replied to a little girl who wrote a letter to him, "Do not worry about your difficulties in Mathematics. I can assure you mine are still greater."

So when you, dear reader, are looking to increase your own intelligence, and increase your personal capacity to use your brain to improve the quality of your life and potentially your work, increasing your book learning isn't really the path you should take. The path you should take is one of inner discovery. That's where you will find all the answers you need.

And on that note, it's time for me to make a personal confession. Because as an example from my own experience which supports this claim, I can say that… although I wrote two complete books on the inner workings of the mind and the {self} works, which explain the source of our pain and suffering, and how to quell that personal pain and suffering, prior to my enlightenment experience, I knew **absolutely nothing** about human emotions and the source of human pain and suffering, or how to quell it.

Don't worry. Everything we discussed in Volumes I and II of this set of books is correct. You will be able to find the studies that support all the information presented, and the groupings of emotions I presented do, in fact, match those of the world's leading emotion scientists (although what is presented here is a little ahead of the curve – and yes, I did publish something very similar to this about seven years ago when it was **waaay** ahead of the curve). But you should know, **because it is important that you can understand the depth of intelligence that is available to you if you dig into your own mind,** that I developed this explanation of our emotions, and the practices associated with calming them, a full decade before any of the science was published that proved it to be completely accurate, and it was handed to me by my subconscious mind through an internal awakening of some sort, which we typically call 'enlightenment'.

Before that experience I had during my meditation that one afternoon, I knew absolutely nothing about the {self}, or the rules that could be used to explain our various individual human emotions. I knew nothing about how the Equation of Emotion worked, or how multiple EoEs could pile up to create our complex and sometimes confusing emotions. I knew nothing about the science that told us we could turn our negative emotions down if we better understood them. **I simply saw it happen,** then the concurring science was published, and I decided the time was right to share this insight with the science to back it. While Einstein might have called it intuition, or an unintentional gedankenexperiment, the fact is that I had to live this knowledge first, seeing it happening, real time, one afternoon in the deep recesses of my mind while I was off being one with God, before I was ever able to understand and explain it. And this capability is available to you, too.

How the question remains; how does this happen for us? From where did this intelligence spring forth to launch us toward the head of the class on something so complex that it's taken us since the days of Aristotle to even get this close? Are we accessing information in our DNA? Or is it that these natural psychedelic chemicals in our brain stimulate the microtubules of our neurons into a state of quantum communication normally closed off from our conscious awareness? Can we both naturally and artificially tap into this intelligence and Consciousness at will with practice and study? It's certainly a potential reality that our brain acts as a receiver of our consciousness rather than a source of it. That's something we don't yet completely understand. Can we change the station on that receiver? There is certainly something more to know. Our bodies are made up of a bunch of dumb atoms. At what point does consciousness turn those dumb atoms into intelligent actions which perform pro-life activities? And how do we more often access that intelligence and Consciousness that drives that whole process, which is something we've proven to ourselves we can do?

I don't know the answer to where my new knowledge came from, but do know that I'm not special to have experienced this dramatic mind expansion called enlightenment, and I think we need to figure out the answers to these question in a hurry, because the results have been nothing but positive regarding my personal existence afterward. Science proves others experience the same positive changes and access to new intelligence. Science doesn't yet understand how this happens though. And the questions of how our higher intelligence comes from within us are definitely questions the human race needs to discover answers to. In agreement with Einstein, I believe that the study of this phenomenon, so more people can experience it, should be one of humanity's top priorities. Not only does tapping into this inner intelligence make us happier as individuals and as a species, but it makes us smarter. Maybe this is why Einstein famously said, "Imagination is more important than knowledge."

The Case for More Research and Why It's You Who Will Need

to Demand It

I think deeper study into the natural psychedelic compounds that open up doors of immense intelligence, and may even show us the path to God, might be a good thing to put on our "To Do" list. I won't come out and say psychedelics are the path to God, because my own path to inner awakening was discovered through meditation and devotion. But neither can I say that a certain mix of psychedelics might not assist us along that path either. We just don't know yet.

Personally, I've never consumed any psychedelics, so I can't speak from experience. I only have the natural experience sourced from within my own brain as reference. Alan Watts, a philosopher and enlightened teacher from the 1960s, experienced enlightenment both through meditation, and also one through a doctor-administered LSD experiment. Although he reported that the experiences were exactly the same, his conclusive findings and remarks were that drugs are not the way to enlightenment. He enjoyed the naturally conscious experiences much more, as that he knew they were completely real. I have to agree with Alan Watts' conclusions that psychedelics probably aren't necessary. And from experience, I can indeed say that we can certainly achieve enlightenment without them. For anyone seeking enlightenment, I would tell them to go engage in meditative disciplines before considering other paths, I would certainly not suggest anyone go off blindly mind spelunking through use of illegal substances. I think the recreational use of psychedelics is the wrong way to go. They're sacred compounds, and spiritual medicines, if anything.

That said, it's interesting to note that Hindus consider the cow to be a sacred animal. And in India, there's a particular species of psychedelic mushroom that is rich in psilocybin which grows exclusively out of cow patties. So… if something that only grows from piles of cow shit then introduces people to God directly, that might explain why the cow is considered sacred. "I ate a cow-shit mushroom and met God. Don't fucking touch the cows, dude." It might also be evidence that psychedelics are a valid path to attaining enlightenment. So maybe if you want to explore that path, find places where these substances are legal, or create the political will to change the laws to make them available for research where they can become legal.

Personally, I think that further scientific research should be done on psychedelics, and I also think it's up to us regular folks to push to make that happen. Because we are the only folks who will ever make it happen. And that road promises to be a difficult and bumpy one. The multibillion dollar pharmaceutical companies who write the drug bills for Congress certainly won't lead the charge. They already spend millions blocking the ability to research these natural substances because of their ability to cure us of our mental ills. If restrictions on these natural substances get loosened to the point they wind up curing us of many of the illnesses that Big Pharma can "fix" today with a profitable pill, Big Pharma eventually goes out of business because of those freebie medicines found growing on the ground.

World governments won't lead the charge either, nor will corporations within the military industrial space. Because if the resulting science supports more wide spread medicinal use of these natural compounds, and more people then wind up meeting God and experiencing the "thou shalt not kill" message first hand, that might kill a profitable business of killing people. People experiencing psychedelics, natural or otherwise, and having experiences during which they feel like they meet God is definitely bad for an industrialized war machine. And certainly wouldn't promote military volunteerism.

So what about the oligarchs? Nope. People in the general populace changing their conscious {self} is scary to people in power who need to maintain the status quo and maintain financial control of a populace. To see people change their mind's {self} and lose their predictable fears is a scary thing. If you take away the fear of death from people, you end all fear of terrorism. You also end them reacting to political threat, which ends your political manipulation of them. And if the populace moves away from materialism, they don't need the rat race anymore. The people currently in power can't have any of that. So they figure if they keep people from meeting God, it keeps people under control, and keeps their profits flowing. That just makes sense.

Maybe it's a crazy idea, but I think it may be time that we as a global populace reassess this global system of mind manipulation and how it all works. I'd like to see us take back control of our lives by taking back control of our minds and eliminating our fear that causes us to harm each other give away our power to evil influences, both within and without. And maybe in a greater sense that's exactly what this set of books on "Mind Hacking Happiness" is all about.

Now… in closing this chapter on the science of enlightenment, there's one more thing you need to know about to increase your chances for experiencing enlightenment.

A Last Bit of Science: Caring for Your Pineal Gland for Enlightenment and for Extending Your life

There's one last thing you need to know about that little pineal gland at the base of your brain that may help you blaze a path to enlightenment, or just ensure your good mental health and happiness; calcification of your pineal gland, which blocks its ability to function properly. Whether or not the pineal produces DMT (which, until we get a sample of DMT from the pineal gland in humans is still in question), the pineal certainly has been proven to produce the DMT-related compound called melatonin. In fact, science strongly agrees the production of melatonin is our pineal gland's main function.

Melatonin, otherwise known as N-acetyl-5-methoxy tryptamine is required for good sleep and REM dreaming, both of which are important for our health. Without sleep, our bodies die. Without dreaming, our bodies die. Melatonin controls our sleep and seasonal rhythms and boosts our capacity to dream. Beyond that, it's an important internal antioxidant which serves to protect our nucleic and mitochondrial DNA, staving off cancer. It interacts with our immune system, acting as an anti-inflammatory agent which reduces the spread of viruses and inhibits the development of chronic health conditions like heart disease. So the pineal gland is a pretty important structure at the base of our brains. Those who experience lower melatonin levels have problems sleeping, and experience other adverse health effects because of the increase in stress and cortisol. Autistic children all have malformed melatonin pathways and abnormally low levels of melatonin in their bodies. Not enough is known about this most important chemical and all the things it does in our bodies, but one thing is certain: all those chemical interactions are **critical life-sustaining functions**.

Here's what you need to know:

There's an unreported epidemic sweeping the United States connected with the calcification of the pineal gland. The condition can be seen in skull X-Rays. It's really easy to spot. Research compiled by Robert Zimmerman of the Radiological Society of North America showed this problem to be so widespread, it's estimated that 40 percent of Americans have some calcification to their pineal gland by the time they're seventeen years old, with calcification showing up in children as young as two years of age.

For a gland that produces a chemical that does, by its effects, determine how healthy we are, including its ability to reduce depression, which can therefore reduce obesity, and all the health problems associated with both depression and obesity, I would think people might be alarmed by the fact that our children are being negatively affected by this very serious health condition. That's a number higher than cancer rates. That's a number higher than heart disease rates. And with autism rates ever increasing year over year, the question certainly needs to be asked, "is there a connection with reduced melatonin production that may be causing a large number of health challenges in modern society?"

Here's the rub: What causes calcification of our pineal glands, therefore reducing its output of melatonin? The answer to that question is simple: Fluoride.

Fluoride has been directly correlated to the calcification of our pineal glands. The big problem here is that we add fluoride to our drinking water in the U.S. Fluoride gets delivered directly to my house through pipes in my home via the public water system of my home town. What's crazy about that is that fluoride is officially classified and listed by the National Institutes of Health and the "The Lancet", the world's most prestigious medical journal, as a **neurotoxin**. Neurotoxins destroy brain cells and kill synapses. Neurotoxins make us dumber and sicker. "The Lancet" specifically identified fluoride as a developmental neurotoxin, meaning children by no means should be exposed to it. And this isn't just alarmist propaganda, it's science. A meta-analysis study done by Harvard University in 2013 showed conclusively that children in areas with highly fluoridated water have "significantly lower IQ scores" than those who live in areas with low amounts of fluoride in their water supplies.

So how much dumber do we want our kids to be? How sicker do we want ourselves to be? How many brain cells and synapses to we voluntarily just want to prune away in our own heads and in the heads of our family? I have a great idea: let's all be dumber while we try to get better jobs, and make more money, and pick a good presidential candidate in the next election.

People lost their minds (and rightfully so) in the United States in 2015 when it was found out the city of Flint, Michigan, had stopped buying clean water from the city of Detroit and started pulling water from the toxic Flint River. This river water caused corrosion issues in the lead pipes of Flint. As a result, those lead pipes started leaching lead into the public water system in large amounts. The city was literally pumping water with high levels of lead into people's water taps and shower heads simply because they wanted to save some money. This caused health issues and developmental problems in the children of Flint who drank that water. It started killing their brain development immediately. Rates of children with unsafe high levels of lead in their blood doubled in less than a year. The fallout of that mess is going to cause millions and potentially billions of dollars to address. To this day, although the city changed back to getting its water from Detroit, experts say the water is still unsafe to drink. The pipes are still leaching lead. They're shipping in millions of bottles of water even still today. And they are taking showers and baths in water with unsafe drinking levels of lead still, at the time this book went to press in 2017, and it's looking like people might serve jail time for that contamination of the water supply.

If you didn't know it, fluoride is in the very same neurotoxin category as lead, arsenic, and mercury. It's been reported by the National Toxicology Program to be a mutagen, which means it's a compound that can cause genetic damage within our cells (which means you pass the damage to any kids you have). Yet we willfully agree to add it into our own water supply.

Here, let me grab your drinking glass of pure clean water, while I also grab my small vial of neurotoxin to mix in with it. You just tell me when to stop at the point I've added enough neurotoxin for you. What? I'm sorry, did you say that you don't want any neurotoxin added to your water? Are you sure? It's completely free. No cost to you, besides what you pay in taxes for it, of course. You do actually pay for this neurotoxin already, so you may as well have some. No? Okay, well . . . let's grab your child's drinking glass. How much neurotoxin would you like me to add to that one?

And that water is most likely coming out of your tap at home, if your city is one of the thousands that add fluoride to the drinking water. Mine is. "Oh, but it's okay in small amounts," they say. They also said that same thing up until 2011, when the Department of Health and Human Services admitted that their previous guidelines were too high for public safety. Personally, I'm not waiting around until they lower them again, or finally just say, "Ya know, maybe we shouldn't put a neurotoxin in our water supply after all. Sorry, everyone, our bad."

Why do we do this? The first answer is typically, "because it helps reduce tooth decay". That was the argument that got us all on board in the 1950s and '60s. But while it's true that fluoride does assist in reducing tooth decay, even the American Dental Association admits that fluoride only helps through direct topical application, having its strongest long term effects on us when it's applied directly to the new permanent teeth of children ages seven to twelve. Besides that, the only benefit the fluoride in our water provides is in the amount of fluoride that actually touches our teeth as it passes through our mouths on the way to our tummies. The bad side effect is that after all that fluoride hits our tummies, it gets into our bloodstream and gets pumped into our brains, and calcifies our pineal gland. Proven science. The same gland that produces the life-sustaining compound called melatonin, and potentially the chemical our body releases to be able to talk to God, dimethyltryptamine.

In the words of Kevin Hart, "I can't make this stuff up, people."

If you already didn't know, the chemical that is added into much of America's water supply is an industrial waste compound that the EPA will not let companies dump into the ground (unless it somehow passes through humans first). We could spend a few hours digging into why we add this industrial waste compound to our drinking water, and the risk analysis we face in doing so as compared to what benefits to our teeth it might provide. We could contemplate the potential for corruption or the potential for some targeted reason that someone somewhere might want our pineal glands to be calcified as witnessed in the X-rays of our kids' heads. But frankly I think it just comes down to stupidity coupled with greed. Simply stated, after doing your own research, even if you wind up agreeing fluoride in our water is a bad thing, it's going to be years for you to get your local government to stop putting it in your water. So for me and my family, I've installed a reverse osmosis water filter in my home to take all that fluoride back out of my water that my local government adds in for me. When it comes to fluoride, I say "thanks, but no thanks". The filter reduces the contaminants of my local public water supply from around 40 parts per million (supposedly a minority of which is the added fluoride) to 0 parts per million.

In addition, I've taken other measures in my diet to add antioxidants in an attempt to keep my pineal function healthy. I want all the melatonin in my system I can get. I love naps. Because of this, I eat fresh blueberries, dark chocolate, and kale shakes mixed with fruit juices. Sometimes I'll take a shot of apple cider vinegar, which not only probably helps with pineal decalcification because of its malic acid properties (although this has not been proven), it also helps support good digestion (which has been proven).

Again, the science around the brain, and the pineal gland is in its infancy. The whole field of neuroscience isn't even walking as a toddler yet. So when we enter this area of discussion, we are forced into the realm of speculation. But speculation informed by good science is better than not speculating at all. At least in my opinion. And I hope yours.

16 Quieting the Mind as a Practice Toward Happiness, Inner Peace, and World Peace

> To the mind that is still,
> the whole universe surrenders.
>
> —Chuang Tzu

There's a story of an old farmer who had worked his simple farm for many years. He was a poor farmer who had only one horse to pull his cart and plow the fields. One day, his horse ran away. Upon hearing the news, his neighbors came to visit. "That is so terrible that your horse ran away," they said sympathetically.

"It is neither good nor bad," the farmer replied. And he went back to work.

The next morning, the farmer's horse returned, bringing with it three other wild horses. "What a wonderful good fortune," the neighbors exclaimed.

"It is neither good nor bad," replied the farmer. And he went back to work.

The following day, the old farmer's son tried to ride one of the untamed horses. He was thrown, and broke his leg. The neighbors again came to offer their sympathy on the farmer's misfortune. "Such a tragedy," they said.

"It is neither good nor bad," answered the farmer. And he went back to work.

The day after, military conscription officials came to the farmer's small village to draft young men into the army. Seeing that the son's leg was broken, they passed him over. The neighbors congratulated the farmer. "How lucky you are," they said.

"It is neither good nor bad," said the farmer. And he went back to work.

Over 2,000 years old, this story of the farmer and his horses has been told a number of times, but the interpretation attached to it rarely changes. This farmer is a great example of a man who doesn't let his mind ruin his life during a number of rather life-changing events. Looking back through the story, we can see that not once did he ever let his mind become attached to anything that wasn't going on in the present moment, nor did he ever let perceptions or judgments about whatever was happening in the moment paint him into a mental corner.

When the farmer's horse ran away, and his neighbors came to console him on his bad luck, and all he replied was, "It is neither good nor bad," the farmer didn't allow his mind to create a negative perception about the horse running away. To him, the situation just was, without the need to paint it as positive or negative. He certainly could have taken time to wallow in {self} pity about his missing horse. He could have worried about how he was going to pull the plow, or get his crops to market without his carthorse. He could have generated any number of negative emotions through Perceptions creating imbalances in his Equation of Emotion. Instead, he didn't create any Perceptions of the event at all. He simply went back to work.

When the farmer's horse returned with three more horses, was that not a good thing for him? Only his mind could determine it so.

But when his neighbors came to congratulate him, his reply was, "It is neither good nor bad." Why did he react this way? Because if he had previously attached to the idea it was a bad thing his horse had run away, he would now have to change that opinion. That also means any time he would have spent worrying about his horse would have been wasted. So why would he change the process of non-judgment that had worked for him the first time? As outsiders, we can see what a great two-day emotional ride it might have been for him to go from perceiving himself to be totally unlucky to then being totally lucky and blessed with good fortune, but he didn't let his mind attach to his good fortune. And, of course, we know what happened next.

The next day was when his son broke his leg. So what now? If the man had previously allowed his mind to attach to the idea he was lucky that his horse ran away to bring back new horses, now he would certainly have to reevaluate that whole assessment, and maybe require him to release the idea his recent life was a lucky string of events but rather an unlucky string. In addition, with the introduction of this new event, he again had the choice to judge that individual event as negative and worry about his son, who might wind up limping for the rest of his life, or be unable to work after the farmer passed away. But all he said was, "It is neither good nor bad." And we can see it was fortunate he took that position, because the very next day his luck changed yet again when the conscription officers came around looking for soldiers to fight in a war, and passed over the son because of his broken leg.

You can see the pattern. Some versions of the story go on and on with additional good and bad turns in the story to make the point. The moral is that regardless what happens in life, your mind has an immense opportunity to waste a lot of your time making judgments and creating thoughts about things that simply are what they are, without the need to be the uncomfortable roller-coaster ride your mind likes to make them out to be.

Changing How Our Minds Work

It's a simple fact that if you want to change the level of happiness in your life, you need to give up needing to change the things around you, and focus on changing yourself, and particularly how your mind works. Happiness comes from within, not when you've aligned all the stars of the universe to be just so, but when you've learned how to manipulate your mind into the space where you have access to happiness without it requiring you to jump through any hoops first. This isn't to say you need to give up on making a better life for yourself and your family and friends. I'm not suggesting that you just get happy with where you are, giving up the drive to change things if you want to. You can still maintain an eye on forwarding your career, or improving your abilities in certain areas (including making an attachment to the idea of gaining a better control over your mind will increase your happiness). You just need to give up feeling bad about your current situation, whatever that situation may be. And extend this state of mind to every situation, even if you wind up deciding to change that situation to make it better. This will relieve you of the negative crap standing in your way of doing what you need to do to make your life exactly what you wish it to be. Of course, you certainly need to be mindful of what's on your mind's {self} list and the things you decide to defend. I've decided to defend my need to make people happier in life so we can all be happier in the world. What's your choice?

To break the machine that has been controlling us for so long, we need to throw a wrench into our negative-Perceptions-creating-a need-for-defense-of-{self} process. But changing how your mind works is a tough thing to do. You are facing years of conditioning, which has left your mind to run free in its own thoughts and emotions. In addition, our present day media has killed your attention span and burned bad patterns into your malleable brain. In the 1940s, the average length of a single shot in a movie before a cut to another shot was 26 seconds. Today, that length of a single shot before a cut has dropped to 6 seconds, and good luck finding a stable camera. It's no wonder that our human attention span at 8.5 seconds is shorter than that of a goldfish's at nine. Your mind is accustomed to being constantly entertained with constantly changing content. It's accustomed to being uncontrolled and ungoverned, thinking what it will, when it will, about whatever it gets distracted with in the moment. And when you look to discipline your mind's chaotic freedom, it like to say, "nope", because you are challenge your mind's own beliefs that it should be unrestricted and liberated enough to run completely amok. But you must remember you are not your mind, and you can prove that to yourself by taking control of your mind. That provides you a closer understanding of what you really are, which is the biggest secret in the universe connected with Self. You have to experience it to know it. And you can't experience it if your mind is making noise. So you need to make it quiet.

Obtaining any type of control and quietness in your mind is certainly the most difficult part of your path to finding happiness. But if there's one recurring theme that keeps popping up again and again throughout this set of books on happiness, it is that happiness is connected with disciplining and controlling the mind into that quietness. Whether it's calming your moment-to-moment inner bullshit engine of negative emotions while you're out and about in the real world doing your everyday life thing, or chasing the mystical states of consciousness that can occur within you when the brain falls into a state of non-thinking awareness, it's a true statement to say that lasting happiness can only be found in the practice of quieting your mind.

You can continue to believe that more money will make you happy. Or when your religion dominates the world, **that** will make you happy. Or when your politics takes over your country and other countries, **that** will make you happy. Or when everyone decides to finally adopt your favorite color as their favorite color, **that** will make you happy. But deep down you know that's all bullshit. If you need to understand the science that proves it, go back and start with Volume I.

In Section I of Volume I, we discussed of the science of your pain and suffering, and we pointed out the disquieting truth that it's the activity of your own mind that causes all your pain and suffering. We talked about your Equation of Emotion, and how it comes from comparing your Expectations / Preferences (within the mind) associated with this nebulous thing we call your sense of {self} (also an invention of your mind), compared to your Perceptions (which again, are inventions of your mind). In Section II of Volume I, we discussed old and new ways of reducing your suffering by manipulating or releasing the variables that create your suffering, which thereby stops your mind from generating so much bullshit for you to deal with. Here in Volume II, we've stepped through the looking glass and discussed how silencing the mind is actually the secret path of all the world's religions, and the practical path to inducing natural mystical states associated with pure bliss and never-ending happiness through enlightenment.

The biggest secret about your personal happiness is that it's found entirely within you. You already have an infinite amount of it, even if you don't know it yet. Start opening those inner doors. You'll find it. It's there. It just got dropped off your mind's inventory sheet a while back.

The reality about finding that happiness, and quieting the mind to get there, is that reading this book (and any other inspiring book on the subject that you can get your hands on) is only your first step. Lao Tzu once said, "A journey of a thousand miles begins with a single step." Feel good in this moment. At this point, you've already taken some steps, so you're already on your way. And thanks to what we've covered here, you now have the whole map of your journey. The next step is to start practicing the disciplines that can be used to better understand your mind's {self}, and practicing the disciplines that can be used to quiet your mind. Now at least you know exactly where you're going.

That said, expect difficulty. Expect challenges. Expect that your mind will not cooperate with you on this quest for happiness. Expect that your mind's {self} will distract you. It will push back sometimes by judging your efforts as "silly" or "weird" or "pointless." It will say that you have something better to do, or other things you should do first. It will keep doing this until the day is done, and you've gone another 24 hours without change, and succumbing to your mind's will of not wanting to change. This is because it knows that if you ever gain control of your mind, that will move toward control and devaluation of the mind's {self}. It seems odd to speak of the {self} as a conscious adversary that stands in the way of your goals, but in reality the {self} sometimes takes actions to defends its {self} even against your own conscious yearning to realize Self. So your mind's {self} can be one of your biggest adversaries to expanding your {self} beyond its current boundaries to attain happiness, and especially to attain enlightenment. Remember the {self} hates change and will attack your efforts to discover your deeper Self. It will attempt to chip away at your resolve to find deeper truth. Controlling the mind takes practice, patience, and a great deal of time to master.

Observing from Meta-awareness

Some good news is that the {self}'s resistive efforts are neutralized when you move your waking awareness into the space of meta-awareness, where you can watch the operation of your mind and see the {self} from a short distance. This shows your subconscious mind that you are not entirely the product of your mind's {self}. This expands and changes your mind's {self} every time you do it.

This is an awesome thing, because your {self} is ultimately the cause of all your psychological pain which can then cause you to create additional pain for yourself and others. When you separate from the mind and distance your awareness from the {self}, you separate from both psychological and physical suffering, and the capability of perpetuating and spreading pain. When you exist in this state, you move toward equanimity in even your life's most challenging situations, regardless of whether you experience them at work, in your family life, in your own thoughts, or in a difficult situation elsewhere. And that helps you and those around you.

Although this book provides an in-depth look at the phenomena of enlightenment and non-dual awareness, you don't have to achieve enlightenment to observe your mind from meta-awareness and realize the benefits of experiencing a dramatic increase in your inner peace and happiness. Even moderate increases in inner peace and happiness can be used to battle stress, reduce worries connected with your societal life, and take a respite from the evils of the mind's {self}. Entering meta-awareness in most situations is not difficult. If you become caught off guard by a negative reaction in your mind, simply notice you are experiencing that negativity, and ask yourself what Perception within your mind has caused that negativity. Then ask yourself what idea of your mind's {self} created the Expectation/Preference that was attacked. By doing this simple mental task, you have entered meta-awareness, and you will gain control back from your mind. Alternatively, you can also handle difficult situations by focusing your awareness on simply experiencing those difficult situations fully without piling additional thought into them. Using Mattieu Ricard's exercise of focusing on the negative reaction itself, rather than what fueled it, will land you in meta-awareness.

Become familiar with that peaceful place that exists within you. It doesn't matter what you observe from meta-awareness. As long as you are observing the world while observing your mind's reaction to the world, you're in that space. The mind classifies, quantifies, and judges everything it perceives. It creates thoughts and observations about everything it experiences. It puts a label on everything that passes through Perception. The portion of you that is closer to Self doesn't need to do all these mind-ly things. It simply observes. It does not label, judge, or quantify anything. It experiences, and enjoys. Even if the mind itself isn't enjoying at the moment.

When you observe from meta-awareness, less and less can upset you. This can be practiced to the point where eventually, you find that very few things can upset you. This brings to your mind a silence of equanimity. Observing from the space of equanimity allows you to realize the quietness of your inner being, and the peaceful and contented state of your true Self. It does take a great deal of practice to master, but it is with practice that things become easier to do. As practicing equanimity becomes easier for you, you can then do it more often.

If you'd like to explore this more, check out our website at MindHackingHappiness.com.

The Inner Peace of World Peace

The inner peace we find at the end of this path is the inner peace that will eventually bring us all to world peace. And make no mistake, without this inner peace, there will be no world peace. Ever. Trying to get people to replace things on their mind's {self} map with attachments of {self} that you think are better, whether that's a different political system, a different financial system, or a different religion… especially when that change is approached with argument and reason… that works against the natural tendency for the mind's {self} to hate and resist change, and it also fights the natural tendency of the {self} to want to be special and unique and different. Trying to make everyone think like {us} is a losing battle, or should I say, a lost war. Our human physiology has already decided the outcome of that type of effort… forever… as far into the future you would like to look. World peace can **only** be attained in the manifestation of an unmolestable mind that renders impotent any attack on a mind's false {self}, including ideas of nation, race, politics, and religion.

If we want world peace, we need to break the mind's system of defense of {self}. And that's the only way it can ever happen. Period.

One of my favorite songs is John Lennon's iconic "Imagine", a favorite shared by millions of people. The lyrics of that song point us right to this truth of not being attached to items of {self}, which then allows us not to be bothered to defend them, leading us to world peace. In the lyrics, Lennon refers to not being attached to ideas about God and religion, ideas of country and patriotism, ideas of material possessions. He points out in the end that some people have already realized this truth of existence, and he hopes we all will come to that realization. When Lennon starts the song "Imagine there's no heaven", he introduces the idea right at the top of the song to imagine a world where people are not attached to the idea of heaven or hell, which suggests having no attachments to our divisive religions. So in the sky, only sky. In addition, with this non-attachment of {self}, there isn't any clinging to thoughts of future or past. There are only people living for today. In the second stanza, not clinging to thoughts of patriotism or national identity allow us to "Imagine there's no countries", and "nothing to kill or die for". In the third stanza, he directly calls out not having possessions or greed, which would indeed solve the world's hunger crisis. Imagine all the people sharing all the world? Mind blowing.

But a completely possible reality if the human race ever learns to get the mind's {self} out of the way. Houston, we are GO for enlightenment.

Enough said about that. Who can follow John Lennon?

This is exactly why the Dalai Lama said that world peace can only come from inner peace. Because at the point the mind and its invention of {self} are quiet, thanks to being rewritten by Self, there is simply nothing more within the mind that your brain needs to defend. When you observe from this silent perspective of equanimity, everything is peaceful. Everything is serene. Nothing is painful. Nothing is bothersome. And there is no other. We are all brothers and sisters in that space. We are all one being. One entity. One piece of the big Consciousness-of-Love puzzle. Sure we all have individual minds, with our unique attachments of mind, but we are all one in being blessed with that same model of physiology that seems to make us all different, but in reality makes us all exactly the same. That makes us all deserving of compassion. All deserving of love. All deserving of forgiveness and warmth for our imperfections and different attachments of mind.

From a personal perspective, in this space of compassion, your boss or co-worker who used to upset you can now be fun to interact with. Take their ability to irritate you away, and what do they have left? It's here that the traffic that used to increase your blood pressure is now enjoyable to exist in, to the point you're even letting people go in front of you. Take away the irritation of traffic, and what does it have on you? It's here that the quirks of your spouse that used to drive you up the wall are simply your spouse. Take away those small irritations, you're only left with appreciating them again. It's in this state of mind that the rebellions of your kids can become an opportunity for constructive communication. Take away your impatience, and you're left with being a better teacher and guide for them. From a higher perspective, we can even view our neighboring countries and cultures as simply different variations of ourselves. And how could you ever approve the order to drop a bomb on yourself, even if you lose your temper with yourself for a short period of time over religion or politics?

It's only when your mind's {self} is making noise that you can't hear the love and peace that emanates from the place there is no {self}. Quieting the mind and attaining inner peace will deliver world peace. And because of how our physiology works, it is the only thing that ever has the chance of doing so.

A Last Word on Self and Happiness

Recalling the two different types of happiness called our temporary hedonic happiness, and our deep meaningful eudaemonic happiness, it's not through the secrets of chasing your shallow happiness that your deep happiness is developed. It's through the development of your deep happiness that your shallow happiness can also constantly flourish from moment to moment. Your deep happiness of eudaemonia is your exit door off the hedonic adaptation treadmill. When you change how your mind works to give up that deep eudaemonic happiness at will, absolutely no one, no matter what they do to you, can take that deep sense of happiness away from you. And because of how your brain works, this state of mind can be trained through the scientific phenomenon of neuroplasticity.

Personally speaking, today, I'm able to observe my mind's movements from meta-awareness within most moments of my everyday life. I see things simply as they are. There are no judgments, no labels, no classifications that bother me. Sure, my mind tries to create that stuff, and I do have fun letting that stuff out in social media posts, and on our podcasts, but deeper within my mind, where my true Self resides, from the space of being aware of the mind's tricks and the fact that its all illusion, I feel that I'm immune to those tricks now. They don't really sway me. But that doesn't mean we can't play with them.

Subsequently, there are few situations that can't be handled very quickly and without emotional turbulence. There are few dilemmas that cause any amount of stress in my life. There's very little of the mind's {self} that needs defending. Don't get me wrong, there's a {self} in this head of mine, and it gets loud from time to time. I even get it out and play with it on my podcasts and social media posts. But it doesn't need defending. It doesn't cause me angst. I can put it away any time I like. Granted, I do feel I have a big advantage because I have the memory of my old {self} being replaced by an experience of a higher Consciousness, but as this book explains, there's a process you can take to get there, too.

In this state of perfect mind control, you can find permanent bliss. Because, again, it's here that you are transitioned from compulsion to choice. Rather than being pushed and pulled by your mind's thoughts to follow your mind's every whim, you can decide what of the mind's muddy mess to engage with and wallow around in for a while before simply deciding not to anymore, and returning to the place within you that is unaffected by mind. And this is fun like you've never experienced it before. It's just like experiencing the ups and downs of life that controlled you previously, except you have the choice of getting off the roller coaster any moment you wish to return immediately to equanimity. Putting on your mind's {self} for a bit to wear it like a costume can be fun if you know you can take it off whenever you wish. It's like playing the part in a play called [Your Name Here], where you pretend to be your {self} for a while, knowing fully well it's all make-believe and designed to be fun. It's at that point that even the anger, fear, or sadness you generate on the stage while in costume can be fun to the person underneath the mask. You may not always have a smile on your face, but you'll always have one on your heart. It's a really way cool way to go through life. And I'll help you get there if I can.

Now… putting our skeptic hat back on for one last moment, it's time to ask one last big question: Having just gone through two books that show us our minds create illusion, what makes this enlightenment stuff real? Are these shifts in consciousness actually real, and are these mind strategies actually real, or am I and the other people who employ it just fooling ourselves? In other words, are these shifts of mind and consciousness congruent with scientific reality, or is it yet another illusion of our minds similar to those we've discussed throughout these two books?

There are two answers to that question. The first comes from scientific evidence, which I think is appropriate. And beyond that, it's scientific evidence of what I've experienced personally.

After being practiced in maintaining meta-awareness for a number of years, I was invited to take a rather expensive and in depth personality test for free. So I did, just for fun. The results of that testing were that my emotional stability scores ranked near 100 percent. My warmth, friendliness, and sensitivity scores also scored very high. One thing that didn't score high, however, was my measure of stress. It came in at a big fat zero. But it's one thing to answer questions and fill out forms, which is what this first test was. It's another thing altogether to see it live on a brain scan. Most recently I found myself lying in an fMRI machine participating in a baseline for a study on meditation and altered mind states. The left shift seen on the monitor in my prefrontal cortex while I was in a state of meta-awareness was substantial. This means there was a lot more activity on the left side of my prefrontal cortex than there was in my right side. To oversimplify the science, the left prefrontal cortex is where happiness and optimism lives, so my brain scan showed I was truly happy, and not just faking it or fooling myself. I thought that was pretty cool.

The second answer to whether or not my shift in consciousness and perception is based in reality is this; **What the fuck does it matter?** If we do this work and our happiness levels increase, that's the whole ballgame, kids. Happiness is indeed "the chief good; the end towards which all other things aim." (Aristotle) If deeper realizations from enlightenment that people have experienced are a hallucination that has improved our lives by changing our mind's inner workings to the point our minds now decide our lives are perfect, then I say; "okay, give me that bullshit hallucination a million times out of a million." I'll happily spend the rest of my existence in this mind space over any other mind space, whether it's real or not. What is real anyway? Reality is just perception. Personally, I'm eternally grateful for the knowledge I've discovered. And I wish for everyone else to have it, too. Especially you.

[And not just because you bought my book. Although I am thankful for that. And I'm so happy that you're so impressed with all this book has delivered, that you're going to share it with everyone you know. Please? Thanks in advance.]

17 The Ancient Wisdom

I hate quotations.
Tell me what you know.

—Ralph Waldo Emerson

I've already told you what I know, so now I'm going to leave you with some quotations. Here's why:

It was only after experiencing an awakening that I started to see a lot of parallels between a number of the sayings preserved from past masters and what I personally learned from my inner experience. In support of my assertion that enlightenment shows, and has shown, many people the very same thing. I wanted to include a number of these sayings that I've not already cited.

Of the Mind

This first saying comes from one of my favorite Zen masters, a man named Ikkyu Sojun. Ikkyu was a Zen monk who, from a very young age, was raised in a Zen monastery to protect him from being killed because he was an illegitimate son of the emperor. At the point he became enlightened, he saw that most of the other monks weren't, and when they gave him a certificate for being enlightened, he ripped it up and trashed the Zen temple, vowing never to return. He then led a life of drinking and whoring, and partying with the rich and famous of society for most of the rest of his life. But late in his life, when the Zen temples fell into disrepair, bringing about a potential end of Zen itself, Ikkyu returned to teaching Zen and used his money and influence with his rich friends to rebuild the temples, infused new students with enlightenment from within themselves, and saved Zen Buddhism for the world.

He said, "Babble about 'God' and 'Buddha' and you will never find the true way."

The reason Ikkyu said this, of course, is that the concepts of {God} and {Buddha} are ideas of the mind that hold us back from attaining the truth that lies beyond the mind itself. Mentally clinging to the {ideas} of {God and Buddha} and all the {associated ideas} that come along with those things turn them into attachments on our {self} map which then stand in the way of the truth. They keep us from getting beyond our mind and experiencing what the reality of God and Buddha are - two names for the same experience of the oneness that is unspeakable. This theme of getting to the experience that is beyond mind is repeated over and over from numerous masters.

"Throw away sacredness and wisdom and people will be a hundred times happier."
Lao Tzu (inspirator of Taoism)

"Only the hand that erases can write the true thing."
Meister Eckhart (Christian master)

"Sell your cleverness and buy bewilderment."
Rumi (Sufi poet)

"Life is something that has to be lived and not talked about."
Carl Gustav Jung (psychologist)

"Words cannot express things;
Speech does not convey spirit.
Swayed by words, one is lost;
Blocked by phrases, one is bewildered."
Mumon (Zen Master)

"You can't know wisdom, you have to be it."
Ram Dass (psychologist and spiritual teacher)

"When you are deluded and full of doubt, even a thousand books

of scripture are not enough.
When you have realized understanding, even one word is too much."

Fen Yang (Zen master)

"The fish trap is meant to catch fish. Once the fish are caught, the trap is forgotten.
The rabbit snare is meant to snare rabbits. Once the rabbit is caught the snare is forgotten. Words exist to convey meaning. Once meaning is understood, the words are forgotten.
Where is the man who has forgotten words? He is the one I wish to speak to."

Chuang Tzu (Taoist master)

Of the Mind's {self}

Regarding what we **think** we are until we awaken, the things we attach to, and the process of simplifying {self} as a road to awakening:

"So long as one does not become simple like a child, one does not get divine illumination. Forget all the worldly knowledge that thou hast acquired and become as a child, and then will thou get the divine wisdom."

Ramakrishna (Indian Yogi)

"Truly I tell you, unless you change and become like little children, you will never enter the kingdom of heaven. Therefore, whoever takes the lowly position of this child is the greatest in the kingdom of heaven."

Jesus of Nazareth (inspirator for Christianity)

"If you would be a real seeker after truth, it is necessary that at least once in your life you doubt, as far as possible, all things."

Rene Descartes (philosopher and polymath)

"Whenever there is attachment, association with it brings endless misery."

Gampopa (Buddhist master)

"Come, behold this world, how it resembles an ornamented chariot, in which fools flounder, but for the wise there is no attachment to it."
The Buddha (inspirator of Buddhism)

"There is no room for God in him who is full of himself."
Hasidic saying

"Trying to define yourself is like trying to bite your own teeth."
Alan Watts (philosopher)

"The mind is everything. What you think, you become."
The Buddha

On the Moment of Enlightenment and Liberation

"To establish ourselves amid perfect emptiness in a single flash is the essence of wisdom."
Dhammapada Sutra (Buddhist text)

"My body and mind have dropped away."
Dōgen (Zen master)

"I awoke only to find that the rest of the world is still asleep."
Leonardo da Vinci (artist)

"The Man who masters himself is delivered from the force that binds all creatures."
Johann Wolfgang von Goethe (German writer and statesman)

"One does not become enlightened by imagining figures of light, but by making the darkness conscious."
Carl Gustav Jung (psychologist)

On the Oneness of Everything and the Illusion of Matter and Spacetime

"From all one; and from one, all."
    Heraclitus (Greek philosopher)

"In royal solitude, you walk the universe."
    Wu-men (Zen master)

"The universe is a single life compromising one substance and one soul."
    Marcus Aurelius (Roman emperor)

"All know that the drop merges into the ocean, but few know the ocean merges into the drop."
    Kabir (Indian mystic)

"The true mystery of the world is the visible, not the invisible."
    Oscar Wilde (writer and poet)

"This moment contains all moments."
    C.S. Lewis (Christian writer)

"To see a world in a grain of sand, and heaven in a wild flower
Hold infinity in the palm of your hand and eternity in an hour"
    William Blake (poet)

"When you make the two one, and when you make the inside like the outside and the outside like the inside, and the above like the below, and when you make the male and the female one in the same, so that the male not be male nor the female female; then you will enter the kingdom."
    Jesus of Nazareth (inspirator of Christianity)

"The real miracle is not to walk on water or thin air but to walk on the earth!"
    Thich Nhat Hanh (Buddhist master)

On Experiencing All Moments as One Moment

"He who sees what is now has seen all things, whatsoever comes to pass from everlasting and whatsoever shall be unto everlasting time."
>Marcus Aurelius (Roman emperor)

"I have realized that the past and future are real illusions, that they exist only in the present, which is what there is and all there is."
>Alan Watts (enlightened philosopher)

On Using This Truth of the Present Moment

"Begin at once to live."
>Seneca (Roman philosopher)

"Spend the afternoon. You can't take it with you."
>Annie Dillard (author)

"Finish every day and be done with it. You have done what you could. Some blunders and absurdities crept in. Forget them as soon as you can. Tomorrow is a new day; you should begin it serenely and with too high a spirit to be encumbered with your old nonsense."
>Ralph Waldo Emerson (American author and Transcendentalist)

"Do every act of your life as if it were your last."
>Marcus Aurelius (Roman emperor)

"What time would it be if all the clocks were stopped?"
>Zen Koan

Of the Truth of the Equation of Emotion

"To set up what you like against what you dislike—this is the disease of the mind."
>Seng T'san (Zen master)

Regarding the Mind Being a Reflection of {self}

"We see things not as they are, but as we are."
    The Talmud (Hebrew text)

Of the Consciousness of the Universe Being in Everyone

"If you don't find God in the next person you meet, it's a waste of time looking for him further."
    Mohondas Gandhi (spiritual leader)

Of the Nothingness of the Universe and the Contradiction of Quantum Physics

"All things in the world come into being from being. Being comes into being from non-being."
    Lao Tzu (inspirator of Taoism)

"This boat is and is not. When it sinks, both disappear."
    Ikkyu

Of the Perfection of the Universe

"Reality and perfection are synonymous."
    Spinoza (Dutch philosopher)

Of the Ultimate Truth of the Universe

"What lies behind us and what lies before us are tiny matters compared to what lies within us."
    Ralph Waldo Emerson (American author and Transcendentalist)

Of the Rarity of Enlightenment

Few among men are they who cross over to the further shore. The others merely run up and down the bank on this side.

The Dhammapada

***

And… Oh Yeah… the Science That God May Exist

History is replete with sayings from the ancient sages who point to the truth of what we've spoken about here in this book. What's the scientific likelihood that they're right? What's the scientific likelihood that there is some sort of transcendent conscious intelligence beyond that of our own consciousness? Well, it's tough to put a number on such things. **That said…** there is a high mathematical probability that something we call consciousness is indeed involved in quantum science, because not one current interpretation of quantum physics leaves consciousness on the sidelines. This means it's a high mathematical probability consciousness is connected with the whole model of the universe. The supporting evidence for this can be seen through observation that our seemingly dumb atoms come together into organic compounds which then become cells, which seem to act intelligently and consciously in a pro-life fashion. Thus, mathematically speaking, because of this observable evidence, there must be a sliver of a chance that consciousness pervades our cells. Additionally, it seems possible that our cellular consciousness provides us some kind of waking consciousness through which we see the world and perceive a larger model of things. The microtubules of our neurons have been proven to interact with quantum vibrations, which may be what spreads consciousness into our cells. This in turn builds consciousness into our cellular structures, which in turn builds consciousness into our organs, which in turn build consciousness into our brain and our waking awareness. So there seems to be a reverse cascade of consciousness at work. If consciousness flows up from below, it might be silly to assume that our top level consciousness is where it all stops. In fact, with our neurons being directly wired into the quantum field, there's a mathematical probability that it doesn't, however slim that mathematical probability is. There's a potential that our consciousness rolls up into higher levels of consciousness that we may not yet be aware of. Many of us may call this consciousness God.

So here's the punchline: All those slim probabilities, multiplied my slim probabilities, multiplied by slim probabilities... when calculated through the filter of an infinite universe... become a **mathematical certainty** once infinity is added to the other side of the equation. So even if the scientific chain of communication we've laid out between our neurons and the quantum soup has only a sliver of hope of being correct, in an infinite multidimensional universe it's a certainty that's already happened. So maybe God does exist, just not in a way we've considered before scientifically.

Maybe? Maybe.

So here we are. You've made it to the end of the book. Now, you have the big picture on happiness, you know how your mind works to steal your happiness, you know how to take control of your mind to allow it to give you more happiness on demand, and the veil has been lifted on that mystical topic called enlightenment (which you don't need to be happy). Now, you've reached the beginning of your journey to take control of your mind to give you happiness anytime you wish. With practice.

Now, if you didn't notice the first time around, this book and the first volume on which it builds contain **a lot** of useful information that has not been published before. And I know for a fact that a lot of it is probably new to you. So if you'd like, now that you've seen the big picture on slight and extreme happiness, go back and read them again. Content like this sticks a little better the second time around, and now that you've seen the big picture, a lot of things will probably pop out at you the second time through. So I make that suggestion for your benefit. I wrote it for you, not me.

There's More!

Okay, time for the {self}ish plugs. If you'd like to get any of the books I've mentioned during our journey for free in their audio version, you can sign up for a free trial at Audible using my link, http://www.mindhackinghappiness.com/freebook . I've been a member since 2006, and it's the one monthly expenditure I will probably never opt out of. If you'd like to get a Muse meditation headband to help you learn how to meditate with audio and visual feedback on your personal electronic device, head to http://mindhackinghappiness.com/muse to check out the Muse meditation headband. It connects to your bluetooth device and helps you learn how to meditate more effectively. Also, don't forget to search for and find the Mind Hacking Happiness podcast, where we'll be discussing various topics connected with consciousness and expanding it. And definitely come by and visit the website for goodies and to share for others how you are using this stuff and what you are getting out of it. Having access to your perspective may help others increase their happiness. www.MindHackingHappiness.com

I hope this book finds you well. And though, no, a book can't make you happier, I hope what we've covered here does provide you the tools to understand your mind better so that you can take control of it and allow your happiness to flourish from within.

Peace.

Printed in Great Britain
by Amazon